Social. & Comm.
J.60d

6/61

D1247772

H. M. HYNDMAN
AND BRITISH SOCIALISM

A Trafalgar Square meeting (1906)

H. M. HYNDMAN
AND BRITISH
SOCIALISM

BY

CHUSHICHI TSUZUKI

Sometime Research Scholar of
St. Antony's College, Oxford

Edited by
HENRY PELLING

OXFORD UNIVERSITY PRESS
1961

Oxford University Press, Amen House, London E.C.4

GLASGOW   NEW YORK   TORONTO   MELBOURNE   WELLINGTON
BOMBAY   CALCUTTA   MADRAS   KARACHI   KUALA LUMPUR
CAPE TOWN   IBADAN   NAIROBI   ACCRA

© *Oxford University Press 1961*

PRINTED IN GREAT BRITAIN

Library
I.U.P.
Indiana, Pa.

335.42   H998

C. 1

PREFACE

THIS book is an attempt to assess the political career of
H. M. Hyndman, the Socialist pioneer. In the days of his
prime, when Socialism was a newly-organized but vigorous
political enthusiasm, it was more identified in the popular
mind with Hyndman than with William Morris, or Bernard
Shaw, or Keir Hardie, who were all his contemporaries.
On the Continent his eminence among British Socialists
was even more readily accorded. Sombart described him
as one of the 'Church Fathers' of Marxism, along with Karl
Kautsky, August Bebel, George Plekhanov, Jules Guesde,
and Antonio Labriola.[1] But his form of Marxism, adapted
as it was to some at least of the social and political traditions
of his country, lost favour after his death, as the Communists
and the non-Marxist Socialists divided the Socialist world
between them. As a result Hyndman himself has long been
neglected and consequently often misunderstood by later
generations. There have been no biographies except for the
uncritical works by Rosalind Travers Hyndman, his second
wife, and by F. J. Gould, his enthusiastic disciple.[2] His own
memoirs, in two volumes, are both entertaining and valuable, but they are wanting in accuracy and completeness.
Further, the official history of the S.D.F.[3] is also very in-
complete and strongly partisan. An attempt to re-examine
his political career, therefore, seemed justified if a fair
estimate were to be made of his life and work.

The sources—especially the unpublished materials—
essential to this study are so scattered that the work would
have been almost impossible to undertake without the help

[1] W. Sombart, *Der proletarische Sozialismus* (Jena, 1924), i. p. 26.
[2] R. T. Hyndman, *Last Years of H. M. Hyndman* (1923); F. J. Gould, *Hyndman, Prophet of Socialism* (1928).
[3] H. W. Lee and E. Archbold, *Social-Democracy in Britain* (1935).

of many other people. Mr. Henry Pelling lent me his collection of photostats and microfilms of letters of Hyndman which are to be found in various libraries in America. He supervised and encouraged my work and in many ways gave me great help. The late Professor G. D. H. Cole read part of my thesis, and his suggestions were extremely useful. I am grateful to Mr. James Joll for constant advice and help, and for special assistance in enabling me to consult most of the Congress Reports of the Second International. Mr. Christopher Seton-Watson very kindly allowed me to consult the correspondence between Hyndman and his father. Professor H. H. Quint of the University of Massachusetts helped me greatly in securing microfilms of the Wilshire Papers. Four old S.D.F. members, Mr. W. P. Coates, Mrs. Zelda Kahan Coates, Mr. Frank Jackson, and the late Mr. Frank Tanner, gave me the benefit of their first-hand know- ledge of the Socialist movement, which was of great value. I am also indebted to the International Institute of Social History in Amsterdam for permission to use Hyndman's corre- spondence with Marx, Engels, and Kautsky, and other documents relating to the S.D.F. The Warden of Wortley Hall, Yorkshire, gave me free access to the Hyndman Library on loan there from the National Council of Labour Colleges. I am also grateful to the staff of the following libraries for their co-operation: the British Museum, Bodleian Library, British Library of Political and Economic Science, Nuffield College Library, and St. Antony's College Library. I could not have carried out this study without financial assistance from the British Council, from Ruskin College, and es- pecially from St. Antony's College which has supported me for most of the period of my research. I hereby make grateful acknowledgment of their generosity.

CHUSHICHI TSUZUKI

EDITOR'S NOTE

S INCE Dr. Tsuzuki had to return to Japan immediately after taking his degree, I undertook to prepare his work for publication. Some abridgment and alteration of style has been necessary, and there are a few short additional passages, but I am confident that those who take the trouble to compare this book with the original thesis in the Bodleian Library will find that no changes of substance have been made, and no sections of great importance or interest sacrificed in the process.

H. M. P.

CONTENTS

LIST OF PLATES

I ❧ SCION OF EMPIRE

I

IT was in the 1880's that 'respectable' people in Britain woke up to the profoundly shocking fact that the revolutionary creed of Socialism, which until this time had been largely confined to the Continent, was making converts in their very midst. In 1881 an organization called the Democratic Federation had been founded, and in 1884 this body had assumed the name of the Social-Democratic Federation and had begun to advocate Marxist principles on the pattern of the French and German Socialist Parties. Worse still, its leaders were able to take advantage of the depression in trade in the middle of the decade, and to place themselves at the head of agitation in London and other cities which provoked rioting and other disorders including the looting of shops.

It was almost equally shocking that the outstanding leader of the Social-Democratic Federation both in this period and through most of its later existence, was not an unlettered proletarian, who might have been expected to bear a grudge against the existing social system, but a man who had been born, as the saying goes, 'with a silver spoon in his mouth' —the son of a wealthy father, related to the aristocracy and equipped with the social advantages of an education at Trinity College, Cambridge. This was no 'angry young man' sowing his political wild oats, but a man of mature years, already in his forties, well-travelled, yet also established in London society. His name was Henry Mayers Hyndman.

As time went on, H. M. Hyndman (as he was almost invariably known, in the rather severe way customary in the period) became regarded by friends and enemies alike as a unique example of devotion to the revolutionary creed. To the gradually growing band of converts to Socialism he was the first of the pioneers, the symbol of incorruptible faith, who would not stoop to the compromises and measures of expediency which, as the movement gradually matured, were more and more common among the leaders. To the much larger body of conservative opinion, which regarded his ideas with aversion, he was the object of a variety of reactions ranging from genuine fear to good-humoured tolerance. Among all who contemplated him, however, there was a measure of bewilderment that such a mixture of incongruities should ever assemble in one man at the same time.

Hyndman, indeed, was a puzzle to his contemporaries, as he has been to many of those who have written about him subsequently. Although he was a convert to the doctrines of Marx, he was a strong believer in the maintenance of the British Empire, and an advocate of heavy expenditure on the Royal Navy. An enthusiast for the most extreme of democratic reforms, he yet prided himself on his own membership of the 'educated classes' and always dressed in an immaculate frock-coat and top hat. Confessing a creed of altruism and brotherly love, he was capable of remarkable vituperation and abuse of those with whom he differed, even if the difference was so slight as to be almost imperceptible to the great mass of his political opponents. Dedicated to the destruction of capitalism, he earned his living and financed his Socialist agitation by speculation in stocks and shares and by company promotion. And towards the end of his long career, with his political ambitions frustrated at every turn, he could yet declare that the greatest satisfaction of his life was being told how unlucky he had been to miss his Blue for cricket at Cambridge.

2

Socialism believes, of course, in the importance of environment rather than heredity: but for all that, perhaps the first thing to appreciate about Hyndman is the character of the inheritance that his family gave him. He was born respectably enough—on 7th March 1842—to the wife of a wealthy merchant, then living at No. 7 Hyde Park Square, in the fashionable West End of London. But it is important to notice that the wealth of the Hyndmans and indeed of his mother's family was derived from enterprise, not in the heart of Britain's commercial empire, but rather at its very frontiers. The Hyndmans originally came from Scotland, but the family had established itself in Ulster in the reign of James I. In the late eighteenth century there was one Hyndman—apparently the great-grandfather of Henry Mayers Hyndman—who was sufficiently radical to become a member of the United Irishmen. With his son Robert Augustus Hyndman, however, the family fortune was made and the radicalism put aside. R. A. Hyndman left Ulster for the West Indies, where he rapidly prospered. By speculating boldly in plantations in Demerara (now British Guiana) just after its cession to Britain at the end of the Napoleonic Wars, he made enough money to become a substantial proprietor on his own account, and the last of his estates remained in his family for two more generations, to be sold eventually by H. M. Hyndman himself.

Not only did the family's wealth come from the West Indies, but many of its members lived and married there. Robert Augustus Hyndman found a bride in the Beckles family, long established on the island of Barbados. His wife was the sister of John Beckles who served as Speaker of the Barbados Assembly for twenty years until his death in 1823. John Beckles was highly esteemed in colonial society and a child of his sister's marriage, born in London in 1812, was named after him. John Beckles Hyndman was educated at

Eton and at Trinity College, Cambridge, and was later
called to the Bar in London. But he also married into a
colonial family, his wife being Caroline Seyliard Mayers,
the daughter of Henry Adams Mayers of Barbados.

Both John Beckles Hyndman and his wife illustrate the
tendency of the West Indian aristocracy to retain close links
with the home country, much closer indeed than was
characteristic of colonists on the American mainland. For
one thing, as there were no good colleges in the Caribbean
colonies, it was customary for wealthy planters to send their
sons to the best educational institutions in England. Thus
Henry Adams Mayers and his brother, John Pollard Mayers,
both went to Cambridge; and Henry Adams Mayers
settled down in England, making his home at Bristol which
had strong commercial ties with the Caribbean. John
Pollard Mayers, however, went back to Barbados and became a member of the island assembly. In 1808, when war
with the United States was imminent, he and John Beckles,
who was also a member of the assembly, took the initiative
in organizing a volunteer corps of loyalists. In 1829 J. P.
Mayers returned 'home' with the appointment of Agent of
Barbados in England. After the 1831 hurricane disaster, he
won praise among the colonists for his 'zealous and laudable
exertions' to obtain relief from the British Government, and
seven years later he was successful in securing the abolition
of a special tax on the colonists.[1]

During this period the Caribbean planters were well
represented in the House of Commons, and one of their
protagonists was John Gladstone, the father of W. E. Gladstone, the future Prime Minister. The 'West Indians'
bitterly opposed the proposals for the abolition of slavery,
although they had to face the opposition of political economists as well as of philanthropists. The parliamentary debates

[1] R. H. Schomburgk, *History of Barbados* (1848), pp. 221, 372, 439, 485;
L. J. Ragatz, *Fall of the Planter Class in the British Caribbean, 1763–1833* (New
York, 1928), pp. 22–23.

on the question were anxiously followed by the planters, and the slaves became restless and sometimes mutinous, thus contributing to the economic decline of the islands. For decline there was: the price of sugar was continually falling, and the planters were running into heavy debts well before the abolition of slavery in 1833. Emancipation was followed in the middle of the century by the advent of free trade, and this finally put an end to their wealth and power. The shrewder of them, including apparently John Beckles Hyndman, had already transferred the bulk of their interest to the home country.

Unfortunately for H. M. Hyndman, however, his father decided to devote most of his fortune to charitable purposes. While still a student at Cambridge he had fallen under the influence of Charles Simeon, the powerful Evangelical who was Vicar of Holy Trinity, Cambridge. In 1836 he decided to set up a fund called 'Miss Catherine Elizabeth Hyndman's Bounty to the Church of England', in memory of his sister, who had lately died. He endowed the fund with some £150,000, which was to be used for the maintenance and extension of the fabric of Anglican churches. His wife, Caroline, was also of religious inclinations, and her brother Henry Mayers, after whom, it appears, H. M. Hyndman was named, took orders in 1846 and later became Rector of Weston in Suffolk.

Only one of Hyndman's grandparents apparently had no West Indian connexions. This was Caroline Seyliard Perkins, his mother's mother, who was a daughter of John Perkins, the owner of Pendell Court, an Elizabethan house at Blechingley in Surrey. When Hyndman was a small boy, he used to stay at Pendell Court, which was then still owned by the Perkins family; and later he recalled a 'nightmare' of his childhood caused by the sight of 'men and women of a new species'—a large number of hungry tramps, perhaps Chartists, who came to demand food and drink at the house one cold day in 1846.[1] In that year Chartist demonstrations

---

[1] H. M. Hyndman, *The Record of an Adventurous Life* (1911), p. 10.

were taking place in many parts of England, and Socialism
was raising its head on the Continent. It was many years,
however, before Hyndman was to make any serious study of
these movements. In his youth he got no further than a
purely personal urge to escape from the stuffy atmosphere
of a conventionally religious Victorian household.

No doubt his childhood would have been much happier
had it not been for the death of his mother in December
1848 when he was only six. All the same, he had already begun to react against the strict régime dictated by his parents'
Simeonite ideas. Like many another Cockney child, his
earliest memories were of feeding the ducks on the Serpentine
and of gazing at the toys on sale at the Soho Bazaar. But he
also recalled his mother's distress at his apparent incapacity
for prayer and pious devotion. He seems to have been a
sensitive yet wilful boy, and his father always found him
difficult to cope with. At the time of his mother's death he
was sent to a boarding school at Headley, near Leatherhead,
Surrey, and thereafter he was constantly being moved from
the care of one private tutor to that of another. He spent
two and a half years with a tutor at Torquay; thence he
was sent to Stockport near Manchester, where he stayed
with a somewhat bibulous clergyman, and had an opportunity to develop some skill at cricket. At the age of sixteen
he heard Ernest Jones, the former Chartist leader speaking
at the Manchester Free Trade Hall, but this event had little
influence on him at the time. Shortly afterwards he made a
trip by himself to the Continent, travelled up the valley of
the Rhine, and stayed at Wiesbaden with an uncle.

The next thing was to prepare for entrance to Cambridge.
The boy spent a further two and a half years receiving
private tuition, this time with a clergyman at Oxburgh in
Norfolk. There he rode to hounds and played cricket, but
also worked hard at mathematics. His tutor, a former Fellow
of Caius, was evidently an able man, and among his fellow
pupils was the future General Sir Frederick Maurice. It

must have been during this period, though when on holiday from Oxburgh, that he played against the great cricketer W. G. Grace, who ran true to form in the match by knocking up 276, partly off Hyndman's bowling. Hyndman was playing for the Gentlemen of Sussex; 'W. G.' for the Gentlemen of Gloucestershire.

In 1861, at the age of nineteen, Hyndman matriculated at Trinity College, his father's college. Here the traditions of academic renown apparently made less impression on him than the fresh opportunities for sport and pleasure. Like many of his contemporaries (who included the Prince of Wales, later King Edward VII), he devoted little of his energies to study. He played cricket, spent much time in idle conviviality and played the flute in the University Orchestra. Strangely enough, probably the only recollections of Hyndman as an undergraduate come from George Meredith, the novelist, who was not a university man himself. They had met in Sussex through a mutual acquaintance, and although Meredith was thirteen or fourteen years older they became close friends. Hyndman invited Meredith to stay with him in his rooms in Rose St., Cambridge, during Newmarket week in May 1864. 'I think of the old days', wrote Meredith over forty years later, 'my visit to Cambridge, your performance on the flute; remembering well the little bit of Beethoven, and your firm stand in the cricket field; some 50!—and the Hauptman duets with my wife at the piano—all as yesterday.'[1]

It was not to be expected that Hyndman's political ideas would develop or change very much at Cambridge. Trinity College, as he later recalled, was 'practically a hot-bed of reaction from the social point of view'; and he shared the view of his friends there that all who were not technically 'gentlemen' were 'cads'.[2] The political tradition of his own family, moreover, was staunchly Conservative. His father

[1] Meredith to Hyndman, 16 Feb. 1908, printed in Hyndman, *Record*, p. 9.
[2] Hyndman, et al., *How I Became a Socialist* (c. 1894), p. 3.

was a member of the Conservative Club, and one of his brothers, Frederick Arthur Hyndman, who went to Oxford, became such an admirer of Disraeli that he later wrote a biographical sketch of his career and reprinted one of his works. A sister, who became a Mrs. D'Albiac, was to be a Dame of the Primrose League.

In the middle 1860's the universities had only just reached the beginning of the era of reform. Liberal ideas were growing popular, however, among some of the younger dons, as also among a section of the undergraduates. Charles Darwin's Theory of Natural Selection, though abhorred by Dr. Whewell, the Master of Trinity, was not without support; George Otto Trevelyan was a leading light at the Union. Hyndman's own tutor, the classical scholar W. G. Clark, was a moderate reformer, and he also attended lectures on political economy by Henry Fawcett. These influences made for some superficial change in his outlook. He became, as he later put it, 'a philosophical radical with a great admiration for John Stuart Mill'.[1] This meant little in practice, however: he was not yet interested in politics, and his new ideas cannot have been much more than a veneer covering a deeply engrained Conservatism.

Hyndman took his degree in 1865, and in the same year was admitted to the Inner Temple and began to read for the Bar. He found the legal profession uncongenial, however; and since the family income was sufficient to enable him to do what he liked, he took little interest in the law but drifted aimlessly through a series of County cricket matches—or, in the winter, whist and billiards. He really was a first-class cricketer, although he missed his Cambridge Blue: he played for the Sussex County Eleven in the years 1863–8. On one occasion he was in the same team as H. G. Wells's father, who was a professional.[2]

In 1866, at the age of twenty-three, Hyndman went off

---

[1] Hyndman, et al., *How I Became a Socialist* (*c.* 1894), p. 3.
[2] Hyndman to Wilshire, 13 Feb. 1902, Wilshire Papers.

to Italy, with no more serious purpose than that of getting acquainted with the land of sunshine and the arts. As it happened, however, his trip coincided with the Italian war for Venice, and because it first aroused his interest in world affairs he later described it as 'the turning-point' of his life.[1] It certainly gave him some experiences which he was to recall vividly throughout his later career.

3

In January 1866 the young man sailed from Marseilles to Leghorn and thence proceeded to Florence, at that time the capital of Italy. From Florence he moved on to Rome, where he was fascinated by living in the 'active past'—under the medieval Papal government of Pius IX. He then went further south to Naples, Salerno, Vietri, and Amalfi. Suddenly in May came the news that Bismarck had provoked war with Austria and that Italy would take advantage of this in order to wrest Venice from Austria. The young traveller, eager to be in the midst of great events, secured himself a job as war correspondent of the *Pall Mall Gazette*, an evening paper of independent Conservative views which had been founded in the previous year.

One of Hyndman's first published letters from Italy appears to have been a note from Naples dated 8th June: in it he described the 'state of general bankruptcy' in the South, which would inevitably hamper Italy's war effort. But he was eager to move to the front, and so he left Naples for Genoa by steamer in the company of some 2,000 Italian soldiers. Arriving at Genoa on 18th June, he reported the great welcome given to Garibaldi, and he then followed the Garibaldian forces in the direction of the Tyrol.[2]

The main Italian army was soon heavily defeated by the Austrians, and Garibaldi himself was wounded; 'that is the

[1] Hyndman, *Record*, p. 26.
[2] *P.M.G.*, 14, 18 June 1866; Hyndman, *Record*, p. 32.

fatal news which seems to have set the world at a standstill', read a dispatch from Lake Garda dated 1st July. However, Austria, having been beaten by the Prussians in the North, offered to cede Venice to Italy through the mediation of France. This proposal to use France as a broker in the deal was resented by the Garibaldini, but the Italian government was not unwilling to accept the offer. Meanwhile, the campaign continued: the Garibaldini took the offensive and on 21st July after a desperate struggle captured the village of Bezzecca, the only victory won by the Italians throughout the whole campaign. The casualties suffered by the volunteers were considerable, and the lack of medical facilities distressed the young war correspondent:

It is monstrous that men should be left to bleed to death for hours without surgical help of any sort . . . and if nobody is made responsible for this carelessness, then for this alone will Garibaldi's campaign of 1866 be a disgrace to the Italian nation. The wounded envied the dead.

After the battle of Bezzecca he visited an emergency hospital in a large church at Storo and helped to tend the wounded Garibaldini awaiting treatment. 'It was not at all the sort of job I liked', he wrote, 'especially as typhoid fever was rife among the injured, and I have a perfect horror of blood and broken bones.' After two hours' work in the church, Hyndman emerged and was at once violently sick. The haunting memory of the 'churchful of shattered human creatures at Storo' was to stay with the young Englishman throughout his life.[1]

In spite of these experiences, Hyndman approved of the aims of Italian nationalism. At the village inn in Storo he met Garibaldi himself and was impressed by the General's 'most unaffected genuineness and frank behaviour'. In August, an armistice was signed, and Italy duly gained Venice through the agency of France. Hyndman now visited several towns in northern Italy and also Trieste and watched

[1] *P.M.G.*, 9, 12, 17, 28 July 1866; Hyndman, *Record*, pp. 36–39.

the entry of the Italian forces into Venice, 'a splendid as well as an historical scene with all the magnificent palaces looking down on the commencement of the new era'.[1]

On his return to England Hyndman decided to make a special study of European nationalism, particularly in the crisis of 1848-9, the Year of Revolutions. His interest in the ill-fated Roman Republic of that year led him to pay several visits to the exiled Mazzini at his humble residence in the Fulham Road, London. In addition, he took the trouble to interview Louis Kossuth, also an exile in London, about his part in the Hungarian Revolution. In spite of these revolutionary contacts, however, he finally gave the stamp of his approval to the parliamentary statecraft of Count Cavour. In 1877, at the age of thirty-five, he wrote an article in the *Fortnightly Review* on Cavour's success in 'the wise application of English methods amid an excitable and far from homogeneous people'. He had come to share Cavour's view that all the conspiracies and insurrections had degraded Italy in the opinion of Europe. He commended the Prime Minister of Piedmont-Sardinia for his decision to participate in the Crimean War, and he blamed Mazzini for having refused to 'sacrifice his long cherished Utopias to the welfare of his country'. Garibaldi, 'the Republican, the devoted follower of Mazzini', was now mentioned merely as 'Dictator of Southern Italy'.[2] In spite of his participation in some of the most stirring events of the Risorgimento, therefore, it was apparent that political opportunism in the end commended itself more to Hyndman than revolutionary bravado.

4

Immediately after his Italian adventure Hyndman returned for a time to his earlier mode of life—his customary round of social entertainments, cricket, and billiards. He

[1] Hyndman, *Record*, pp. 39-48.
[2] Hyndman, 'Cavour', *Fortnightly Review*, n.s. xxii (1 Aug. 1877), 219-43.

was still interested in journalism, however, and had made several new friends in the profession. Among those he met in Italy was Boyd Kinnear, who two years later stood as a Radical candidate for Parliament. Kinnear invited Hyndman to visit him during the contest, which was for the constituency of Fifeshire; and Hyndman appears to have thoroughly enjoyed the 'fierce heckling' and 'well-educated ruffianism' of the electoral campaign. Kinnear was defeated by his Conservative opponent, and blamed the result on 'wholesale bribery and intimidation' by his successful opponent.[1] This was the first General Election after the Second Reform Act; but Hyndman became convinced of the defects of this 'system of pseudo-democracy'—a limited electorate which could still easily be influenced by bribery and by issues which seemed remote from the vital problems of the people.[2]

New horizons were now beckoning to Hyndman, however—or was it simply the old pioneering spirit of his forbears? For by 1868, perhaps under the influence of his Cambridge contemporary Charles Dilke, he had become interested in the problems of Empire. Why should not Britain strive to achieve a closer union with Australia, Canada, and other 'democratic Colonies', just as Italy had accomplished the unification of her component parts in the peninsula? Such was Hyndman's main idea at this time, which also finds expression in Dilke's *Greater Britain*, published in the same year. Early in 1869 on the excuse, genuine or imagined, of an impairment to his health—he was later to be something of a hypochondriac—Hyndman left for Australia in order to see the Empire at first hand. It was a journey which developed his nascent political interest still further—an interest which so far at least was neither intense nor sustained, but likely to be aroused by the experience of seeing new lands and different social systems.

[1] *The Times*, 26 Nov. 1868.   [2] Hyndman, *Record*, pp. 95–97.

II ✦ TORY RADICAL

I

Hᴙᴅᴍᴀɴ arrived at Melbourne after a monotonous voyage of 104 days. He soon went inland and stayed with one of his Trinity friends at Glenormiston, Victoria, where he took part in hunting kangaroo and rounding up cattle. It was while he was staying in the rich district of Camperdown that he observed this vast land being quickly absorbed by squatters or land grabbers with the assent of a legislature which they virtually controlled. At an informal gathering of local squatters, Hyndman ventured to propose the resumption of the land from the large land owners. As yet he had no fine theories about the evils of land monopoly such as Henry George was to develop on the basis of observations in California less than a decade later. He was, however, apparently willing to commit himself to radical political aims. On his return to Melbourne he took a job as leader-writer on the *Argus*, and plunged into local politics in support of free and secular education. But after only a few months of life in Melbourne, and in spite of his liking for the variety of its club and business life, he went on his travels again, in the direction of New South Wales and Queensland.

When he travelled north in Queensland, the climate was so hot and unbearable that he came to the conclusion that the policy of 'White Australia' was untenable and that the northern territory could safely be left to colonization by the Chinese. This was on the eve of the mass immigration of the Chinese to the sugar plantations and goldfields in Queensland,

and there was even talk of a possible invasion by the yellow
race. Hyndman met Charles Pearson, the author of *The
Yellow Danger*; he saw the Chinese working in goldfields
abandoned by white diggers, and later prepared an article,
'Les Chinois hors de la Chine', for the *Revue des Deux Mondes*.
In spite of his view of the dangers of competition by cheap
Asian labour, he seems to have had a high opinion of the
Chinese and their future.

His stay in Sydney was quiet and uneventful except for a
trip to Armadale, where he studied ranching. There followed
a hazardous voyage to Levuka and other ports in the Fijis,
then still under native rule. An old topsail schooner on
board which Hyndman was travelling got caught in a
hurricane while crossing the shark-infested waters, and
narrowly escaped shipwreck. In the Fijis Hyndman witnessed the activities of Wesleyan missionaries propagating
what he described as 'a terribly woe-begone Calvinistic
creed' at the expense of the natives' tribal dances and their
other enjoyments. On the other hand, he formed a high
regard for the Catholic missionaries, who adapted themselves
well to the customs of the inhabitants. He came to know the
Rev. Lorimer Fison, a Wesleyan missionary, on the island
of Viti Levu. Fison was then studying tribal relationships
among the Polynesians in response to an inquiry sent from
the Smithsonian Institute of the United States on the
initiative of Lewis H. Morgan, whose celebrated work,
Ancient Society, was to come out in a few years' time. Hyndman, though interested in what Fison showed him, failed at
the time to understand the significance of the research which
Morgan was then undertaking. Later, when he saw how
much use Engels was able to make of Morgan's work in his
Origin of the Family, his respect for Morgan grew.

Hyndman was always interested in native life. He felt
that Westerners should not despise those whom they took
no pains to understand. He was indignant at the high-
handed manner in which some of the Europeans treated the

natives. In the 1860's, tropical agriculture had been introduced to the South Pacific; just as the establishment of plantations had led to slavery and the slave trade in the West Indies and North America, so the same cause was now producing similar effects in the Pacific—a traffic in hapless Polynesians in order to supply a labour force for the sugar plantations of Queensland and the cotton plantations of Fiji. Hyndman described the recruiting agents in the Fijis as men of 'general loose living, unscrupulous trickery, and frequently downright brutality', but he took a more tolerant view of the trade itself. Indeed, shortly afterwards, he insisted that it was not fair to regard the colonists as responsible for abuses involved in the recruiting of native labour; in any case, such abuses—kidnapping and manslaughter, for instance—were, in his opinion, 'grossly exaggerated'. During the eight months he was in the Fijis, said Hyndman, no British warship visited the islands and if any party was to be blamed it was the British Government for neglecting the task of maintaining order in the South Pacific.[1]

In the autumn of 1870, Hyndman left the Fijis to return to Australia; after a further visit to Sydney and Melbourne, he crossed the Pacific eastwards by way of Auckland and Honolulu, and landed at San Francisco. Thence he travelled through the United States on the Central and Union Pacific Railroads, which had been completed only a few years before. After having satisfied his curiosity for the peculiarities of American life by visiting various 'dangerous dens' in New York in the company of a police detective, he sailed for England on board the liner *Manhattan* and arrived in London in February 1871.

Hyndman returned from the Antipodes with a firm belief in the beneficent mission of Empire. Not long after his return the question of the annexation of Fiji came up again. The islands had been offered to Britain in the 1850's by their native ruler, but the British Government, then weary

[1] *P.M.G.*, 19 June 1871; Hyndman, *Record*, pp. 141, 150.

of fresh responsibility, had refused the offer. Growing disturbances arising out of the labour traffic, however, forced
Britain to annex the islands at last in 1874. 'I cannot but
rejoice', wrote Hyndman at the time, 'that so magnificent an
archipelago has been placed under the British flag. Fiji is
really the key to the South Pacific, and merely as a naval or
coaling station it is worth the partial sacrifice which may be
entailed at first.' He was against 'little Englanders' and
was of the opinion that the policy of refusing annexation was
'utterly untenable for a progressive people such as ours'.
He demanded 'a well-understood and definite policy of
extending the boundaries of the Empire', but not such a
process of reluctant annexation as was forced by 'unscrupulous marauders and enterprising settlers' in the South
Pacific. 'I cannot but think', wrote Hyndman, 'that in the
Pacific, as elsewhere, we ought never to shirk annexation
when it is plain that it will benefit any portion of the empire,
without materially damaging the inhabitants of the country
annexed.'[1]

At the same time, Hyndman's professed Radicalism does
not appear to have been much strengthened by his visit
to the then rapidly developing Australian colonies. We
find a clear indication of his views in his later comments
on the conflict of powers between the two Houses in
Victoria. 'The late troubles in the Assembly seem to be-
token a political collapse as imminent', he wrote in 1876,
'and the 800,000 inhabitants of Victoria bid fair to show
even more conclusively than the larger population of the
United States how great is the danger which a community
runs when it permits the lowest class of voters to have the
entire monopoly of the polling booths.'[2] Thus Hyndman
evidently still regarded the suffrage as a privilege suitably
reserved to the educated upper and middle classes of the
community.

[1] *P.M.G.*, 9 April, 21 Oct. 1874.   [2] Ibid., 15 April 1876.

2

Events in Europe now drew Hyndman's attention, for the Franco-Prussian War had taken place in his absence, and the Paris Commune lived its brief life shortly after his return to London. He had known and loved the French capital since 1858, and he admired the gallant action of its citizens. He 'entirely agreed' with the articles of the English Positivist Frederic Harrison in defence of the Communards,[1] and he may have had some influence in ensuring that the *Pall Mall Gazette* was one of the few London papers which did not express hostility to their struggle. Under its editor Frederick Greenwood, the paper was perhaps more anti-Gladstonian than Conservative; and now and then it allowed, as Hyndman put it, 'free expression to out-and-out democratic opinions'. He himself wrote anonymous articles and criticism for its pages, besides occasional letters signed 'H'. He had a high opinion of Greenwood and shared his hostility to Gladstone. Greenwood was very interested in the politics of Egypt and the Near East, and it was he who suggested to Disraeli that the British Government should buy the four million pounds worth of shares of the Suez Canal Company offered for sale by the spendthrift Khedive Ismail. Hyndman in his own words 'saw the whole of that Suez Canal business very close indeed', and the transaction which was concluded in 1875 and which later proved of great strategical importance seems to have further strengthened Hyndman's interest in imperial problems.[2]

Hyndman had secured election as a Fellow of the Royal Geographical Society, and it was in this capacity that he called attention to what he regarded as the shameful aspects of Henry M. Stanley's work of African exploration. The same strong sympathy with native populations at the mercy

[1] Hyndman, *How I Became a Socialist*, p. 5.
[2] J. W. Robertson Scott, *Story of the Pall Mall Gazette* (1950), pp. 199f., 235; Hyndman, *Record*, pp. 163–4.

of the white man which he had already displayed in the
Pacific came to the fore on this issue. Stanley had been sent
on a second expedition to Central Africa by the proprietors
of the London *Daily Telegraph* and the New York *Herald,* in
order to explore the chain of great lakes. A despatch of his
published in the *Daily Telegraph* in October 1875 told a story
of a three days' battle with the Waturu, and in another
letter published the following month he referred to the
shooting of natives at Bambireh. The *Pall Mall Gazette* of
2nd December published a letter signed 'F.R.G.S.' in
which bitter criticism was expressed of 'the unscrupulous
slaughter of miserable negroes merely for the sake of getting
more quickly from one part of their country to another'.
A few days later the same 'F.R.G.S.' again denounced
Stanley for having 'killed numbers of natives in Central
Africa nominally in the cause of science and Christianity but
really for the sake of personal aggrandisement or for the
benefit of adventurous journalism'. At a meeting of the
Royal Geographical Society held about a year later Hyndman sought to move a resolution condemning Stanley's
methods of dealing with the natives. He was called to order
and silenced by the chairman of the meeting, but he published his resolution in the *Pall Mall Gazette* together with
some extracts from Stanley's letters.

In January 1878, having completed his explorations,
Stanley returned to England and was welcomed by the Royal
Geographical Society at a banquet, at which he replied to
Hyndman's criticisms, which he described as 'almost libel-
lous'. Hyndman responded in a letter to the *Pall Mall Gazette*
in which he said that Stanley had committed such grave
mistakes as 'would tarnish the fame of a Columbus', and
Hyndman and a sympathizer, Colonel Henry Yule, published a joint pamphlet explaining the grounds for protesting
against Stanley's 'system of exploration by private war'.[1]

---

[1] *P.M.G.,* 2, 8 Dec. 1875; 15, 29 Nov. 1876; 11 Feb. 1878; H. M. Hyndman
and H. Yule, *Mr. Henry M. Stanley and the Royal Geographical Society* (1875).

On questions of diplomatic policy, however, Hyndman
found himself more in accord with Conservative opinion.
He was very suspicious of Russia, believing that the most
important issue in foreign affairs was the 'sharp political
struggle between Russia and England . . . as to which should
for the future predominate from the Euphrates Valley to
the China Sea'.[1] At first he regarded China as a possible
ally; and he thought it advisable to reach an agreement
with the Chinese government in order to 'counterbalance
any Muscovite intrigues in Afghanistan'. Later, as China
appeared to have been reconciled to Russia by a compromise on her territorial claims, he favoured the occupation
of Burma by Britain, and a more vigorous policy in the Far
East, because 'it would seem that Pekin at once becomes a
more important centre than Teheran or even Constanti-
nople'.[2] The pro-Russian attitude of Afghanistan Hyndman
regarded as 'openly hostile', and when in 1879 British troops
entered the country, he supported the military action 'for
the safety of the Empire', and bitterly denounced the
Gladstonian anti-imperialist agitation. When two Japanese
ironclads built in Britain sailed for the Pacific, he feared
that these might be used in the interests of Russia.[3]

Hyndman declared that 'the domination of the sea' was
'a necessity' without which Britain could not maintain
adequate food supplies and would experience 'bread riots
of the most dangerous kind'. He emphasized the 'overwhelming importance' of equipping British vessels with
'heavy armour-piercing guns' and of establishing an ex-
tensive system of coaling stations all over the world, because
Russia would tear up the Declaration of Paris and would
seize even neutral shipping in the event of war with Britain.
'Our force in the China seas . . . was quite out of proportion
to the interests we are bound to protect; while in American

[1] *P.M.G.*, 8 July 1878.
[2] Ibid., 13 July 1875, 7 Nov. 1878, 30 April, 30 Sept. 1879.
[3] Ibid., 18 Aug. 1877; 6, 22 March 1878, 13 Sept. 1879, 21 Jan. 1880.

and Australian waters we were and are worse off.' Every
nation in the world, he said, was making serious preparations
for war while Britain was becoming more and more dependent upon foreign countries for its food supply. He went
so far as to declare that if Britain was slow to build a powerful navy 'we might have such an awakening as befell France
in 1870'.[1]

Meanwhile, the Bulgarian atrocities in 1876 had brought
about Gladstone's stormy agitation to chastise 'the unspeakable Turk'. Hyndman thought that 'the desire to
emancipate Christian populations' could never justify any
attempt to support 'the growing and aggressive despotism
of Russia'.[2] When Russia declared war against Turkey
he raised his voice in the *Pall Mall Gazette* and demanded
active intervention by the British Government:

> We cannot afford as a mere matter of business . . . to see
> Russia in possession of Constantinople or mistress of Asia Minor.
> Either would endanger our route to the East. . . . Whenever and
> wherever we go to war to check Russia, whether six months or
> twelve months hence, on the Danube or on the Euphrates, at
> Adrianople or Damascus, we shall do so because we believe it is
> cheaper and better for us in the long run to fight than to let
> matters take their course.[3]

In later articles, however, he took a somewhat less belligerent
line, saying that his ultimate aim was 'to avoid fighting at
all' and that what he had meant in his previous letter was
that the most complete preparation for war would be the best
preventive of it. He was not, however, satisfied with the
'Peace with honour' which Disraeli brought home from the
Congress of Berlin. 'To say that a harbourless, famine-
stricken island like Cyprus makes amends to us for the gains
of Russia is not only untenable but ridiculous', he wrote.
As soon as peace was restored, Hyndman went on to advocate war preparations in order to preserve it; as peace was

---

[1] *P.M.G.*, 13 Dec. 1876, 8 Jan., 6 Aug., 15 Nov., 9 Dec. 1879.
[2] Hyndman, *Record*, p. 180.   [3] *P.M.G.*, 26 April 1877.

'the greatest English interest', he said, 'no effort should be omitted to make war with us an almost hopeless game'.[1]

It will be seen that Hyndman's views as expressed in the *Pall Mall Gazette* were those of a keen advocate of imperial power—keener even than Disraeli. His attitude to the possibility of war with Russia seemed to verge on alarmism. This was a characteristic that was frequently to reappear in his later assessments of the political situation both at home and abroad.

3

Hyndman's family had been closely connected with British rule in India. A Colonel Hyndman, probably his great-grandfather's brother, had fought against the French in Mysore, disarming Reymond's force at the Court of the Nizam of Hyderabad in 1802. Colonel John Perkins Mayers, his uncle, commanded an element of Sir Hugh Rose's column which restored British supremacy in Central India at the time of the Indian Mutiny. 'Blow them from guns! Blow them from guns!' wrote Hyndman after he had become a Socialist: 'How well I remember, as a lad of sixteen, the clamour of the highly civilized people of this island for the wholesale use of that attractive form of capital punishment during and after the Mutiny.'[2] His concern with India at the time was largely motivated by his fear of Russia and her southward advance in Central Asia, but he developed a considerable sympathy for the inhabitants of India and he was even ready to support their nationalist aspirations provided that they did not conflict with the maintenance of British authority.

He came to know Tom Palmer, the Eurasian son of the head of a banking house in Hyderabad, who was then acting as London agent for the Nizam. At Palmer's request, Hyndman in 1875 wrote a pamphlet upholding the claims

[1] *P.M.G.*, 24, 25 May 1877, 13 July, 6 Sept. 1878.
[2] *Justice*, 9 May 1908.

of the Nizam to recover the Berars, provinces which he had
lost to the British in 1853. Hyndman proposed to benefit the
position of the Nizam by putting an end to the levy of troops
which had been forced on him by the British Government
and which had caused him considerable financial difficulties.
He also urged that it was desirable to 'foster a loyalty to the
English Government by opening a career . . . to able
natives'.[1] Hyndman's contact with Palmer and his sympathy
with the Nizam led him to re-examine the whole question
of British rule in India. He began a serious study of Indian
affairs; as he put it, 'Every minute of my spare time was
given to India, and volumes of Blue Books on India filled up
the house'. He came to the conclusion that European administration was inferior to native rule. As a remedy for the
severe famine of 1876–8, he advocated a drastic retrenchment
of Indian government expenditure, and he was particularly
indignant at the British Government's decision to impose the
cost of the Afghan war upon the Indians.[2]

Hyndman was now regarded as an 'Indian reformer'. In
a pamphlet on the famine published in 1877, he declared:
'The natural inclination of free men to make others free . . .
will make itself felt in India.' 'Mankind is not so widely
different even in Asia,' he said, and

a wise, firm, economical and liberal rule may . . . render the
races which are subject to it proud of the Empire. . . . The same
Liberalism which has produced such marvellous results in
Europe should be cautiously introduced into Asia. Such liberal
policy means no connivance at anarchy, no relaxation of order,
no real weakening even of the European leadership which is
absolutely needed, if the population as a whole is ever to be
raised above its present level.

He suggested a series of immediate measures—'a light
permanent taxation'; drastic cuts in the 'frightful waste' of

---

[1] Hyndman, *The Nizam of Hyderabad, Indian Policy and English Justice* (1875),
p. 32.
[2] *P.M.G.*, 20 Dec. 1878, 18 March 1879; Hyndman, *Record*, p. 174.

government expenditure; the employment of more Indians
in the administration; and the development of the country
by private capital from Britain. His conversion to this
attitude, he declared, was based on the belief that 'the truest
and the widest Liberalism' as he understood it was 'the best
Conservatism'.[1]

During the course of his Indian studies, Hyndman came
across *The Poverty of India*, a booklet by the early nationalist
leader Dadabhai Naoroji, who was then living in England.
He made use of Naoroji's statistics to show the low income
level of Indians—'the gaol rate of nourishment' as he called
it in an article entitled 'The Bankruptcy of India', published
in the *Nineteenth Century* of October 1878. 'The famines which
have been devastating India', Hyndman declared, 'are in
the main financial famines.' He maintained that they were
caused by the 'drain' of Indian wealth amounting on an
average to £21,000,000 a year, which he calculated from the
trade figures of the previous twenty years. The remedies he
suggested were similar to those he had proposed in his
pamphlet about Hyderabad. The main line of policy he
advocated was to give the Indian ryots an opportunity to
improve their conditions so that they might become 'our
best customers'.[2] He was very critical of the new taxation
introduced by the Indian government: 'Our present rule in
India,' he said, 'is warranted to perpetuate famines *ad
infinitum*. The spots which bring them about are those in
our administration—not those of the sun.'[3]

Hyndman's article, 'The Bankruptcy of India', attracted
considerable attention, and first brought its author to the
notice of a wide political audience. Several critics attacked
it, however, for its 'exaggerations' and 'inaccuracies'.[4] *The*

[1] Hyndman, *The Indian Famine and the Crisis in India* (1877).
[2] *Nineteenth Century*, iv (Oct. 1878), 585–608. See also his further article in
the same journal, v (March 1879), 443–62.
[3] *P.M.G.*, 16 April, 18 July, 1878.
[4] Thus Erskine Perry in *Nineteenth Century*, John Morley in *Fortnightly Review*,
and Juland Danvers in *Frazer's Magazine* (all of Dec. 1878).

Times maintained that such a 'drain' from India, though 'to some extent economically injurious', was 'inseparable from the conditions of our rule in India', and it taxed Hyndman for his 'short-sighted philanthropy', since native administration, as proposed by Hyndman, would ruin 'our great experiment' by 'corruption, weakness, and oppression'.[1] On the other hand, Hyndman's arguments were welcomed in India and they gave a certain confidence to the Indian nationalist leaders in their struggle against British rule. Many years later an Indian writer could quote extensively from Hyndman's article to show that 'India does pay a tribute, which the Imperialists call compensation for service rendered'.[2] Hyndman was not a trained economist nor a particularly careful scholar, nor had he ever been to India; it should not, therefore, be surprising if inaccuracies or even exaggerations had crept into his figures on the 'drain'. Nevertheless, it was true that British investment in India in this period was not of the sort likely to bring about immediate improvement in the conditions of the bulk of the people; and the Indian trade 'gap' was met by the remittance of bullion, which often had a depressing effect on the Indian economy. In fact, Britain was drawing 'income' from India—perhaps to spend it in the development of other areas of the world.[3]

Hyndman continued to express his views about India in the *Nineteenth Century*. In an article entitled 'Bleeding to Death', he advocated 'a native state administered under British supervision' as an ideal form of government in India under existing circumstances. He strongly recommended decentralization and 'relentless economy' in the Indian government, and his rather narrow obsession with Indian finance was carried so far as to defend the opium trade as an important source of revenue for India. In his opinion, 'Indian opium holds much the same position with respect to

[1] *The Times*, 8 Oct. 1878.
[2] Lajpat Rai, *England's Debt to India* (New York, 1917), p. 102.
[3] L. H. Jenks, *Migration of British Capital* (1938), pp. 225–30.

Library
I.U.P.
Indiana, Pa.

335.42 H 998

C. 1

native Chinese opium that fine French brandy does to
fusel-oil gin'.[1]

Hyndman's discovery of the economic exploitation of
India under British rule was a big step forward in his
evolution towards Socialism: it helped, as he later said, to
prepare his mind to 'accept the true solution'.[2] But it did
not mean that he was any the less of an imperialist: on the
contrary, he now realized the necessity for launching a new
imperial policy—one which had features foreshadowing the
eventual development of the self-governing Commonwealth
of Nations. 'A true imperial policy—which I for one cordially
welcome,' said Hyndman:

> means a constant endeavour on the part of the whole nation to
> secure liberality, welfare, and contentment in every part of the
> British dominions, to knit together the various communities
> under our flag, and to exercise far and wide that continuous
> influence in favour of the principles that have made the greatness
> of this country—justice, freedom, and respect for each one's
> rights.[3]

He firmly believed that the 'natives of India have no desire
to change our rule for that of Russia, even if they could
do so'.[4]

For a while in 1879 Hyndman entertained the possibility
that his reform policy might be adopted by Disraeli's
Government; but the Liberal victory at the General Election
in 1880 dashed all his hopes of immediate reform in India.
This was, he said, 'the saddest disappointment of my life',
and what followed only strengthened his conviction that the
Liberals were worse than the Conservatives in their imperial
policy.[5] Although he broadened the scope of his political
interest in later years, he did not forget the problems of

[1] *Nineteenth Century*, vi (1880), 174n.
[2] Hyndman, *How I Became a Socialist*, p. 6.
[3] *Nineteenth Century*, iv (Oct. 1878), 607.
[4] Hyndman to Naoroji, 17 Oct. 1878, quoted in R. P. Masani, *Dadabhai Naoroji* (1939), p. 198.
[5] Hyndman, *Record*, p. 179.

India, and he found that they provided an inexhaustible fund of material for his later analyses of world affairs.

4

In February 1876, at the age of almost thirty-four, Hyndman married Matilda Ware, the daughter of William Ware of Newick, Sussex, a yeoman farmer. It is not easy to obtain any impression of Mrs. Hyndman's personality or of her influence on her husband, but it seems that they enjoyed a happy married life together. Although she did not bear him a child, she assisted him loyally throughout the ups and downs of his business and political life until her death in 1913. The marriage followed a little over two years after the death of Hyndman's father, from whose remaining wealth his eldest son received a substantial legacy: together with what he had been left by his mother, his fortune amounted to about £21,000. All this effected a change in his attitude to life: now nearing middle age, he was abandoning the leisurely existence of occasional journalism and taking up a new career in business. A photograph of him probably dating from the early 1870's shows that he already had the round face and flowing beard that were to become well known to London political audiences in later years. He was a man of medium height and sturdy build, with a fair complexion and blue eyes.

In 1874 Hyndman in conjunction with a brother, probably Hugh, invested some of their respective inheritances in the mining industry of the American West, and he himself thereafter made several visits to the United States to further their prospects. Since the gold rush of the late forties, the search for mineral wealth had spread into the wide area of the Rockies and the Great Basin. It soon became rare, however, for a man without capital to make his fortune in this way, and the miners' frontier grew more and more into a preserve for mining companies, as capital poured in from

H. M. Hyndman as a young man
(probably 1871)

the East and from across the Atlantic. Hyndman and his brother tried their luck in a Californian mine employing Chinese labour; and he also took an active part in ventures in the Salt Lake Valley of Utah. Towards the end of his life he made an attempt to write a novel based on his personal experiences in Utah; his hero ran away with an American girl who had been living with a Mormon and took her to London, where he fought a parliamentary election in an East End constituency. The story unfortunately was never completed.[1]

The life that Hyndman experienced at the mining frontier was febrile and cosmopolitan: 'at the diggings, college graduates rubbed elbows with illiterates, ministers and rogues worked side by side over sluice boxes, Southern planters swung their picks beside Yankee abolitionists, drunken jailbirds mingled with pious deacons'.[2] For this motley throng Hyndman formed a good deal of respect. 'I know them well', he later wrote, 'I have employed them, and a finer set of men as a whole do not exist.' From the miners' frontier later emerged a militant trade union movement, that of Bill Haywood and his Western Miners' Federation, but at the time when Hyndman was in the West the violence which he met with was mostly occasioned by disputed claims on land. He seems himself to have had difficulty in keeping the peace on his own property in the face of rough-and-ready frontier democracy or what he described as 'equity by revolver'.[3]

Hyndman has left little record of his own financial success or failure in these adventures. The possibilities of vast gain appealed to his gambling instinct: but evidently they were not realized. In May 1873, the *Wall-street Journal* warned British investors against 'another of those "Silver Mines in Utah" which have no silver in them'. In September 1874,

[1] Hyndman in *Daily News*, 23 Feb. 1904; Hyndman, *Record*, pp. 181–6; R. T. Hyndman, *Last Years of H. M. Hyndman*, p. 76.
[2] R. A. Billington, *Westward Expansion* (New York, 1949), p. 620.
[3] H. M. Hyndman, *Further Reminiscences*, pp. 340–1.

the year which saw the beginning of Hyndman's interest in
American mining, the Emma Silver Mining Company of
Utah, which had been worked by English managers and had
been highly successful, went bankrupt, and its failure
attracted wide attention. In July 1880, when Hyndman paid
his last visit to America, Flagstaff Silver Mining, another
British enterprise in Utah, was being wound up. It was
unfortunate for Hyndman that he had no sooner started his
search for mineral wealth than the industry began to suffer
from universal depression. It was stated that out of more than
a hundred mining companies which had been set up in
1870-1 and whose names had appeared in the *Investor's
Monthly Manual*, only ten were in existence in 1880, of which
only five were paying dividends. If the two Hyndmans made
any money out of their ventures in America, it cannot have
been very much.[1]

5

Meanwhile, however, Hyndman was getting more and
more interested in British politics. The growth of agitation
in Ireland—largely due to the agricultural depression—
aroused him to a contemplation of the possibility of home
rule, although at first he had no hesitation in rejecting the
idea. 'Wherein,' he asked, 'is Ireland worse off today than
Scotland in regard to her influence in Parliament?' He
bitterly criticized Parnell, the new leader of the Irish party,
for having 'listen[ed] unmoved to murderous outcries'. He
expanded his views on the question in an article in the
Fortnightly: significantly, his only economic remedy for the
island's ills was a proposal for state-aided emigration.[2]

Hyndman's whole political attitude derived from his conception of the importance of the Empire and of the need for

---

1 Hyndman, *Further Reminiscences*, pp. 181–3; *The Times*, 2 June 1873; R. G.
Raymer, 'Early Mining in Utah', *Pacific Historical Review*, viii (1939), 86–87;
Investor's Monthly Manual, 31 July, 25 Dec. 1880; R. L. Nash, *A Short Inquiry
into the Profitable Nature of Our Investment* (1880), p. 103n.

2 *P.M.G.*, 18 Oct. 1879; *Fortnightly Review*, n.s. xxvii (Feb. 1880), 208–26.

imperial reorganization. Parliament, he thought, should be
thoroughly reformed in order to give representation to the
colonies:

> Englishmen have no more idea of giving up India or the
> colonies than they have of surrendering Ireland to the control of
> Mr. Parnell. . . . To organize satisfactorily any complete scheme
> of general defence, to harmonize the details of a Customs Union
> . . . require that our representatives should be brought more
> directly into contact with the diverse portions of the empire. . . .
> Representatives of India, of Australia, of Canada, of New
> Zealand might give vigour to the now flagging energies of the
> oldest and noblest House of Assembly in the world. . . . People
> have decided once for all that they will have no more of the
> disintegrationist policy of which Mr. Gladstone so unfortunately
> constituted himself the champion.[1]

This passage strikingly anticipates the proposal for an
Imperial Zollvereim that Joseph Chamberlain was to
popularize twenty years later.

When a Dissolution took place in 1880, Hyndman determined to stand for Parliament, and announced his candidature for Marylebone as an independent. The imperial
policy which he had outlined in his writings in the *Pall Mall
Gazette* was given special prominence in his election manifesto, and the 'free Colonies' were now described as 'the
special heritage of our working classes'.[2] Hyndman decided
to seek the support of the 'working classes' in his constituency, and so he approached the Marylebone Radical
Association to ask for its endorsement. He negotiated with
one Joseph Lane, a member of the Association, who had
belonged to the English section of the First International.
'After many conversations,' Lane wrote many years later,

> . . . I told him it was a waste of time to talk to him. Land Nation-
> alization he thought too extreme; was opposed to Home Rule;

[1] *P.M.G.*, 27 Aug. 1879.
[2] *Marylebone Mercury*, 13 March 1880; Lee and Archbold, *Social Democracy in Britain*, pp. 275–6.

on the Suffrage Question he made a remark I have never for-
gotten or forgiven. He asked me if I meant to say that a loafer
at the East End of London was to be placed on an equality with
myself.[1]

This rebuff was serious enough, but a further damaging
blow to his candidature came from Gladstone, himself an
elector in the constituency, who denounced him as a Tory.
At one campaign meeting that he himself held—it was in
St. George's Hall, Langham Place, on 16th March—
Hyndman spoke of 'a really liberal policy at home and the
maintenance of the Empire abroad', but the audience
refused to hear him, seized the platform from Boyd Kinnear,
who was acting as chairman, and passed a resolution in
favour of the two Gladstonian Liberal candidates. This set-
back was too much: and as a result Hyndman felt obliged
to withdraw from the contest.[2] Thus Hyndman's first attempt
to contest a parliamentary election ended in a miserable
failure. Yet the failure was in fact to be the prelude to a
political career which increasingly absorbed his energies
and his wealth.

[1] Joseph Lane, *The Father and Founder of the Modern English Socialist Movement*
(1912).
[2] *Daily News*, 13, 17, 18 March 1880; *Marylebone Mercury*, 20 March 1880.

III ~ FOUNDING THE DEMO-CRATIC FEDERATION 1880-1884

I

By the time when Hyndman approached the Marylebone voters at the 1880 General Election, he had already acquired some knowledge of the Socialist movement on the Continent through certain German acquaintances in London—some of them being the victims of Bismarck's anti-Socialist legislation. He came to know Rudolph Meyer, formerly Bismarck's private secretary, from whom he learned a great deal about the relationship between the German Chancellor and Ferdinand Lassalle, the aristocratic Socialist pioneer. Bismarck and Lassalle had had in common an interest in opposing liberal tendencies and in endeavouring to strengthen the authority of the State; and they had come to some sort of understanding, for a time at least. In 1880 Hyndman's friend George Meredith published *The Tragic Comedian*, a novel based on Lassalle's eventful private life; and this appears to have added to Hyndman's interest in the German Socialist.

Lassalle, who had stirred the German workers to organize themselves into an independent political party, was, as Hyndman remarked, 'essentially a national Socialist, who wished, above all things, to raise the Fatherland to a high level of greatness and glory'. 'This national turn,' said Hyndman:

was . . . a help rather than a hindrance to an agitator who wished to rouse his countrymen from a long and apparently hopeless apathy. He [Lassalle] took up, in fact, the programme of the English social agitators of the Chartist times, and applied it with additions to Germany, hoping to bring about the success of his ideas by peaceful and constitutional means, through the ballot and universal suffrage.[1]

Lassalle had learned Socialism from Marx, but had given it a new twist on matters of practical politics. Hyndman in his turn consciously followed the example set by Lassalle, and learned how to combine Socialist sympathies with patriotic aspirations. He took to the study of the Chartist movement, and shortly afterwards sought counsel both from Marx and from the closest British equivalent of Bismarck—Benjamin Disraeli.

Hyndman met Marx through Karl Hirsch, a veteran German Socialist who in 1878 had founded the Brussels *Laterne,* one of the organs of the German Socialists in exile. Early in 1880 Hirsch took Hyndman to Marx's residence at 41 Maitland Park Road, Haverstock Hill. Hyndman expressed pleasure at meeting the author of *Das Kapital*— which however he had not yet read—and Marx replied that he had read Hyndman's articles on India and had commented on them favourably in his newspaper correspondence. Thus Hyndman made the direct acquaintance of the founder of modern revolutionary Socialism and soon became an occasional visitor at his home.[2] Marx's way of conducting a conversation was to stride up and down the room, talking volubly. He must have been rather taken aback when Hyndman imitated him, parading to and fro on the other side of the room and conversing with equal vigour.[3]

In the summer of 1880 Hyndman's mining interests again took him to America. There still being no English translation of *Das Kapital,* he took with him a French version lent to him by H. A. M. Butler-Johnstone, a friend of his who for

---

[1] Hyndman, *Historical Basis of Socialism* (1883), pp. 417f.
[2] The earliest extant letter from Hyndman to Marx is dated 25 Feb. 1880. See Karl Marx Correspondence.
[3] Hyndman, *Record,* p. 275.

many years had been an independent Conservative M.P.
On board the Cunarder *Algeria* and during his stay at Salt
Lake City, which was his destination, he tackled its 351
pages. The picture of Hyndman among the Mormons
struggling with the Theory of Surplus Value, is a bizarre
one; his thoughts must often have strayed from the future
prospect of the Dictatorship of the Proletariat to the present
behaviour of the Latter Day Saints, among whom the
practice of polygamy still existed. But at all events, he enjoyed his reading: 'I have learned more from its perusal, I
think, than from any other book I ever read', he wrote to
Marx from America, and he also conveyed his impression of
American capitalists—'brutal' and 'half-educated' and with
'no halo of hereditary distinction'.[1] In a letter to John
Morley which was subsequently published in the *Fortnightly*,
he referred to the nascent Socialist movement of the Eastern
cities and to Dennis Kearney's anti-Chinese agitation in
California. All was not well in America, he concluded, and
there was scope for new political beginnings. 'Below the
surface of American politics are grave difficulties', he wrote,
'and such a party as that which sprang up in favour of the
rights of labour would have something to say for itself if
organized aright and on sound principles.'[2]

In October Hyndman returned to England, and resumed
personal contact with Marx. He invited him and his daughter, Eleanor, to dinner more than once at his home in
Devonshire Street. He expounded to him the idea of reviving
the Chartist movement, and found Marx not entirely
sympathetic. One reason for Marx's attitude was that
Hyndman himself did not by any means yet accept the
whole of Marx's ideas. Hyndman could not stomach the
Marxian conception of revolution, preferring instead the
Lassallean idea of constitutional transformation. He had
written to Marx as early as February 1880; 'The object

[1] Hyndman to Marx, 1 Oct. 1880, Karl Marx Correspondence.
[2] *Fortnightly Review*, xxix (1 March 1881), 351.

which I think every Englishman should have is to bring
about the coming mobilization, political and social, without
troublous dangerous conflict.'[1] Marx wrote in one of his
letters to Hyndman (after the latter had read *Das Kapital*):

If you say that you do not share the views of my party for
England I can only reply that that party considers an English
revolution not *necessary*, but—according to historic precedents—
possible. If the unavoidable evolution turn into a revolution, it
would not only be the fault of the ruling classes, but also of the
working class.[2]

To this Hyndman replied:

What you have said and say about the situation here is most
true. Revolution is possible, since the recent foolish action of our
Government in many directions I had almost put probable.
But what I mean is I do not wish to push men on to what must
be violence when they might easily attain their objects by
peaceful action in common.[3]

Hyndman determined to do his best to forestall the threatened revolution. In an article entitled 'The Dawn of a
Revolutionary Epoch' which he published in the *Nineteenth
Century* in January 1881, he pointed to the growth of Socialism in Germany and France, and warned that Britain would
not be immune from the same tendency. 'In some of the giant
northern towns,' he declared, '. . . are all the elements of
the fiercest and, under certain conditions, the most un-
controllable democracy the world has ever seen.'[4] In
America too, he pointed out, 'hatred of the capitalist class is
growing up'. Yet he still felt that the British workers would
not accept 'the subversionary doctrine of the Continental
agitator' so long as constitutional means were open to them.
To ensure that constitutional means were open was in his
view the true object of political action.

---

[1] Hyndman to Marx, 25 Feb. 1880, Karl Marx Correspondence.
[2] Marx to Hyndman, 8 Dec. 1880, quoted in Hyndman, *Record*, p. 283.
[3] Hyndman to Marx, 13 Dec. 1880, Karl Marx Correspondence.
[4] *Nineteenth Century*, xix (1881), p. 14.

In the early spring of 1881 Hyndman made an important further move. He arranged to pay a visit to Disraeli—Lord Beaconsfield as he now was—who, having attained the climax of his career by securing 'Peace with Honour' at Berlin, had retired from active political life. The interview lasted three hours: Hyndman spoke and Disraeli listened. Democratic reorganization of the Empire and 'Peace with Comfort', said Hyndman, could be brought into effect only by the Conservative Party. He elaborated this idea at some length, and the veteran statesman (at least according to Hyndman's account) seemed anxious to draw him out rather than to make comments of his own. Finally, however, he delivered his verdict:

'You can never carry it out with the Conservative party. That is quite certain. Your life would become a burden to you. It is only possible through such a democracy as you speak of. The moment you tried to realize it on our side you would find yourself surrounded by a phalanx of the great families who would thwart you at every turn: they and their women. And you would be no better off on the other side.'

'But this party system,' I rejoined, 'need not go on for ever?'

'No, but private property which you hope to communize, and vested interests which you openly threaten, have a great many to speak up for them still. I do not say it to discourage you, but you have taken upon yourself a very—heavy—work indeed, and' (smiling), 'even now you are not a very young man to have so much zeal and enthusiasm. It is a very difficult country to move, Mr. Hyndman, a very difficult country indeed, and one in which there is more disappointment to be looked for than success. But you do intend to go on?' I said I did. 'Then I shall have the pleasure of seeing you again.'[1]

This, however, was not to be: for Beaconsfield was dead within a few weeks, and Hyndman found himself moving more and more into a position of independence from both major political parties.

[1] Hyndman, *Record*, pp. 244-5.

2

The new Liberal Government which took office in 1880 was soon seriously embarrassed by the Irish question, expecially when it found that the preservation of law and order there necessitated a special measure of coercion. In this situation, Hyndman's views of the Irish question, which had formerly been unionist and imperialist, now began to take more account of the economic aspects of the problem. He began to denounce the tenant evictions as an incitement of civil war,[1] and his sympathy with the poverty-stricken Irish peasantry led him to accept a programme of Irish self-government within the Empire, just as his studies of Indian famine had convinced him of a similar need for India.

The enactment of the Coercion Bill in the winter of 1880–1 was hotly opposed by a small minority of Radical opinion, which felt itself thoroughly estranged from the Government. Two Radical working men, F. W. Soutter and Samuel Bennett, formed an Anti-Coercion Association, which from December 1880 began to issue a small weekly paper, the *Radical*. From its first issue the paper also advocated independent labour representation as a step towards social equality, and its appeal was directed primarily to working-men's associations in the Metropolis. There were various Radical clubs in London—some of them under local denominations but some with titles such as 'The Patriotic', the 'Magna Charta Association', and the 'Manhood Suffrage League'. Hyndman made the acquaintance of these clubs, and also of the Social-Democratic (Rose Street) Club, which had come into existence as a result of the merger of Lassalean and Marxian German Socialists in London. The Rose Street Club had an English section, and one of its active members was a working man called John E. ('Jack') Williams, who was also a member of the Irish Land League. 'It was in the course of this [anti-Coercion] agitation', he later recalled:

[1] *P.M.G.*, 24 July 1880.

that I first met Hyndman at the Rose Street Club. Hyndman first communicated with the English section there with a view to forming a definite Democratic Party. . . . I am bound to say that most of us there were a bit suspicious of him as a middle-class man at first.[1]

Poor Hyndman! His gentlemanly airs were always against him. He persevered, however, and sought to prove his democratic sentiments. An opportunity occurred in January 1881, when the Yorkshire miners went on strike in protest against their employers' practice of making them 'contract out' of the Employers' Liability Act. This strike developed into rioting and necessitated the calling in of troops; and Hyndman in a letter to the *Pall Mall Gazette* took the miners' side, maintaining that the strike was 'in the interests of all England'.[2] To Marx he wrote at the time:

Matters are ripening in the North of England. This weather will push them yet faster. Poor creatures with the pits closed and their children crying for food and warmth! . . . We shall be into revolution before we know it. That indeed is coming but I do want it to come peacefully. I am going to see some of the leaders of the working classes. . . . The movement has begun for which you have so long waited: now it has to be guided to grow.[3]

Looking round for allies, Hyndman approached Joseph Cowen, the Radical M.P. for Newcastle-on-Tyne. Cowen had demonstrated his political independence by opposing his own party on such vital issues as the Eastern Question and Irish Coercion; and as a result he was at loggerheads with the local 'caucus' of Joseph Chamberlain's National Liberal Federation, which tried to force him to relinquish his seat. Cowen accepted Hyndman's invitation, apparently seeing in it the opportunity to form an opposition group to Chamberlain's organization. Cowen's personal popularity

[1] J. E. Williams in *Justice*, 21 July 1894, reprinted in Hyndman and others, *How I Became a Socialist*, p. 39. See also *John E. Williams and the Early History of the S.D.F.* (1886).
[2] *P.M.G.*, 28 Jan. 1881.
[3] Hyndman to Marx, 15 Jan. 1881, Karl Marx Correspondence.

probably enabled Hyndman to win further support for his project. On 28th February he wrote to Marx: 'We are going to try and hold a little conference between the members who have opposed the Coercion Bill and some representative working men. Mr. Cowen and his friends have agreed to this and so have the working men.'[1] On 2nd March, the meeting of which he wrote was duly held. It consisted of representatives of various London clubs, and took place at the Rose Street Club. A resolution was passed urging 'the necessity of the formation of a New Party, the grand object of which should be the direct representation of labour.'[2]

Three days later a second preliminary meeting was held in the more respectable surroundings of the Westminster Palace Hotel, which provided a congenial atmosphere for the middle-class element in the proposed organization, although the representatives of the working men's clubs also attended. Besides Cowen, who was in the chair, and Hyndman himself, there were present several independent Radicals, such as the Positivist, Professor E. S. Beesly of University College, London, who had presided over the inaugural conference of the First International, Henry Crompton, a barrister-at-law and also a Positivist, Dr. G. B. Clark, an active Radical and later M.P. for Caithness, and Lloyd Jones, the veteran Co-operative leader who had been associated with Robert Owen. Hyndman's friend Butler-Johnstone, the former independent Conservative M.P., was also there. Professor Beesly and Lloyd Jones expressed doubt about the immediate prospects of Labour representation; but Hyndman and Dr. Clark stressed the necessity of having 'a centre of organization', and a resolution to this effect, moved, by Butler-Johnstone, was carried *nem. con.*[3] 'Our

---

[1] Hyndman to Marx, 28 Feb. 1881, ibid.
[2] *Radical*, 5 and 12 March 1881; *Echo*, 3 March 1881. For a recent brief account of the preliminary meetings, see Mira Wilkins, 'Non-Socialist Origins of England's First Important Socialist Organization', *International Review of Social History*, iv (1959), 199–207.
[3] *Observer*, 6 March 1881; *Echo*, 7 March 1881.

little meeting last evening was very successful', wrote
Hyndman to Marx.[1]

Hyndman's evidently skilful progress in the negotiations
for forming the new party now, however, began to meet
considerable obstacles. Cowen, whose career had been based
on adherence to 'principles' as against 'organization', did
not appear to be able to accept the emphasis placed upon
organization in the new movement. At the same time,
Hyndman's own attitude was regarded with some suspicion.
On the one hand, many of the Radicals who were hostile
to Conservatism regarded him as 'an ultra Jingo'.[2] On the
other hand, at least one Conservative agent in Labour
circles saw in him a dangerous rival. This was Maltman
Barry, a former member of the First International, who
seems to have been for some time in the pay of the Conservative Party. Barry denounced the 'secrecy and mystery'
about the new movement which in his opinion had become
'the patented monopoly of a limited company'.[3] This was
probably because he himself was kept outside the small
group of sponsors of the new movement.

A third preliminary conference was held at the Westminster Palace Hotel on 19th March. This time Hyndman
was in the chair, and it was evident that a good deal of
middle-class support was already being lost to the movement. Cowen did not attend, and Beesly came apparently
with the sole purpose of foiling Hyndman's efforts. After
considerable discussion, however, the meeting managed to
pass a resolution in favour of a new body, to be called 'The
Democratic Federation', with a programme including adult
suffrage, land nationalization, and legislative independence
for Ireland.[4]

Finally on 8th June the new organization held its inaugural conference at the Memorial Hall in Farringdon

[1] Hyndman to Marx, 6 March 1881, Karl Marx Correspondence. See also
his letter in *Echo*, 7 March 1881.
[2] *Weekly Dispatch*, 12 June 1881.   [3] *Radical*, 12 March 1881.
[4] *Observer*, 20 March 1881; *Daily News*, 21 March 1881.

DH

Street, which nineteen years later was to see the foundation of the Labour Party. Hyndman took the chair, and in his opening speech he deplored the lack of harmony among the various Radical bodies. The absence of Cowen who pleaded the necessity of his attending a celebration in Newcastle in honour of George Stephenson, the railway pioneer, gave point to his remarks. Many of those who were present seemed to have merely sectional issues to promote. Helen Taylor, the step-daughter of John Stuart Mill, and Herbert Burrows, a civil servant in the Excise Department, who were both prominent Radicals, spoke in favour of women's suffrage; Justin McCarthy, the Irish Nationalist M.P., pleaded for Irish Home Rule. Hyndman was reported to have bitterly opposed 'such disloyalty' as the suggestion that the abolition of the hereditary monarchy should be an item of the new body's programme. It was almost certainly on his initiative, however, that the conference declared in favour of 'federal Parliaments' and 'an Imperial Parliament' which would include representatives of the colonies.[1]

The Democratic Federation was thus launched under middle-class leadership. The *Radical*, the organ of the working men's clubs in London, warned against 'the corrupting element of patronage' which this involved—presumably referring in particular to the fact that Hyndman seemed prepared to finance the organization.[2] It was more than a month later that the paper published the 'Object' and 'Programme' of the Federation, which read as follows:

OBJECT. To unite the various organizations of Democrats and workers throughout Great Britain and Ireland for the purpose of securing equal rights for all, and forming a centre of organization in times of political excitement. To agitate for the ultimate adoption of the programme of the Federation. To aid all social and political movements in the direction of these reforms.

[1] *Manchester Guardian*, 9 June 1881; *P.M.G.*, 9 June 1881; *Reynolds's Newspaper*, 12 June 1881; *Weekly Dispatch*, 12 June 1881.
[2] *Radical*, 11 June 1881.

PROGRAMME.

1. Adult Suffrage.
2. Triennial Parliaments.
3. Equal Electoral Districts.
4. Payment of Members and Official Expenses out of the Rates.
5. Bribery, Treating, and Corrupt Practices, to be made acts of Felony.
6. Abolition of the House of Lords as a Legislative Body.
7. Legislative Independence for Ireland.
8. National and Federal Parliaments.
9. Nationalization of the Land.[1]

The first four points were a reminder of the Chartists, for with the exception of the substitution of 'triennial' for 'annual' Parliaments, they were the four remaining points of the Charter which had not yet been enacted.

Hyndman elaborated his own views by distributing to each of the delegates at the inaugural conference a copy of a book he had written entitled *The Text-book of Democracy: England for All*. The book contained, as he said, a fuller exposition of the political views which he had put to Disraeli.[2] The Empire was to be reorganized on the basis of decentralization and self-government except for matters such as imperial defence and customs. In two chapters dealing with labour and capital Hyndman made an attempt to summarize Marx's *Capital*, and for this he made an acknowledgment of his indebtedness to 'a great thinker and original writer'— whom he did not name. His reform programme, however, was mainly political, and he was doubtful about the immediate expediency of nationalization even of the land. On the one hand he appealed to the working men of Britain and Ireland to unite; but on the other hand he still had his hopes of the 'truer patriotism' of the upper classes: 'If reforms are to be peaceful those who are rich and powerful must lead the way.' His conclusion ran: 'We, perhaps, alone among the peoples can carry out with peace, order, and contentment those changes which Continental revolutionists

[1] *Radical*, 16 July 1881.   [2] Hyndman, *Record*, p. 248.

have sought through anarchy and bloodshed.'[1] In short, Hyndman's *England for All* was a text-book of English 'Tory Democracy' rather than of Continental Social Democracy; and Marx's theory of Surplus Value seemed merely an intrusion.

As we have seen, Hyndman had kept Marx informed of the progress of the earlier negotiations for the new party; but Marx had nevertheless formed an unfavourable impression of his new disciple. In April he wrote to his daughter Jenny:

> Yesterday . . . an invasion from Hyndman and spouse, who both have too much staying power. I don't dislike the wife, for she has a brusque unconventional and decided way of thinking and speaking, but it is funny to see how admiringly her eyes fasten upon the lips of her self-satisfied garrulous husband.[2]

This may have been Hyndman's last visit to Marx, for their extant correspondence concludes at this point. Some time after the publication of *England for All*, Marx privately criticized Hyndman for not mentioning his name in the book. 'Vis-à-vis myself', he wrote to Sorge:

> The fellow wrote stupid letters of excuse, for instance that 'the English don't like to be taught by foreigners', that 'my name was so much detested', etc. With all that, his little book—so far as it pilfers the *Capital*—makes good propaganda, although the man is a weak vessel, and very far from having the patience —the first condition of learning anything—of studying a matter thoroughly.[3]

Engels, it seems, was even more emphatic in disavowing Hyndman whom he regarded as an 'ambitious . . . ex-Conservative'. Although Hyndman sought to make his acquaintance, they did not meet, for Engels preferred to avoid contact. This led Hyndman to suspect that Engels

---

[1] Hyndman, *England for All* (1881), pp. 31, 194.
[2] Marx to Jenny, 11 April 1881, K. Marx and F. Engels, *Correspondence 1846–1895* (1934), p. 389.
[3] Marx to Sorge, 15 Dec. 1881, Marx and Engels, *Correspondence*, p. 397.

might be afraid of him as a rival in the financial patronage of Marx.[1]

Engels had been an occasional contributor to the *Labour Standard*, a weekly newspaper sponsored by George Shipton of the London Trades Council. Although this paper ignored the foundation of the Democratic Federation, in July it published an anonymous article by Engels advocating an independent working men's party.[2] The idea was occurring simultaneously to various people at the time; and Hyndman's efforts to organize Radical opinion independently of the Liberals were not unique. A 'Democratic League of Great Britain and Ireland' was set up at Manchester in April 1881, and a group of 'Social Democrats' meeting at Hamilton in Lanarkshire in June resolved to form a 'Scottish Labour Party' with a programme including the 'nationalization of the means of industrial production'.[3] One of the secretaries of the latter body was a young man called Robert Banner, who was converted to Socialism by an Austrian *émigré* in Edinburgh called Andreas Scheu. Engels was in contact with Scheu, and thus had reason to believe that Hyndman was not the only possible founder of a British Socialist organization.

Hyndman still hoped to establish contact with Engels, and when in 1881 Hyndman republished a lecture of Thomas Spence, the eighteenth-century radical, on land nationalization, together with properly acknowledged quotations from Marx, he sent a copy to Engels. The latter, however, replied rather tartly: 'I shall be very happy to make your personal acquaintance as soon as you shall have set yourself right with my friend Marx whom I see you can now afford to quote.'[4] But they never did become formally acquainted.

[1] Engels to E. Bernstein, 3 May 1882, *Marx and Engels on Britain* (Moscow, 1953), p. 514; Hyndman to Engels, n.d. (June or July? 1880), Engels Correspondence; Hyndman, *Record*, p. 279.

[2] *Labour Standard*, 25 July 1881, reprinted in *Marx and Engels on Britain*, pp. 479f.

[3] *Labour Standard*, 18 July 1881.

[4] Engels to Hyndman, n.d., Engels Correspondence.

Although Marx died in 1883, Engels remained hostile, and his attempts to establish a Marxian Socialist movement in Britain in opposition to Hyndman were to continue for more than a decade, almost until his own death in 1895.

3

As yet, however, the Democratic Federation was in no way committed to Marxism. During its first year of existence, the Irish question continued to overshadow all other issues. At the inaugural conference, the Rev. Harold Rylett, a member of the Irish Land League, had invited the new body to send delegates to Ireland. Accordingly a deputation including Hyndman went across St. George's Channel, and on its return it published a report on the condition of the Irish peasantry. In October Parnell was arrested and imprisoned in Kilmainham gaol, and the Irish Land League, having replied to this by issuing a 'No Rent' manifesto, was immediately suppressed by the Government. On 23rd October the Federation held a special open-air meeting—its first—in Hyde Park. Hyndman defended the Land League as follows,

> This Land League of Ireland is a perfectly legal trade union.
> . . . But the Landlords' League and the Emergency Committee have 40,000 English bayonets and 13,000 armed police to push evictions. . . . The Government have overthrown the Constitution, and resorted to revolutionary measures. The people have but one weapon left—a passive and orderly resistance to the exaction of rent.[1]

Hyndman himself had joined the Irish Land League, and when the National Land League of Great Britain was formed he served as a member—the only English member—of its executive. When a further Coercion Act was passed after the Phoenix Park murders in 1882 a second Hyde Park demonstration was held by the Federation on 11th June, and it was apparently a considerable success, the attendance being

[1] *Radical*, 29 Oct. 1881.

estimated at nearly 30,000.[1] All the same, Hyndman was
obliged to admit the following year that 'this confounded
affair about the Phoenix Park murders has thrown back all
movements terribly as far as surface action goes'.[2]

The Irish agitation of the Federation brought Hyndman
into close contact with Henry George, the American author
of the stirring radical work *Progress and Poverty*. In the autumn
of 1881 George had visited Ireland to propagate his gospel
of the 'Single Tax on Land'. Early in the following year he
travelled on to London where he stayed with Hyndman for
a month and, as a recent biographer says, 'experienced
for the first time a very expensive way of living'. Hyndman
seemed 'hopeful of converting Mr. George to his views'
while George 'thought Socialism in his friend was weakening'.[3] Both were wrong: but they had much in common on
immediate policy. In February George sent an account of
an interview with Hyndman to the *Irish World* of New York
in which Hyndman was reported to have said:

I regret . . . that the Irish leaders did not boldly declare, in
opposition to the trimming policy of the Government, that the
Nationalization of the Land of Ireland, under the administration
of direct representatives of the Irish people, is, and can be, the
only real solution of the Irish Land Question.[4]

It was under George's inspiration that Hyndman dug out
and republished the work on land nationalization by Spence.

Hyndman, however, soon felt obliged to state his differences with the doctrine of Henry George. In an article on
'Coercion and Revolution' he said:

Mr. Henry George . . . has himself, as I venture to think,
misapprehended the crucial problems of our industrial system.
More nationalization of the land by itself would benefit the
workers of a country very little. . . . Dr. Karl Marx . . . shows

[1] *Radical*, 17 June 1882; *Reynolds's Newspaper*, 18 June 1882.
[2] Hyndman to Henry George, 14 March 1883, George Papers.
[3] C. A. Barker, *Henry George* (New York, 1955), p. 356; Henry George, Jr.,
Life of Henry George (1900), p. 368.
[4] *Irish World*, 18 March 1882.

clearly that the capitalist class rob the working class by means of
the surplus value . . . more than the landlord class do by their
monopoly of land.[1]

In spite of these differences, he remained on better personal terms with George than with Marx. They kept up a
correspondence, with Hyndman every now and then in-
sinuating a phrase about the evils of capitalism. In March
1883 after a bomb had exploded in a Whitehall office,
Hyndman wrote:

Last night the great explosion in Westminster occurred of
which you will have heard by telegram. . . . I do not approve
of these unorganized anarchist attempts. Still, when the capitalist
and landlord class perpetually use force it is absurd for them to
cry out against the use of force. . . . This is a class war and
horrible bloodshed will come of it anyhow.[2]

In 1884 George again came over to Britain and toured the
whole country advocating his doctrine of 'the land for the
people'. In January 1885, shortly before his departure, he
again met Hyndman, but both of them had to recognize
that there was no more room for alliance between the Single-
Tax policy and Socialism.[3] Four years later when Hyndman
and George met in a debate held in St. James's Hall,
Hyndman denounced his former ally as a reactionary,
maintaining that the revenue from the Single Tax, if
introduced, would go into the hands of the capitalists.[4]

If the Irish agitation had brought the Democratic Federation to notice, however, it had also frightened away some of
its supporters who were Gladstonians. In September 1881
a by-election took place in Tyrone, an Irish county constituency, and there were candidates both of the Liberal
Party and of the Land League, as well as of the Conservative

---

[1] *Radical*, 15 April 1882.
[2] Hyndman to George, 16 March 1883, George Papers.
[3] See their 'dialogue' on 'Socialism and Rent-Appropriation', *Nineteenth
Century*, xvii (Feb. 1885), 369–80.
[4] A verbatim report was published under the title, *Single Tax and Social-
Democracy*.

Party. The Federation at once set up an election committee, with Hyndman as chairman, to assist the Land League candidate. Parnell was naturally active in the same cause, denouncing the Liberal Government's policy towards Ireland. The Liberal candidate, however, declared himself to be an opponent of coercion, and consequently a local Tenant-right Association decided to support him. This did not deter Hyndman's committee from issuing a manifesto criticizing 'the hollowness and hypocrisy of capitalist Radicalism'. As a result all Radical working men's clubs which had been affiliated to the Federation immediately withdrew from it in protest, with the single exception of the Stratford Radical Club.[1] Shortly after the election, Hyndman wrote to Helen Taylor:

The fight has begun. The Liberal wirepullers, specially paid for that purpose, are at work taking the Clubs from us. . . . For my part I have thrown in my lot with the Federation finally. . . . Charles Murray and all the old '48 men are heartily with us. . . . The Irish, too, we could fully rely upon if only they could shake off their religionism a little. . . . The only hope for the workers is to nail the 'no compromise' flag to the mast.[2]

Thus the Federation was reduced to a small middle-class group largely deprived of the support of working men. Prince Kropotkin who visited London in the autumn of 1881 observed in his memoirs:

The only active outspoken representatives of the socialist movement were Mr. and Mrs. Hyndman, with a very few workers grouped round them. They had held . . . a small congress, and we used to say jokingly—but it was very nearly true—that Mrs. Hyndman had received all the congress in her house.[3]

As for Engels, it was probably with some satisfaction that

[1] *Justice*, 4 Aug. 1884. For the Tyrone election, see *The Times*, 22 Aug.–9 Sept. 1881; the voting result was: Dickson (L) 3,168, Knox (C) 3,084, Rylett 907.
[2] Hyndman to Helen Taylor, 2 Oct. 1881, Mill-Taylor Correspondence. Charles Murray and his brother James were former Chartists.
[3] P. Kropotkin, *Memoirs of a Revolutionary* (1908), p. 412.

he was able to report that the Federation at this time appeared to be 'of no account whatever'.[1]

4

The setback caused by the 'Tyrone Manifesto', however, led to fresh attempts at organization on the part of the little party's leaders. The 'Democratic League of Great Britain and Ireland', the Manchester group already mentioned, was 'captured' by the concerted effort of Hyndman, Burrows, and Helen Taylor, and became affiliated to the Federation in May 1882. By the time of the Federation's first annual conference on 31st May, it had succeeded in organizing six provincial groups—at Manchester, Liverpool, Edinburgh, Glasgow, Nottingham, and Dulwich. All the same, there seemed to be little activity by the branches, and it looked as if the organization was in decline. Hyndman, however, remained optimistic about the prospects and the work that the Federation could do for the Empire. Writing to Naoroji, the Indian nationalist, he said:

Nothing can be done for India unless we have a revolution here. . . . The mass of the people here are in a deplorable state and worse, I sometimes think, than your starving ryots and famished labourers of Bombay and Madras—for they have at least the sun.[2]

Towards the end of the year the Federation began to win some new recruits, not indeed from 'the mass of the people', but from some young professional men attracted to politics by Henry George's propaganda. One of them was J. L. Joynes, a master at Eton, who visited Ireland with George in 1881, and with him was arrested by the authorities. He lost his job at Eton after publishing an account of this episode, and subsequently became even more extreme in his

---

[1] Engels to Bernstein, 3 May 1882, *Marx and Engels on Britain*, p. 513.
[2] Hyndman to Naoroji, 2 Aug. 1882, Masani, *Naoroji*, pp. 200–1.

views.[1] Another new recruit was H. H. Champion, an invalided Royal Artillery officer, who had served in the Afghan war and had been converted to Socialism by reading both Henry George and Marx. These two, together with R. P. B. Frost, an old school friend of Champion's at Marlborough, were instrumental in June 1883 in founding the *Christian Socialist*, which declared itself to be the monthly organ of the Land Reform Union. This paper nominally supported Henry George, but was in fact largely at the service of the Federation.

In the winter of 1882–3 the Federation won two still more notable recruits—Ernest Belfort Bax and William Morris. Bax had been a journalist in Germany, and had studied music and philosophy there; he had read *Das Kapital* as early as 1879. In 1881 (while still in his twenties) he published an article on Socialism and then studies of Wagner, Hegel, and Marx in a journal called *Modern Thought*. His article on Marx was highly praised by Marx himself on the ground that it 'stands up against Brit. Philistinism'.[2] Unfortunately, his writings were generally found too abstruse and dull for popular taste. William Morris, already well known as a designer and poet, was a specially important acquisition for the Federation. Besides being twenty years older than Bax—he was now forty-eight—he also had a completely contrasting turn of mind: in him the artist predominated over the intellectual, and he later admitted that he 'suffered agonies of confusion of the brain over reading the pure economics' of *Das Kapital*, though he enjoyed its historical parts. Converted emotionally rather than by reason, he found in the Federation an outlet for his 'hatred of modern civilization'.[3]

Meanwhile, as we have seen, the Federation's working-class support had become very limited. The only organized

[1] J. L. Joynes, *Adventures of a Tourist in Ireland* (1882).
[2] *Modern Thought*, Dec. 1881; Marx to Sorge, 15 Dec. 1881, Marx and Engels, *Correspondence*, p. 398.
[3] Morris in Hyndman *et al.*, *How I Became a Socialist*, p. 18.

group of working men still affiliated was the Stratford Radical Club. Towards the end of 1881 this group changed its name to the 'Labour Emancipation League' and adopted a Socialist programme calling for the collectivization of the means of production and the establishment of 'a National Citizen Force'. Its leader was Joseph Lane, who had already shown suspicion of Hyndman, and had attended an International Anarchist Congress held in London in 1881.

In spite of the heterogeneity of its membership, it was clear that the Federation was at least making its way towards a definite Socialist programme, though the details of such a programme might cause disagreements. Early in 1883 Hyndman gave six lectures on 'Practical Proposals for Pressing Needs' at the Federation's headquarters. These proposals were incorporated in a declaration of principles adopted at the second annual conference held in June, which was then published in a pamphlet entitled *Socialism Made Plain*. The nationalization of the means of production and distribution was for the first time adopted as a plank of the Federation's programme. At the same time the manifesto advocated the immediate adoption of what Hyndman called 'stepping stones to a happier period': better housing for artisans and agricultural labourers, free compulsory education for all classes together with free meals for children, an eight-hour day, cumulative taxation, state appropriation of railways, national banks, abolition of the national debt, nationalization of the land, and 'organization of agricultural and industrial armies under State control on co-operative principles'. The statement was signed by the members of the new executive including Hyndman (Chairman), Morris (Treasurer), Champion (Hon. Secretary), Burrows, Helen Taylor, the Austrian *émigré* Andreas Scheu, Joynes, Jack Williams, the old Chartist James Murray, and James Macdonald, a West End tailor.

The adoption of the manifesto led to the resignation of

almost all the remaining non-Socialist members including
Dr. G. B. Clark. Meanwhile, the working-class element of
the Federation was being strengthened by a few new recruits. Two were of exceptional ability: Harry Quelch,
an unskilled labourer with a 'heavy and gloomy' manner[1]
who nevertheless, had distinct literary gifts and became quite
proficient in the French language; and John Burns, a
working engineer who soon became an outstanding speaker
and a leader of public agitation. The programme, of course,
failed to satisfy everybody: and the members inclined to
anarchism were critical of Hyndman's 'stepping stones',
which would involve parliamentary politics and political
opportunism. Nevertheless, the Federation had now become
an avowedly Socialist body and this helped to give it a
certain distinctive character.

Hyndman meanwhile, energetically carried on with his
propaganda. In November 1883 he published a book entitled *The Historical Basis of Socialism in England*, and this
time he took care to acknowledge his debt to 'the famous
German historical school of political economy headed by
Karl Marx'. A chapter dealing with 'International Labour
Movements', however, showed that the author was still
under the influence of his conception of imperialism. 'To
my mind,' he said, 'we have to base the first real Socialistic
combination upon the common interests and affinities of the
great Celto-Teutonic peoples in America, in Australia, in
these islands, and possibly in Germany.' He also declared:
'I am quite content to bear the reproach of Chauvinism in
regard to what I say about the English-speaking and
Teutonic peoples.'[2] There had thus been little change in
Hyndman's political views since he had written *England for
All*.

[1] Bax's comments in his introduction to Harry Quelch, *Literary Remains*
(1914) p. 13.
[2] Hyndman, *Historical Basis*, pp. 194n, 433.

5

The next step for the Federation was the publication of a regular journal. Providentially, there appeared a donation of £300 from Edward Carpenter, a former Cambridge don who had given up his fellowship to live the simple life in a cottage near Sheffield, where he wrote verse in the style of Walt Whitman. Hyndman and his colleagues used the money to start a weekly paper, which they called *Justice* and subtitled 'Organ of the Social Democracy'. Its first number appeared on 19th January 1884, and within a few weeks Hyndman became its editor. The paper was soon placed under a boycott by the wholesale newsagents, and the members of the Federation were obliged to organize its sale themselves. Led personally by Hyndman, they began to sell copies in the streets. Carrying bundles of the paper they paraded through Ludgate Circus, Fleet Street, and the Strand, calling out '*Justice*, the organ of Social Democracy, one penny!' Jack Williams who took part in this unusual demonstration, wrote many years later:

There was Hyndman, in his immaculate frock coat and high hat; there was Morris, dressed in his usual blue serge suit and soft hat; Joynes in his aesthetic dress; Champion looking every inch the military man; Frost looking every inch the aristocrat; Quelch and myself in our everyday working clothes. I am sure we made an impression on that day.[1]

The policy of *Justice*, as stated in its first number, was to support the Socialist movement in Britain by declaring its independence from existing parties and by rejecting the personal influence of Gladstone, Chamberlain, and Churchill. The manifesto pointed out that there were two sides to the Federation's domestic propaganda: one was to preach discontent among the workers, and the other was to show the educated classes that Socialism had a scientific basis and was striving to put an end to the existing anarchy.[2]

[1] *Justice*, 15 Jan. 1914.   [2] Ibid., 19 Jan. 1884.

Hyndman had already been trying hard to convert the middle classes to his views. In various writings he bitterly criticized what he regarded as the hypocrisy of philanthropists such as Samuel Smith and Octavia Hill.[1] A few journals, in particular, the *St. James's Gazette* and the *Pall Mall Gazette*, provided space for his observations. In the former he wrote a brief summary of *Das Kapital*, and when Marx died in March 1883 he contributed an obituary. In the *Pall Mall Gazette*—edited by John Morley and then by W. T. Stead, in place of Greenwood, whose hostility to Gladstone had annoyed the proprietor—he published a list of proposed reforms under the title of 'Revolutionary Socialism'.[2] On 30th January 1884, he visited Oxford and gave a talk on 'Constructive Socialism' at a meeting of the Russell Club, a society of Radical undergraduates. On 5th February he appeared at a debate of the Cambridge Union Society to propose a motion in favour of Collectivism. On both occasions his audience was largely hostile, but it was at least significant that for the first time Marxian Socialism was being publicly advocated at the two major universities.[3]

This Socialist propaganda naturally did not pass without critical comment. Herbert Spencer and Charles Bradlaugh, two formidable protagonists of individualism, launched counter-attacks upon Hyndman's views. In an article dealing with the Federation's manifesto, 'Socialism Made Plain', Spencer declared that 'All Socialism involves slavery'. In reply to this Hyndman wrote a pamphlet in which he retorted that Spencer ignored 'the palpable slavery' under capitalism.[4] Moreover, Hyndman suggested that many of Spencer's own arguments, derived from the theory of evolution, led to conclusions in support of Socialism. Bradlaugh was a more formidable opponent, if only

[1] See, for instance, Hyndman's pamphlet, *Socialism v. Smithism* (1883).
[2] *St. James's Gazette*, 18 Jan., 19 March 1883; *P.M.G.*, 29 Oct. 1883.
[3] *Oxford Magazine*, 6 Feb. 1884; *Cambridge Review*, 6 Feb. 1884.
[4] H. Spencer, 'The Coming Slavery', *Contemporary Review*, xlv (April 1884), pp. 461–82; Hyndman, *Socialism and Slavery* (1884), p. 6.

because of his oratorical ability and popularity with London audiences. He gave four lectures at the Hall of Science, London, in order to 'define and confute German, French, Russian, Italian, American, and English Socialism', and he also accepted a challenge from the Federation to debate with Hyndman at St. James's Hall on 17th April 1884. Bradlaugh was clearly a more skilful speaker than Hyndman, and it was generally agreed that after two hours' debate the champion of individualism had won the day. But Hyndman and his supporters had no reason to regret the engagement. Bradlaugh's great popularity and his willingness to discuss Socialism inevitably brought Socialist ideas to a wider public, and the result was that several well-known followers of Bradlaugh including Mrs. Annie Besant began to take an interest in the new movement.[1]

It must have been comparatively easy to acquaint the reading public of the educated classes with some at least of the principles of Socialism. Many vehicles of propaganda were available—lectures in public halls, newspaper correspondence columns, and articles in magazines. Most of the leaders of the Federation were themselves of the educated classes, and could address their equals in their own language. To win support among the working class, however, required a different method of agitation, and would have proved exceptionally difficult for the leaders of the Federation had it not been for the state of trade in the middle eighties. Although there had been a recovery from the deepest depression of the previous decade, by 1884 the country was again entering a period of slump, and sporadic strikes against wage-cuts were reported in a number of inductrial centres. Here was an opportunity for the Federation to take advantage of.

In February 1884 Joynes, Williams, and Macdonald were commissioned to go to Blackburn and work among the

---

[1] See the verbatim report of the debate, *Will Socialism Benefit the English People?* (1884); *Justice*, 19 April, 1884.

weavers, who were on strike. Then in the summer, when the miners in Staffordshire and Worcestershire struck against wage-cuts, Herbert Burrows went to the scene to assist their cause. Hyndman also visited these two centres of discontent, and the result was that branches of the Federation were formed, one at Blackburn and several among the Midland miners. In September, the Federation issued a manifesto to the trade unions, calling on them to join 'the Socialist party' while emphasizing the uselessness of isolated strike action: 'Until the time comes—and it is coming—when strikes can be organized and universal throughout not one country but many, it is wiser for the workers to suffer, to protest and to remember.'[1]

Although the mid-Victorian prosperity had come to an end, the 'Great Depression' with its falling prices seemed, theoretically at least, to have a favourable impact on the conditions of the workers. At a meeting of the Statistical Society in November 1883, Robert Giffen of the Board of Trade delivered an address on 'The Progress of the Working Classes in the last half-century' and drew an optimistic conclusion as to the improvement in their circumstances. Hyndman did not agree: he admitted that the position of the 'aristocracy of labour' was better than it had been, though subject to the uncertainties of employment; but the 'fringe of labour' had greatly increased, and 'never in my memory was the misery among the very poor so serious as it is today'.[2]

Hyndman's attitude to the 'aristocracy of labour' was a hostile one, and because it was only this 'aristocracy' which was yet organized in trade unions, he saw little future for the working classes as a whole within the existing trade union movement. Furthermore, he believed at this time in the Lassallean 'iron law of wages', which maintained that under Capitalism any increase in the wages of a section of the working classes would be at the expense of the other sections. In recent years, Marxist writers have criticized Hyndman

[1] *Justice*, 6 Sept. 1884.   [2] *The Times*, 23 Nov. 1883.

for the rigidity of his views on this question.[1] The criticism has some justification; but Hyndman must not be credited with too much theoretical consistency. At other times he would grant the possibility of a general increase in workers' wages 'if only they would combine'; and he was prepared to allow the possibility that 'the trade unions will lead the way'.[2]

Further, Hyndman never opposed the adoption of 'palliative' reforms, as some Socialists did, on the grounds that they would mollify the workers and so delay the revolution. For him, they were 'stepping stones' leading in the right direction. In June 1884 he spoke at Regent's Park on the necessity of the eight-hour day; and he emphasized that the shorter working week was 'most immediately important'.[3] He often talked about an imminent revolution, but he did not propose to initiate it himself. It is true that in an article entitled 'The Revolution of To-day' published in the first number of To-day, a Socialist magazine, Hyndman predicted that the date of 1889, the centenary of the French Revolution would be celebrated as the dawn of the Socialist revolution. Less sanguine leaders of the Federation did not agree, and Bax referred to the idea as 'a surmize' for which the Socialists as a whole should not be held responsible. But in fact, Hyndman's fixing of the date in this way was simply a mixture of optimism and expediency, for the sake of propaganda. He had not really altered his view that the type of revolution he really wanted was a peaceful revolution through Parliament. At a meeting in Sheffield in June 1884 he declared himself 'a Socialist unarmed with revolvers or any other dynamite than mental dynamite'.[4] He was no advocate of force for the solution of domestic political problems; and it was only the unexpected events of the following two years which were to make him, for a time at least, hope for a sudden violent revolution as a short cut to Socialism.

[1] Dona Torr, Tom Mann and his Times (1956), p. 213; E. P. Thompson, William Morris (1955), p. 390.
[2] Justice, 15 March, 5 July 1884.   [3] Ibid., 28 June, 5 July 1884.
[4] Ibid., 7 June 1884.

IV ~ RIOTS AND RUCTIONS

I

As the Democratic Federation transformed itself into a Socialist body, differences of opinion over Socialist tactics soon divided its leaders. On the one hand was a 'right' which believed in some sort of parliamentary action; on the other hand was a 'left' which favoured a peaceful 'social agitation', aimed, however, at a genuine revolution in the future. The words 'right' and 'left' were not used at the time: but they afford a convenient classification for what were in reality two distinct tendencies.

The leader of the 'right' was, of course, Hyndman himself. He naturally took cognisance of the growing agitation for franchise reform—the extension of the household suffrage to the counties—which was then being conducted under the active leadership of Joseph Chamberlain. Although the Federation held no demonstration of its own, it took advantage of a big franchise rally of Radical and Liberal working men held in Hyde Park on 21st July 1884. Hyndman, Champion, Burns, and Williams addressed the crowd, which had really come to hear the Liberal trade union leaders, Henry Broadhurst and Joseph Arch. Some of the Socialists of the 'left', however, took little interest in the franchise agitation: J. L. Mahon, a young engineering apprentice from Scotland, insisted that the key to political power was property and argued that even under adult suffrage, the propertied classes would be 'at the horses' heads'.[1]

[1] *Justice*, 15 Nov. 1884.

The 'left' opposition to Hyndman soon began to make its strength felt inside the Federation, for it contained such prominent members as Morris, Scheu, and Joseph Lane of the Labour Emancipation League. At the annual conference of the Federation held in August 1884, it was readily decided to change the name to 'Social-Democratic Federation' (S.D.F.). Lane, however, caused disagreement by demanding that the programme of his Labour Emancipation League should be adopted as the party programme. To this there were certain objections from the 'right', but Scheu managed to persuade the conference to accept Lane's demand in principle. A committee was set up consisting of Lane, Bax, Morris, and Champion; and these four men drafted a new party programme which, as Morris triumphantly pointed out, was 'not parliamentary'.[1] It was identical with the programme of the Labour Emancipation League except in details of phraseology, and it eliminated the purely political reforms in the earlier programme of the Democratic Federation, such as payment of members and proportional representation. The 'left' felt that it had thus won the first round of its struggle against Hyndman's leadership.

Another point at issue was Hyndman's attitude towards foreign policy. The Federation had been united in condemning the British occupation of Egypt. Morris and Hyndman wrote a joint article in which they denounced the military operation as 'the Bondholders' *Battue*'. But the despatch of General Gordon to Khartoum to suppress a Sudanese revolt and his precarious situation in the besieged town enlisted Hyndman's patriotic sympathies. He felt, as most Englishmen did, that every effort not even excluding a further military campaign should be made to relieve the beleaguered outpost. Bax, however, protested against the sudden appearance of 'the old Adam of Jingoism' in Hyndman, and a weekly meeting of the Federation unanimously

[1] Morris to Scheu, 13 Aug. 1884, P. Henderson (ed.), *Letters of William Morris* (1950), p. 211.

adopted a motion proposed by Morris opposing any new expedition 'under the pretence of rescuing General Gordon'.[1]

Meanwhile, an attempt to restore the links between different European Socialist parties intensified the difference between the 'right' and 'left' of the Federation. The French Socialists, who had recovered from the set-back caused by the failure of the Paris Commune, had been attempting to hold an international conference, but there was a split in their own party between the revolutionary Marxists led by Jules Guesde and Paul Lafargue, Marx's son-in-law, and the Possibilists under Paul Brousse, who were not averse to an alliance with 'bourgeois' political groups in order to secure immediate reforms. Early in 1884 when the Guesdists held an annual congress of their own at Roubaix, the Federation sent Bax and Quelch as fraternal delegates. The congress accepted a proposal from the Federation to hold an international conference in London in 1885. In July, however, the Belgian Socialists, who were closer to the Possibilists in their outlook than to the Marxists, intimated their desire to hold the proposed international congress of 1885 at Antwerp. Bax, who was more or less the spokesman of the Marx-Engels family group inside the Federation, urged resistance to the Belgian suggestion, although Hyndman favoured it. Hyndman had on his side a Socialist journalist called Adolph Smith Headingly, who had long been a personal enemy of Marx and Engels, and who was in close touch with the French Possibilists. Hyndman published in *Justice* a letter from Headingly criticizing the Marxist influence, 'the authoritative domination of a clique, a family circle' as he put it, in international Socialism.[2] In August 1885 Headingly represented the Federation at the Antwerp conference, at which the Belgian Labour Party was formed. The projected London conference, however, was never held.

[1] *Justice*, 26 Jan., 9 Feb., 10, 17 March, 24 May 1884.
[2] Ibid., 27 Dec. 1884.

These differences over Socialist tactics, foreign policy, and
international co-operation widened the schism between the
'left' and the 'right'. But the dispute also had its personal
side. As we have seen, Hyndman and Headingly had been
at odds with Marx and Engels, and the differences remained
after Marx's death. Hyndman refused to speak at a meeting
arranged to take place at Marx's grave in 1884; and when
in the same year Engels published *Der Ursprung der Familie*
Hyndman remarked that as Marx and Engels had objected
to Hyndman's *England for All*, an abstract of *Das Kapital*,
Engels ought to have been the first man to criticize his own
work which, according to Hyndman, was merely an abstract
of Morgan's *Ancient Society* with some additions. There was a
rumour that Hyndman himself was busy translating *Das
Kapital*. An authorized translation undertaken by Samuel
Moore, a friend of Marx and Engels, had been delayed, and
in order to beat Hyndman to it, Edward Aveling, who was
the lover of Marx's daughter Eleanor, was adopted as a co-
translator under Engels's supervision. Their translation
appeared in 1887, but *To-day*, then under the editorship of
Hyndman, had already started serializing a translation of
the first ten chapters by 'John Broadhouse' (Hyndman
himself) from the 'original' which was probably in fact the
French edition.[1]

Hyndman's quarrel with Engels accounted for much of his
distrust of Aveling, although there were plenty of other
grounds for this. A Doctor of Science (London), Aveling had
been Vice-President of Bradlaugh's National Secular Society.
Equipped with a considerable intellect and fluency, he was
a man without recognizable principle. In 1884 he was
accused by Bradlaugh of causing 'irregularities' in the
accounts of the National Secular Society; and Hyndman
accordingly sought to raise the question of his suitability for
membership of the executive of the S.D.F., to which he had

---

[1] *To-day*, Oct. 1885–May 1889; Engels to Laura Lafargue, 18 April 1884,
15 March 1886, *Correspondance Engels-Lafargue* (Paris, 1956), i, 192–3, 342.

been elected.[1] Engels, on the other hand, was committed to the defence of the man who was virtually Marx's son-in-law.

The mutual animosity between Hyndman and Engels was, however, also due in part to political differences. 'Mr. Hyndman, whenever he could do so with impunity, has endeavoured to set Englishmen against "foreigners" ', wrote Eleanor Marx to Wilhelm Liebknecht.[2] There was, of course, some truth in this, although at the same time, if the Federation was to be a success as a new political party it had to look for British rather than cosmopolitan support. But Andreas Scheu regarded Hyndman as a 'chauvinist', and Morris, who had co-operated with Hyndman in the preparation of the *Summary of the Principles of Socialism* and also in lecture trips to Oxford and Cambridge, was now coming round to agree with this view. The similarity in their occupations—for Scheu was a furniture designer—may also account for the ease with which these two saw eye to eye on political questions.

Thus there was a rising tide of criticism, both political and personal, against Hyndman's leadership. But the opposition was not united; in fact, there were at least three groups among the critics of the 'left'. There was Joseph Lane and his anti-political Labour Emancipation League, in which anarchist influence was steadily growing; there was the faction led by Bax and Aveling, supported from outside by Engels and representing the Marx–Engels family group; and finally there were those associated with Morris and Scheu. All, however, were agreed that Hyndman as the editor of *Justice* and chairman of the Federation had obtained dictatorial powers and was pursuing what Scheu called 'persönlich Machtpolitik'.[3] In 1884 Hyndman gave added weight to this view by buying *To-day*, a little monthly

---

[1] Morris to Scheu, 8, 13 Sept. 1884, Scheu Papers.
[2] E. Marx to W. Liebknecht, 12 Jan. 1885, E. Marx correspondence.
[3] A. Scheu, *Umsturzkeime*, iii (Vienna, 1923), p. 57.

which Bax had been editing, and assuming control of it. 'Hyndman is thinking to buy up all the little movement here', wrote Engels to Kautsky in June.[1]

2

It was no novelty for Hyndman to be putting a lot of money into the Federation's activities. At its foundation he had to pay the rent of the Federation's headquarters and the £2-a-week salary of its first secretary. 'But that very fact cripples me in the chair', he wrote to Helen Taylor: 'Any strong action would appear like an attempt on the strength of mere money help—an idea most repugnant to me.'[2] In fact, however, there was plenty of strong action by Hyndman. *Justice* was founded, as we have seen, with the help of a generous donation from Edward Carpenter, and Hyndman was only one of the three registered owners of the paper, the other two being William Morris and Jonathan Taylor of Sheffield (presumably a nominee of Carpenter's). Moreover, it was Morris who either directly or indirectly paid the weekly loss of the paper. Yet Hyndman, as its editor, was in a position to dictate the day-to-day policy of the Federation. He dealt rudely with Helen Taylor herself: he criticized her devotion to the London School Board, 'that feeble middle-class body' as he put it, and wrote a censorious letter to her telling her that it was her 'duty' to work solely with the Federation. 'As to *Justice*', he continued:

. . . mistakes have been made possibly: we are human, all of us; but you yourself cannot deny that no journal since you ever had anything to do with politics has done so much good, set so many people thinking as *Justice* has done during the last six months. . . . There are people around us that I dislike, and have good reason to dislike, more than you do. But in such a life's work as this we must take bad and good together. . . . The future is too glorious to be associated with meanness of any kind.[3]

[1] Engels to Kautsky, 22 June 1884, *Labour Monthly*, xv (Oct. 1933), 645.
[2] Hyndman to Helen Taylor, 16 Oct. (1881 ?), Mill-Taylor Correspondence.
[3] Hyndman to Helen Taylor, 25 July 1884, ibid.

Helen Taylor replied by describing Hyndman's letter as 'hopelessly arrogant' and by telling him that he was conducting *Justice* 'in a manner to make it an engine of public demoralization' owing to its anonymous attacks on those whom he did not like.[1]

At a meeting of the Federation held in January 1884, Hyndman pointed out that the Federation had no permanent President and that he was merely the chairman of the executive council, subject to annual re-election, holding a position the main purpose of which was to preserve continuity in business. His opponents such as Lane and Scheu, however, maintained that his 'personal Presidency' gave him domination of the Federation. At an executive meeting held in the summer, Morris, who took the chair in the absence of Hyndman, was compelled to remonstrate against the repeated attacks on Hyndman. At this point Morris was attempting to play the part of 'a moderator and patcher up' of the conflicting influences inside the Federation. At one angry moment he wrote that he could not trust Hyndman any longer, but he soon put aside his resentment and decided that 'the days of personal dictation' were over.[2]

Morris's policy was not without effect at first: in September Hyndman appeared to have agreed to some concessions —the chairmanship was to be by rotation, and his wife was to withdraw from the executive of which she had been a member. Morris wrote to Scheu: 'There is no appearance at present of the risk of our falling under personal rule: therefore it would be a great mistake to try to break up the Federation for there is no definite cause of quarrel.'[3] Moreover, it was Hyndman's supporters who seemed to be doing the real work. Bernard Shaw observed in a letter to Scheu that he himself had been put off joining the Federation by

[1] Helen Taylor to Hyndman, n.d., ibid.
[2] Morris to Scheu, 18 July, 13, 28 Aug. 1884, Henderson, *Letters of Morris*, pp. 203-4, 210, 212; Mackail, *William Morris* (World's Classics ed. 1950), ii, pp. 117, 133.
[3] Morris to Scheu, 28 Sept. 1884, Scheu Papers.

Hyndman's 'stories of capitalist greed and oppression', and
suggested that

But for Frost and Champion, who, though nominally Hyndmanites, practically boss the Federation between them by
sticking together and working (they have kicked up a flourishing
agitation at the east end) the whole body would have gone to
pieces long ago. . . . Morris, now that you are no longer at his
elbow, wanders along between Hyndman and Aveling rather
uncertainly.[1]

In the meantime the centre of the dispute was shifted to
Scotland where Scheu had set up a semi-independent body
called the Scottish Land and Labour League. Scheu had
founded the League in Edinburgh, but he was anxious to
spread its influence to other towns, especially Glasgow. He
pressed Moses McGibbon, a Glasgow Socialist, to co-operate
with him, but he was too late: Hyndman had already got in
touch with McGibbon and arranged to speak in Glasgow.
Hyndman's visit (on 1st December 1884) led to the formation
of a Glasgow branch of the S.D.F. with W. J. Nairn, a
staunch supporter, as its secretary.[2] Two days later Hyndman appeared in Edinburgh where he spoke on the 'Progress
of Socialism'. In reporting Hyndman's speech Scheu made
special reference to the emphasis he had placed on revolution
not by force but by 'gentle persuasion'.[3] Meanwhile,
Scheu's Scottish League sent a delegation to Glasgow with
a view to arriving at some understanding. To frustrate this,
Hyndman sent a letter to McGibbon dated 9th December,
in which Scheu (according to his own account) was severely
criticized.[4] Morris who had seen the work of the Scottish
League at first hand when he had been in Edinburgh in
November was now determined to support Scheu in his

[1] Shaw to Scheu, 26 Oct. 1884, Scheu Papers.
[2] *Justice*, 8, 15 Nov., 6 Dec. 1884; B. Glasier, *William Morris and the Early
Days of the Socialist Movement* (1921), pp. 29, 33. Glasier was wrong about the
date of Hyndman's visit. E. P. Thompson who relies on him puts it in October
and consequently gives a rather exaggerated picture of what he calls Hyndman's 'intrigue'. E. P. Thompson, *William Morris* (1955), pp. 407ff.
[3] *Justice*, 13 Dec. 1884.   [4] Scheu, op. cit., p. 60.

struggle with Hyndman. As the Glasgow branch was reluctant to come in line with the League, Morris paid a flying visit again to Edinburgh on 14th December, and on the following day he attended a meeting of the Glasgow Socialists with the hope of arbitrating between Edinburgh and Glasgow. At this meeting, however, a letter from Hyndman attacking Scheu was read, and Morris was heckled by Nairn on his knowledge of Marxian economics which he was forced to admit was rudimentary.[1]

The struggle now centred around *Justice*, the symbol of Hyndman's 'autocratic' rule. Hyndman, for his part, was willing to have Morris terminate his regular subsidy of the paper, which he had initiated in his capacity as Treasurer of the Federation, provided that he (Hyndman) could retain editorial control. But he firmly rejected a demand from the Avelings for the editorship to be placed under the control of the executive. 'I don't believe in a committee being placed in control of a newspaper,' he said. 'I wouldn't go to sea with a council in command of a ship.'[2]

By now the elements of the 'left' had become increasingly united in their exasperation with Hyndman, and nine out of the nineteen members of the executive formed a hostile front against him under the leadership of Morris. They availed themselves of an opportunity for attack at a meeting on 16th December. A Hyndmanite motion to expel W. J. Clark, a member of the 'left', on the ground of his being an anarchist was defeated by 9 to 7. Hyndman's letter to Glasgow, already mentioned, was also discussed. Every one of the 'left' members who were there criticized Hyndman; Morris spoke (according to his own account) 'temperately'; but the issue was in the open, and the 'left' had as its clear purpose 'the shaking off of Hyndman'. Morris was putting 'spur into the Aveling's side . . . by telling him one or two

[1] Morris to J. A. Morris, 14 Dec. 1884, Morris to R. Thompson, 1 Jan. 1885, Henderson, *Letters of Morris*, pp. 219, 227; Glasier, op. cit., p. 32.
[2] *Daily News*, 13 Jan. 1885; Hyndman to Morris, 27 Nov., 8 Dec. 1884, B.M. Add. MSS. 45345.

things he doesn't know'.[1] On the 18th the 'cabal' as Morris called his opposition group met at the Avelings' house and decided to ask Scheu to come down to London in order to appear in person at a renewed executive meeting on 23rd December. Scheu did so, and on the 23rd a vote of confidence in him and of no confidence in Hyndman was hotly discussed. The meeting adjourned for four days without decision. On the following day (Christmas Eve) Morris wrote:

As Hyndman considers the S.D.F. his property, let him take it and make what he can of it, and try if he can really make up a bogie of it to frighten the Government, which I really think is about all his scheme; and we will begin again quite clean-handed to try the more humdrum method of quiet propaganda.[2]

It appears that the 'left' decision to withdraw from the Federation was taken about this time, while Scheu was still in London. As we have seen, Scheu, having his organization in Scotland, had been in favour of secession, though Bax seems to have held that the 'left' should capture control of the Federation. This might have been practicable, as the opposition had won over J. Cooper, a member of the executive who had been wavering between Hyndman and Morris, and had thus secured a bare majority on the executive council.[3] At the adjourned meeting on 27th December, the motion of confidence in Scheu and no confidence in Hyndman was carried by 10 votes to 8. Hyndman did not vote, but Quelch, who was in the chair, was allowed to take his side. At the close of the meeting the ten 'left' members of the executive—the Avelings, Robert Banner, Bax, W. J. Clark, Cooper, Lane, Mahon, S. Mainwaring, and Morris —issued a statement announcing their resignation and criticizing Hyndman's 'arbitrary rule'. The group had already decided to launch a new Socialist paper, the

---

[1] Morris to Scheu, 18 Dec. 1884, Henderson, *Letters of Morris*, pp. 220-1.
[2] Morris to Mrs. Burne-Jones, 24 Dec. 1884, ibid., pp. 222-3.
[3] Morris to Scheu, 28 Dec. 1884, ibid., pp. 224-5.

Commonweal; and on 30th December they founded a new organization, the Socialist League. On the same day the nine remaining members of the executive—Burns, Burrows, Champion, Frost, Mrs. Hicks, Hyndman, J. Murray, Harry Quelch, and Williams—issued a counter-statement denying the accusations against Hyndman and calling a general meeting of the S.D.F. to discuss the whole matter.[1]

At this general meeting, which was held on 22nd January, the Hyndmanites dominated the proceedings, although Morris was present. John Burns spoke up warmly, saying that the whole thing was 'an organized attack on H. M. Hyndman, who at least had shown some sincerity for Socialist principles, by advocating them at street corners on sixty-six consecutive Sundays'. He declared that the majority of the executive had resigned 'because they were afraid of the members'. Jack Williams and Helen Taylor both expressed criticism of Aveling. The meeting adopted a resolution proposed by James Macdonald declaring that the charges of 'absolutism, Jingoism and political opportunism' brought out against Hyndman were 'unworthy of the consideration of all men who had at heart the emancipation of labour.'[2]

With the formation of the League, the internal dispute came to an end. The Socialist League took away from the Federation the two branches organized and run by Morris at Merton Abbey and Hammersmith, and also the Leeds branch and Robert Banner's branch at Woolwich (where the young Scot had now settled). The Labour Emancipation League and the Scottish Land and Labour League also detached themselves. For some time the Socialist League seemed to be a formidable rival to the S.D.F., but it was always a little weaker in membership. Towards the end of the decade, however, it was disrupted by disagreements between Marxists and anarchists, and when the former were defeated and withdrew in 1888, it fell entirely into the hands of the

[1] Ibid.; *Justice*, 3 Jan. 1885.　　　　[2] *Justice*, 31 Jan. 1885.

anarchists, and thus ceased to divide the very limited
strength of Marxism in Britain.

3

The split was a hard blow both to the S.D.F. and to
Hyndman. Morris, who had provided generous financial
support as well as the prestige of his name, had now gone;
and even on a basis of counting heads, any sizeable loss of
membership (which had been estimated at only 500 in
December 1884)[1] must have depressed those who were
dreaming of a mass Socialist party. *Justice* received the worst
damage from the split, for it suffered the competition of the
much more attractive *Commonweal*. The weekly loss of £10
on its publication could henceforth be covered only by
extraordinary self-sacrifice on the part of the remaining
members of the Federation. Assistance came from compositors of the Modern Press, which was owned by Champ-
pion. Champion had introduced an eight-hour day there,
and some of his workers, impressed by this liberality, now
offered to work overtime without payment. Helen Taylor
provided an old press, and Hyndman himself worked with
the compositors setting 'stereo' in a dingy basement. A
'*Justice* Distribution Corps' again paraded in the London
streets. An impressive appeal for support for the paper was
signed by ninety-four working men including twenty
compositors.[2]

Yet the Federation was still by no means predominantly a
working-class organization. The departure of the 'left'
brought it closer to the Fabian Society, a little group of
young intellectuals, which had come into existence in January 1884, and which had declared the Federation 'worthy
of sympathy and support'.[3] There was little difference of

[1] Morris quoted in a letter from Engels to Bernstein, 29 Dec. 1884, E.
Bernstein, *Briefe von Engels* (Berlin 1925), p. 161.
[2] *Justice*, 25 April 1885.
[3] E. R. Pease, *History of the Fabian Society* (1916), p. 38.

policy between the Federation and the Society, which had not yet worked out constitutional ideas. Hubert Bland, his wife Edith (E. Nesbit, the novelist and writer of children's books), Frederick Keddell, and a few other Fabians had joined the S.D.F. and they mostly kept up their allegiance throughout the turbulent days of the split. John Hunter Watts, also a Fabian, became Treasurer of the Federation in place of Morris. He presided at an 'extraordinary' conference of the S.D.F. held in April 1885, at which it was decided to restore the old political programme of the Democratic Federation and to 'take political action in whatever way circumstances may suggest'. 'With a political programme,' declared Hyndman, 'we develop into a party.'[1]

The Federation had other opportunities to express its views in co-operation with other bodies. In January 1885 it sent three working men—Burns, Williams, and Macdonald —as delegates to the 'Industrial Remuneration Conference' held in London in January 1885, at which the problems of industry and poverty was discussed by leading economists and representatives of various political and labour organizations. About the same time a vigorous campaign for free speech began in Dod Street in the East End, where the police had decided to remove an established speakers' pitch. Several S.D.F. speakers in turn were arrested. 'We are stopped from speaking because of our opinions', wrote Hyndman in the *Standard*, a Radical paper.[2] Metropolitan Radical clubs as well as the Socialist League and the Fabian Society readily co-operated with the S.D.F. in the fight for free speech. A successful joint demonstration of the Federation and of the League was held in Dod Street on 27th September, but the campaign ended in a petty quarrel between the two bodies over priority in speaking.[3]

In November 1885 the Socialists faced the opportunity of a general election, which was fought on a new extended franchise. In view of their numerical weakness, Hyndman

[1] *Justice*, 11 April 1885. [2] *Standard*, 9 Sept. 1885. [3] *Justice*, 17 Oct. 1885.

and his colleagues did not expect to make much impact on
the voters unless they secured non-Socialist allies. Hyndman
himself would have been quite happy to split the Liberal
Party so that the Radicals would have been forced to join up
with the Socialists.[1] The disadvantages of fighting without
Radical support were shown clearly by the result of the
London School Board election, which preceded the General
Election. Three S.D.F. candidates had polled 4,301 votes
between them, but Burrows, who though an S.D.F. member,
was put up by the Tower Hamlets Radical Club, alone
received 4,232 votes. There was, however, a possibility of
securing help from another quarter. In October, *Justice*
published a letter from Maltman Barry, who was evidently
working for the Conservatives:

> The Irish party will return to St. Stephen's 80 or 90 strong.
> They will sit astride the Parliamentary beam, a foot in each
> scale, prepared and able to compel compliance with their just
> demands. Does the spectacle not rouse the ambition and stir
> the emulation of Socialists? . . . Seize the opportunity while it
> is within your grasp.[2]

Shortly afterwards Champion came to an executive meeting
with an offer of money, the source of which was not disclosed, to finance S.D.F. candidatures. The proposal was
accepted 'for consideration' only at first, but a cheque for
£340 from Barry was cashed by Champion and the money
given to Hunter Watts, the Federation's Treasurer. The
S.D.F. had already arranged a candidature by John Burns
of Nottingham; it now hastily put up two candidates in
London, Jack Williams at Hampstead and John Fielding at
Kennington. Hyndman and Champion went off to Birmingham to try to persuade Chamberlain to secure the withdrawal of Liberal and Radical opposition from these two
constituencies. Hyndman also suggested to Chamberlain
that John Bright be withdrawn from Birmingham so that

[1] *Justice*, 14 Nov. 1885.   [2] Ibid., 17 Oct. 1885.

Hyndman himself could stand against Randolph Churchill.[1] Chamberlain rejected these proposals, probably fully realizing the electoral weakness of the S.D.F. He was justified in the outcome: for the Federation's London candidates polled only 27 votes in Hampstead and 32 in Kennington, although John Burns fared distinctly better at Nottingham with 598 votes.

These miserable totals did not provide the full extent of the Federation's discomfiture: it was soon under attack from various quarters for its acceptance of 'Tory Gold'. The details were first disclosed by Hunter Watts in a letter published in the *Pall Mall Gazette*.[2] The Fabians were particularly disgusted. 'Out of our wonderful show of 50–70–80 or a hundred thousand men at Dod St.,' said Bernard Shaw:

the polling has proved that not a hundred were Socialists. The Federation are convicted of offering to sell their fictitious numbers to the highest bidder (in money, not in reforms). The [Socialist] League have no feeling in the matter except one of gratified spite at the disgrace of their rivals. All England is satisfied that we are a paltry handful of blackguards.[3]

Hyndman and his colleagues issued a statement defending their action on the grounds that the election campaign was merely propagandist and that the source of its finance was not a matter for the concern of the membership—as Hyndman put it in the cynical words of the Emperor Vespasian, *'pecunia non olet'*. But there was much criticism from within the Federation, and Jack Williams, one of the defeated candidates, declared, 'We cannot trust the middle-class men of our movement any longer.'[4] The executive council, now condemned by the rank and file, was replaced by a general council, a larger body consisting of branch representatives. The losses to the party caused by the 'Tory Gold' affair were almost as serious as those caused by the split in

[1] Shaw to Scheu, 14 Dec. 1885, Scheu Papers; H. H. Sparling to Scheu, 8 Dec. 1885, Socialist League Papers.
[2] *P.M.G.*, 4 Dec. 1885. [3] Shaw to Scheu, 14 Dec. 1885, Scheu Papers.
[4] *P.M.G.*, 5 Dec. 1885; *Justice*, 12 Dec. 1885.

FH

the previous year. A general meeting of the Federation held
on 10th January 1886 could do little to allay the feeling of
resentment among the members. As their number dropped,
the size of *Justice* had to be reduced. Nearly all the Fabians
who had joined the S.D.F. withdrew, though one, Frederick
Keddell, later became Treasurer of the Federation. Several
leading members who were advocates of political action—
but not on Hyndman's terms—withdrew from the S.D.F.
and formed yet another organization, the Socialist Union,
with a monthly journal of its own, the *Socialist*. Its most
prominent members were James Macdonald, the West End
tailor, and C. L. Fitzgerald, a retired Army officer. The
S.D.F. Bristol branch, of which Ramsay MacDonald, the
future Labour Prime Minister, was a very junior member,
also seceded from the national body, renamed itself the
Bristol Socialist Society, and threw in its lot with the
Socialist Union. The Union itself, however, was unable to
maintain its precarious existence as a small centre group
between the S.D.F. and the Socialist League. Early in the
following year it quietly disappeared from the scene, though
the Bristol Socialist Society continued in existence as an
independent body. It was not long before James Macdonald
was back in the ranks of the Federation.

4

As a result of the election 'scandal' of 1885 the policy of
political action lost support even among the parliamentary
Socialists of the S.D.F. Indeed, the swing of the pendulum
had gone too far to the 'right'. But the reverse of its course
was equally disconcerting. The S.D.F. seized upon an
unexpected opportunity for agitation among the workers,
occasioned by a sharp increase in the number of the unemployed. This new policy and its implications inevitably
brought in its train fresh dissensions among the members of
the Federation.

During the winter of 1885–6, the S.D.F. branches in London were active in organizing demonstrations of the unemployed. A procession of men out of work was jeered at by some members of the Reform Club as it passed through Pall Mall, and Hyndman declared in *Justice* that 'vows of vengeance were registered after such treatment'.[1] On 8th February, later to be known as 'Black Monday'—it was only two days after the appearance of Hyndman's article—the famous West End Riot took place. The S.D.F. took advantage of a meeting of the unemployed in Trafalgar Square called by the Fair Trade League, whose remedy for unemployment was the introduction of tariffs. Before the Fair Trade meeting was due to begin John Burns addressed the crowd, and drew off several thousand people to the north side of the Square. Here the Federation held its own meeting, in the course of which there were several speeches including what *The Times* described as 'a violent harangue' from Hyndman.[2] A resolution was put and carried demanding the absorption of the unemployed by useful public works, especially housing, and by the shortening of hours of transport workers. A considerable crowd then marched down Pall Mall with Burns in the lead waving a little red flag. Again there was the appearance of jeering from the Reform Club, and retaliation began in earnest. The crowd smashed the windows of several clubs on the way including the New University Club, from which Hyndman had shortly before been expelled. Even worse, a number of shops were looted as the crowd moved west through Piccadilly towards Hyde Park. The Federation leaders were incapable of controlling the mob, but they did their best. When the procession reached its destination, they advised the crowd to 'disperse quietly' saying that the time for revolution had not yet come.[3] But the damage had been done: about 200 claims for compensation, amounting in all to £11,000, were later

[1] *Justice*, 6 Feb. 1886. [2] *The Times*, 9 Feb. 1886.
[3] *Justice*, 13 Feb. 1886.

recorded. A report in *The Times* declared that the day's
work was more alarming than the Chartist demonstration
in 1848, and the paper demanded severe punishment for
'men like Hyndman'.[1] Queen Victoria also expressed her
'indignation at the monstrous riot' which, she said, was 'a
momentary triumph of socialism and disgrace to the capital'.[2]
Engels did not take this view: he thought that Hyndman had
mistaken the 'Lumpenproletariat' for the unemployed and
had fallen into a police trap, thereby doing 'irreparable
damage to the movement'.[3] Morris on the other hand feared
that it was likely to 'rehabilitate' Hyndman and to enhance
his prestige as a leader of the movement.[4] The immediate
upshot of the affair was the prosecution for sedition of
Hyndman and his colleagues Burns, Champion, and
Williams, who had all spoken at the Trafalgar Square
meeting. Hyndman evidently realized at once the propaganda value of this. 'We do not pose as martyrs or go in for
advertisement,' he declared shortly after receiving his
summons: 'But whatever may happen to us . . . I hope that
every month of our sentences . . . will mean so much the
more complete an overthrow for them.'[5] On 17th February
the four Socialists appeared at Bow Street Police Court.
Morris and Bax came to offer bail for them, and they were
released pending trial. On 21st February the S.D.F. again
called an unemployed demonstration in Hyde Park, and
Hyndman spoke to a large crowd. He warned his audience
against any renewed disturbance: 'I say no mere shooting,
no mere looting of shops, can alter a great economic problem. You can only solve this great economic difficulty by

1 *The Times*, 10 Feb. 1886.
2 Queen Victoria to W. E. Gladstone, 11 Feb. 1886, *Letters of Queen Victoria
1886–1901* (1930), i, p. 52.
3 Engels to Laura Lafargue, 9 Feb. 1886, *Correspondance Engels-Lafargue*,
i, p. 336; Engels to Bebel, 15 Feb. 1886, Marx and Engels, *Correspondence*,
p. 447.
4 Morris to Dr. Glasse, 10 Feb. 1886, R. P. Arnot (ed.), *Unpublished Letters
of William Morris* (1951), p. 2.
5 *Daily Telegraph*, 17 Feb. 1886.

educating and organizing yourselves for victory in the future.'[1]

The trial began at the Old Bailey on 8th April, with the Attorney-General, Sir Charles Russell, acting as prosecutor. Hyndman and Champion defended themselves, and the Radical barrister and journalist W. M. Thompson, later the editor of *Reynolds's Newspaper*, was counsel for Burns and Williams. Both Hyndman and Champion did a good deal of cross-examining of witnesses, and Champion put a number of questions to Joseph Chamberlain, who was in the witness box for a time. All the prisoners made speeches from the dock; and Hyndman, the last to expound his views, re-counted his conversion to Socialism, as a result of his travels in the Pacific and in America. He said that Socialism was 'a matter of economics', and quoted from the writings of Adam Smith, John Stuart Mill, and Henry Fawcett.

The judge, Mr. Justice Cave, had given a good deal of latitude to the defendants, and after four days of hearings he gave what the prisoners themselves later described as 'an absolutely impartial summary of the evidence both as to fact and motive'.[2] The jury thereupon delivered a verdict of 'Not Guilty', though adding a rider to the effect that Burns and Champion (but not Hyndman or Williams) had used 'highly inflammatory language'. The defendants 'then left the court, and were loudly cheered in the forecourts as they departed'.[3]

The verdict was undoubtedly a just one. There had, indeed, been no seditious conspiracy. But in the alarm and excitement of the disturbances it was possible that a jury would be anxious to convict. It was undoubtedly an impressive success, not only for the Socialists, but also for all those who believed in the possibility of peaceful change. The prisoners themselves said that the conduct of the trial 'did much to restore confidence in the administration of justice',

[1] *Daily Telegraph*, 22 Feb. 1886.   [2] *Justice*, 17 April 1886.
[3] *The Times*, 12 April 1886.

and they concluded that 'In the centre of capitalism, therefore, the Social Revolution may yet be accomplished by the
peaceable demonstration of organized force'. Dadabhai
Naoroji, Hyndman's old friend, who had come to London
shortly before, wrote in his diary that Hyndman's trial 'had
strengthened his position immensely, and a great revolution,
peaceful as far as possible, was pending'.[1]

The S.D.F., however, had still not won its struggle for free
speech in public places. Hyndman was anxious to keep the
initiative now secured for his organization, and this led to
friction with other bodies, particularly with the Socialist
League. He went so far as to declare in a letter to Morris
that 'the further we act apart on the same lines, the less
likely are we to come into any collision'.[2] The S.D.F.
evidently now felt itself strong enough to stand alone. Indeed,
as Engels wrote at the time, Hyndman was strengthening
his position vis-à-vis Morris 'because he has a definite
programme and a definite line of political action, to both of
which Morris seems to object'.[3] It must have been about
this time that Hyndman had a tête-à-tête discussion of
the Socialist programme with Lord Randolph Churchill,
who was the Chancellor of the Exchequer, and obtained
from him a promise to do all he could for the achievement of
the 'palliatives'.[4]

A major crisis in the free speech campaign came with the
Lord Mayor's show of 1886. A month beforehand the general
council of the S.D.F. had issued a manifesto calling on 'the
unemployed of London' to 'leave your slums and follow
that pageant along the thoroughfares in silent and solemn
order'. The police were concerned about this proposal, and
instructions were given to shopkeepers along the route of
the procession to barricade their windows. In the end, the

political organizations were forbidden to parade behind the show, and to enforce this troops and police were ordered to patrol the procession route. Accordingly, the S.D.F. refrained from joining in as had originally been arranged: but they had to have their demonstration somehow. As soon as the Lord Mayor's gilded coach had disappeared down Northumberland Avenue, therefore, stalwarts of the Federation led by George Bateman, an ex-soldier, rushed to Trafalgar Square, occupied the plinth, and in the presence of a dense crowd passed a resolution demanding the relief of the unemployed. The *Pall Mall Gazette* declared indignantly that the S.D.F.'s 'flagrant defiance of constituted authority' was 'crowned with signal success'.[1]

Two weeks later the Federation called another unemployed demonstration in Trafalgar Square. Hyndman spoke from the balustrade to a huge crowd which overflowed into near-by streets, and declared that if all the political factions were against the S.D.F. it would be 'so much the worse for them', for 'we flourish: they decay'.[2] Indeed, the S.D.F. appeared to be a power in the metropolis; at the time of the rioting in February, it was said that the circulation of *Justice* was between 3,000 and 4,000 and that Hyndman could probably muster some 10,000 supporters in London.[3] Even Engels remarked on the S.D.F.'s 'very powerful tail' and admitted that the Federation had become 'sensible': adding, however, 'How long that will last, of course nobody can tell. Hyndman *est capable de tout*.'[4]

Hyndman himself realized how he had benefited from the course of events. Although he did not advocate a violent revolution, he became convinced that the threat of revolution was a more powerful weapon to influence politics than anything that the S.D.F. could do at election time. The Federation wisely took little part in the General Election of

[1] *Justice*, 9 Oct., 6, 13 Nov. 1886; *P.M.G.*, 10 Nov. 1886.
[2] *Justice*, 27 Nov. 1886.   [3] *Daily Chronicle*, 15 Feb. 1886.
[4] Engels to Laura Lafargue, 24 Nov. 1886, *Correspondance Engels-Lafargue*, i, pp. 408-9.

1886, and on New Year's Day 1887 Hyndman declared in
Justice that political action was 'after all quite secondary'
and that there was 'more chance of getting revolutionary
political change through vehement social agitation'. In an
article in the *Contemporary Review*, he warned that the
English workers, peaceful and law-abiding as they were,
would 'not be patient for ever'.[1] Meanwhile, in order to
achieve a semblance of military discipline at the Federation's
demonstrations, some of its members were learning to drill
in Harry Quelch's backyard at Bermondsey, and the rumour
got about that this was for the purpose of military insurrection.

And so the agitations went on. In 1887 various meetings
were held to demand relief for the unemployed; and for one
of them, which was held in front of St. Paul's Cathedral,
Hyndman wrote a 'Socialist sermon'. A new crisis occurred
in the autumn when the Metropolitan Police decided to
forbid the holding of public meetings in Trafalgar Square,
the 'Forum of the London Democracy', as Hyndman called
it. This move, restrictive as it was, led to such a widespread
protest movement that the Federation entirely lost the
initiative. Radicals of all descriptions rallied to the defence
of 'free speech', and the great meeting known as 'Bloody
Sunday', held on 13th November 1887, was organized as
an Anti-Coercion Demonstration with the S.D.F. taking
little part. On this occasion columns of marchers descended
from various quarters upon Trafalgar Square, their advance
being resisted and broken up by police on foot and on horse-
back. Fighting took place in various places, and sixty people
were taken to hospital and another 150 detained by the
police. John Burns and Cunninghame Graham, the Radical
M.P. for North-West Lanark who had lately become a
Socialist, were arrested and later sent to prison. One
member of the Socialist League, by name Alfred Linnel, was
mortally injured during the skirmishing; and when his

[1] *Contemporary Review*, lii (July 1887), 136.

funeral took place, Hyndman followed the long procession
through London streets, and felt a 'sensation of something
akin to fear' as he contemplated the quietness of the crowds
on this occasion, thinking that they were 'the most dangerous
of all when fairly exasperated by petty tyranny'.[1]

On the initiative of W. T. Stead, the editor of the *Pall Mall
Gazette*, a 'Law and Liberty League' was now formed with
'the establishment of popular control over the Metropolitan
Police' as its ultimate aim, and with the immediate task of
helping the victims of the free speech fight. Hyndman and
his colleagues co-operated with the League at first, but they
must have realized that this 'middle-class affair' would
steal the Federation's thunder. At a meeting held in February 1888 to welcome Burns and Cunninghame Graham
on their release from prison, Hyndman made various unkind
remarks about several Radicals who were present, and he
was hooted down, the meeting ending in a free fight between
Radicals and Socialists. The Federation therefore, decided
to try and make its own propaganda activities quite distinct
from those of the Radicals. It could only do this, however,
by assuming a more definitely revolutionary tone—and this
at a time when some of its ablest members regarded it as too
revolutionary already.

The internal politics of the Federation at this juncture are
hard to unravel. But there is some reason to believe that
Hyndman was having difficulty in dominating his colleagues
as he had done earlier. For one thing, there was the aftermath of the 'Tory gold' affair, for which he was blamed along
with Champion. Champion had previously resigned the
secretaryship of the Federation, which had passed to a rather
colourless twenty-year-old clerk called H. W. Lee; and
Hyndman now transferred the editorship of *Justice* to Harry
Quelch—an unskilled labourer, but an altogether stronger
and abler character than Lee. Quelch could certainly write
well, as his contributions to *Justice* show.

[1] *Justice*, 19 Nov., 24 Dec. 1887; *P.M.G.*, 14 Nov. 1887.

Hyndman also found that he could no longer provide much financial support for the Federation. In the course of 1886 he was harassed by a libel action against himself for some criticisms in *Justice* of conditions in Welsh slate quarries. The case was in the end withdrawn after hanging over his head for several months.[1] His financial situation suffered in other ways also from his absorption in politics: for instance, he and Champion had to contribute to the legal expenses of their trial. Significantly, just at this time he found it necessary to sell his spacious house at 10 Devonshire Street and move into rooms in Buckingham Palace Road.

In these circumstances, one or two other leaders of the Federation began to bulk larger both in its activities and in the formulation of its policy. Among the compositors, for instance, there was a man called James Blackwell, who had visited America and seen something of the violence of labour politics there. He declared on his return that peaceful political action was useless and that the revolution must be 'a forcible one'.[2] His views were shared by another compositor, A. P. Hazell, and Harry Quelch himself was probably in sympathy.

At the same time, there were several members of the Federation who deplored this tendency to toy with violent measures. The most prominent of them was Champion, who had apparently thoroughly learnt the lesson of 'Black Monday', 1886. As a former artillery officer, he had some conception of the effectiveness of modern weapons of war, especially against an untrained rabble. Some of the working-class members of the Federation agreed with him, among them being Tom Mann, who was like Burns a member of the Amalgamated Society of Engineers. Mann was interested in the agitation for an eight-hour day by legislative enactment, and Champion's Modern Press in 1886 published a pamphlet of his entitled *What a Compulsory Eight-Hour Working Day*

[1] *Justice*, 23 Jan., 6 Feb., 5 June, 17 July, 18 Dec. 1886.
[2] Ibid., 13 July 1886.

Means to the Workers.[1] In October an Eight Hours League was formed with sections in London and Newcastle; Mann became Honorary Secretary of the London section and began to set up branches of the League. But Hazell, under the pseudonym of 'Summat Stronger of Clerkenwell', criticized the 'fuss' about the 'Eight-Hour palliative movement'. Overwork would continue as long as capitalism lasts, he said, and legal restriction of working hours would strengthen the 'aristocracy of labour'. Hyndman intervened and chided Hazell for his criticism, but maintained that the formation of a separate organization was 'foolish and injurious'.[2]

In 1887, Champion was becoming increasingly dissatisfied with the attitude of Hyndman and of the extremists who were influencing the Federation's policy. He was beginning to find his work for the S.D.F. unpleasant owing to the 'personal jealousy and ineptitude' of its members.[3] His own idea was that a 'Labour Party' should be organized by strengthening the independent elements in the Labour Electoral Committee which had been set up by the Trades Union Congress in 1886. In May 1887 he founded a little paper of his own, which he called *Common Sense*, and soon he was openly attacking Hyndman. In an article entitled 'The Future of Socialism in England', he criticized 'the vacillating tactics and absence of definite policy' which, he said, has been responsible for the slow progress of the S.D.F. whose paying membership then stood only at 689. He proposed that the S.D.F. should widen its basis so that all those who would accept Socialist principles could work together; to this end a parliamentary committee of 'specialists' should be set up.[4]

As it happened, the conflict between parliamentary and

---

[1] Dona Torr suggests in her *Tom Mann* (i, 218) that Mann's pamphlet was ignored by *Justice*. In fact, the paper published a favourable review in its issue of 26 June 1886.
[2] *Justice*, 8 Jan., 5, 12 Feb. 1887.
[3] Champion to T. Davidson, 6 July 1887, Davidson Correspondence.
[4] *Common Sense*, 15 Sept. 1887.

non-parliamentary methods was also reaching a crisis inside
the Socialist League. Champion found that J. L. Mahon,
who had been organizing for the League in the North of
England, was sympathetic to his views. Mahon rejoined the
S.D.F. in 1887, having resisted the blandishments of Engels,
who had proposed to finance his efforts in the North on
condition that Aveling should be accepted as a leader of
the movement.[1] In May 1888 Tom Mann, who was then
unemployed, was sent to Newcastle as S.D.F. organizer, and
he at once joined forces with Mahon to conduct propaganda
work in the Northumbrian coalfields. The arrangement may
have been sponsored by Champion and it was perhaps
approved of by Hyndman as a way of removing Mann from
the London scene.

In 1888 Mann moved to Bolton in Lancashire at the
invitation of the local S.D.F. branch, and from there he
wrote to John Burns, who was also of the Champion party:
'Naturally I have lost hope as regards S.D.F. tho' I am sanguine concerning one or two districts. The Hazell Blackwell
Hyndman policy will not do for me, let those who like it go
for it.' A few weeks later he again wrote: 'I had hoped that
Hyndman was changing for the better. I much regret that
differences should have been accentuated instead of blended
. . . He [Hyndman] complains of the Council being composed
of "delegates" . . . I can't feel enthusiastic about the matter.'[2]

The conflict between the two groups in the Federation
came to a head at its annual conference in August 1888.
Burns bitterly criticized a resolution in favour of replacing
the general council or delegate council by a revived executive
council, saying that the change would give more room to
the further development of 'cliqueism' and 'despotism'.
Champion and his associates also raised the issue of political
action, and this led to a heated discussion. The existing

---

[1] Mahon to Engels, 22, 23 June, 21 July 1887, printed in E. P. Thompson,
op. cit., pp. 863–6.

[2] Mann to Burns, 25 June, 19 July 1888, Burns Papers, B.M.Add.MSS.
46286.

leadership was victorious, however, and an executive council was re-introduced as a part of the Federation's structure. The only gesture to the opposition was the publication of a manifesto advocating 'direct political and parliamentary action'. But this, it appeared, meant that the S.D.F. would support only candidates prepared to wage 'the class war' in Parliament.[1] Political action was thus very grudgingly accepted, and no disavowal of violence was made.

Shortly after the annual conference, it became clear that the breach between Hyndman and Champion could not be healed. Hyndman had temporarily resumed the editorship of *Justice* (Quelch being ill at the time), and he now attacked Champion, saying that he had been 'made use of by abler and more unscrupulous intriguers than himself to discredit and injure our cause'. He specifically named Maltman Barry, whom he described as a 'notorious agent of reaction'.[2] Champion appealed to the general council for support, and secured the approval of the majority; but with the new executive in existence this was no longer sufficient. He therefore decided to leave the Federation, and with the assistance of Tom Mann and John Burns he began to organize his own agitation among the industrial workers. The loss of this able little group was far more serious in its consequences to the Federation than any of the previous splits, for it meant that the men who were later to come to the fore in both industrial and political leadership of the working class were initially hostile to Hyndman and hence to the S.D.F.

5

We have now seen how, in the four years after its final acceptance of Socialism in 1883–4, the S.D.F. had gone through a series of crises, its policy gradually moving from parliamentary reformism to a militant semi-revolutionary attitude. Now, however, the pendulum began to swing back

---

[1] *Justice*, 11 Aug., 1 Sept. 1888.   [2] Ibid., 20 Oct. 1888.

again. Hyndman, distressed by the loss of Champion, seems to have sensed the danger of complete isolation and slowly returned to a more practical policy. He began to take an interest in the problems of London government. A Cockney by birth himself, he placed great emphasis on the political importance of the metropolis. 'The worst mistake the Chartist leaders made,' he once said, 'was that they neglected London until too late.'[1] Henry George's Mayoralty campaign in New York in 1886 and the success of the French Possibilists at the Paris municipal elections in the following year stirred him to emulation. He wrote a pamphlet entitled *A Commune for London* in which he suggested the establishment of a 'Great Central Council of the Metropolitan Municipality'. 'London,' he said, 'with its enormous concentration of wealth, population, and active commerce, must lead England safely along the path to the new period.'[2]

The S.D.F., however, was powerless without allies to make any impression on the London electorate. Herbert Burrows, who had represented the Federation on the executive of the Law and Liberty League, formed a link between the London Radicals and the S.D.F. At the London School Board election in November 1888, the S.D.F. in conjunction with the Metropolitan Radical Federation, the London Secular Society and the Fabian Society, set up a Central Democratic Committee, which issued a joint manifesto advocating free and secular education, free meals, and popular control of state-aided schools.[3] Annie Besant, the Fabian, who had joined the S.D.F. shortly before, and the Rev. Stewart Headlam, also a Fabian, were elected, and Hyndman wrote on the 'glorious victory' in *Justice*. The elections for the London County Council, the new administrative body to be set up in 1889, provided another occasion for activity by the Federation on behalf of municipal reform.

---

[1] *Justice*, 3 July 1886.   [2] Hyndman, *A Commune for London*, n.d., p. 15.
[3] *Link*, 6 Oct. 1888. The London Secular Society did not commit itself to the last two items in the programme.

The S.D.F., like the Fabians, was willing to advocate 'Gas and Water Socialism', though it thought that the L.C.C. should also eventually undertake the organization of industrial production and distribution. John Burns stood as a candidate for the L.C.C. at Battersea and was elected, but he was still at loggerheads with Hyndman and resigned from the S.D.F. in June 1889. Hyndman's return to interest in political action evidently had not patched up the disagreement between himself and his opponents—a disagreement aggravated as usual by personal distrust and suspicion.

Hyndman's own views of policy in 1888 are best illustrated by a letter which he wrote to H. A. Barker, a member of the 'parliamentary' faction of the Socialist League. He was, he said, willing to admit the importance of winning the '8 hours day or something like it, as well as other minor measures, before the general movement for a Social Revolution'. 'If we don't,' he said, 'there will be an upheaval of embittered ignorance, not an organized revolt of educated and determined men when the time comes for action.'[1] Apparently, therefore, he did not conceive of an effective and successful revolution taking place in the near future. This was the distinction between his position and that of the anarchists, who wanted to initiate an immediate revolution. It was significant that when in 1888 Mrs. Parsons, the wife of one of the executed Chicago anarchists, came over to England and made a tour under the sponsorship of the Socialist League, the S.D.F. not only boycotted her meetings but also criticized the speaker for her 'intemperate' language.

At the same time, Hyndman felt that there was a vast gulf between himself and 'reformists' of the Fabian type. The Fabians had now altogether disavowed any but constitutional methods and had become very selective in their economic thinking. When in 1887 the Moore and Aveling translation of *Das Kapital* was published, Hyndman naturally rallied to Marx's defence against criticisms of the work

[1] Hyndman to Barker, 16 March 1888, Socialist League Papers.

voiced by Bernard Shaw and by Mrs. Besant.[1] Although he had admitted that 'some portions' of the *Communist Manifesto* 'have become obsolete', he was not willing to allow any criticism of Marx's Theory of Surplus Value. In 1889 he wrote an article on this subject in which he attacked the views of the 'bourgeois' economists Wicksteed, Jevons, and Kirkup.[2] And he wrote to Sidney Webb: 'I do not despair of converting you to the truth of Marx's Theory even now.'[3]

Thus in the matter of Socialist theory Hyndman claimed to be an orthodox Marxist, and in tactics he believed that the true Marxist path lay between the apostles of imminent revolution and the reformists. He believed both in 'the final clash' and in 'stepping stones', and managed to reconcile millenarianism with concessions to opportunism. Upon this somewhat uneasy basis of conviction the Federation launched foward into the last decade of the nineteenth century—a tiny caravan of missionaries struggling through a quagmire of theoretical and practical difficulties.

[1] *P.M.G.*, 24 May 1887. For Shaw and Hyndman on Marx, see *P.M.G.*, 7, 11, 12, 16 May 1887.
[2] *To-day*, April 1889; *International Review*, July 1889.
[3] Hyndman to Webb, 25 May 1889, Webb Papers.

V ❧ NEW UNIONS AND 'INDEPENDENT LABOUR'

I

I T is generally said that the S.D.F. was hostile to trade unionism, and there is some evidence to support this view. As the Webbs pointed out, there were certain resemblances between the Owenites of the 1830's and the Social Democrats of the 1880's, in their criticism of what they regarded as the futility of the craft unions.[1] Hyndman in his most militant phase predicted 'the fast-approaching bankruptcy of the most powerful trade unions in the world': this was when a financial report of the Amalgamated Society of Engineers had shown a marked decline in its balances in 1885 and 1886. He thought that the unions could not cope with the new industrial situation created by the introduction of new machinery, and he appealed 'to the skilled artisans of all trades, to make common cause with their unskilled brethren, and with us Social-Democrats' so as to facilitate the advent of a Co-operative Commonwealth.[2]

It may be suggested, however, that Hyndman and *Justice* played some part in preparing the minds of the workers for the great revival of unionism which took place at the end of the eighties. In 1888 *Justice* published a series of articles on the conditions of workers in various trades, and on the need for their organization; and in the same year the first battle in the campaign to organize the unskilled workers was led by

[1] S. and B. Webb, *History of Trade Unionism* (1950 ed.), p. 409.
[2] *Justice*, 18 June 1887.

members of the Federation. The match girls employed at
Bryant & May's who revolted against their wretched conditions were, as a *Times* editorial remarked, 'egged on to
strike by irresponsible advisers . . . those pests of the modern
industrial world'.[1] Mrs. Besant and Herbert Burrows had
held an interview with the girls and published its result in
the *Link* under the heading of 'White Slavery in London'.[2]
Early in July the girls came out on strike and attracted wide
sympathy for their cause: the strike fund reached £360 in a
fortnight, and it became possible to found a permanent
organization for them. Mrs. Besant and Burrows became
Secretary and Treasurer respectively of this body, the Union
of Women Matchmakers as it was called.

The revolt of the lowest strata of the working class now
spread like wildfire, and again the members of the S.D.F.
were busy fanning the flames. In October when 400 men
went on strike at Tilbury Docks, H. W. Hobart of the
London Society of Compositors, a member of the S.D.F.,
assisted Ben Tillett, secretary of the Tea Operatives Union,
who took charge of the strike. Then in March 1889 a gas
worker called Will Thorne, a member of the S.D.F. who had
served as secretary of the Canning Town branch, took the
initiative in organizing the men of his trade with the immediate object of obtaining the eight-hours day. Sunday after
Sunday the agitation went on, and early in July the gas
workers in London were granted the shorter working day
without a strike. The Gasworkers and General Labourers'
Union, of which Thorne became general secretary, decided
to enroll all comers irrespective of trade. Their decision,
though in part dictated by the unskilled and seasonal
character of the work, may have owed something to Socialist
propaganda for united activity by all workers.

The victory of the gasworkers was followed in August by
the great strike of the London dockers. In this struggle
Tillett secured the co-operation of the Championites—

---

[1] *The Times*, 14 July 1888.   [2] *Link*, 23 June 1888.

Champion himself and also Burns and Mann. The dockers' cause was supported by the Liberal and Radical press from the beginning, and as the Championite influence was so considerable—Burns becoming the main popular leader of the strike—there was little opportunity left for the Federation to take part in the work of the main strike committee. Quelch, however, with the support of Will Thorne, organized strikers south of the Thames through a separate South Side Strike Committee. To the main strike committee the S.D.F.'s attitude was naturally equivocal: although through allocations and donations it contributed nearly £140 to the strike fund, it strongly criticized the leaders' call for a general strike throughout London in sympathy. *Justice* issued a special edition attacking the 'most treacherous manifesto' drafted by 'middle-class political tricksters', by which it meant Champion and his associates.[1] There is no doubt, however, that this move by the dockers' leaders was an error. Engels described it as 'a declaration of despair', which would alienate 'all the sympathies of the shopkeepers and even of the great mass of the bourgeoisie who all hated the dock monopolists'.[2] On 1st September the strike committee wisely withdrew the manifesto and this was soon followed by the mediation by Cardinal Manning and the Lord Mayor, which led to the Dock Companies accepting the demands of the men.

Although Hyndman supported the strike, he regarded the growth of unionism as unimportant compared with the opportunities provided for the advancement of Socialism. He and his sympathizers often stated the view that the dockers' demand for a wage increase of a penny an hour was a trivial matter compared to the grand aim of Social Democracy, and they attempted to propagate the pure doctrine of Socialism among the strikers. John Burns, however, took a

[1] *Justice*, 7 Sept. 1889.
[2] Engels to Laura Lafargue, 1 Sept. 1889, *Correspondance Engels-Lafargue*, ii, p. 317.

more opportunistic attitude, and made no protest when the
police seized a red flag carried by a member of the S.D.F.
in a procession of the dockers. Indeed, the Socialists, as
Champion remarked, had been welcomed by the strikers
'not because of their Socialism but in spite of it',[1] and both
Burns and Mann felt obliged to play down their own Socialist
sentiments during the strike.

There was no doubt that in its size and organization this
was the most spectacular industrial struggle of the period,
and it gave such encouragement to other unskilled workers
that even the strike leaders had to issue a statement depre-
cating 'the rash action taken by unorganized workmen, not
directly connected with the dock work, of coming out on
strike'.[2] The S.D.F., however, had by now realized the
opportunities provided by the growth of militancy among
the workers. It sought to win a position for itself by assisting
sporadic strikes of unorganized workers such as printers'
labourers and East End tailors. It recruited the navvies and
the laundresses, hoping that these groups would become
nuclei of a general union. In September when the engineers
and other labourers at the Thornycroft torpedo works at
Chiswick came out on strike, Jack Williams and John Ward,
both S.D.F. members, recruited for a so-called National
Federation of Labour Union among the strikers. In less than
two months thirteen local branches were set up, mostly in
South-West London, besides several single-trade branches
among railway workers, leather dressers, waiters, and
mathematical instrument makers. The 'general union'
movement also spread through the East End, and a Federation of East London Unions was formed under the auspices
of eight separate trade unions and with Jewish unionists as
its core.[3] Another new body of some importance was the
Labour Protection League, which developed out of the

---

[1] H. H. Champion, *The Great Dock Strike in London* (1890), p. 11.
[2] H. L. Smith and V. Nash, *Story of the Dockers' Strike* (1889), p. 177.
[3] *Justice*, 31 Aug., 7, 28 Sept., 12 Oct., 9 Nov. 1889.

South Side Strike Committee of the dock strike. The League was formed in September 1889, and within two months it had set up twenty-three branches and had a certain following in the Chatham dockyard and the Woolwich arsenal works.[1]

The Dockers' Union on the north side kept a jealous watch on the spread of the general union movement. As we have seen, the Gasworkers' Union opened its door to allcomers, and its motto, 'One Man, One Ticket, and Every Man with a Ticket', characterized the idealistic aims of a general union. 'To this idea', wrote Thorne, 'opposition immediately came from both Tom Mann and Ben Tillett. They wanted to put a "ring fence" around the docks.' As it was customary for many men to work at the gas works in winter and at the docks in summer, the decision of the Dockers' Union not to recognize the union tickets issued by the Gasworkers led to much friction, and the inter-union rivalry threatened to cause demarcation strikes.[2] The Dockers' Union has been described as typical of new unionism, but it persistently opposed the idea of the general union, which was the practical expression of class solidarity. As Quelch pointed out, the new movement thus lapsed into 'the old unionism applied to unskilled labour'.[3] It was, however, the only way to survive, as Quelch discovered with the decline of his own organization.

Nevertheless, the tide of new unionism affected almost every aspect of the country's industrial life and added nearly 200,000 workers to the total trade union membership within a year after the dockers' strike. Hyndman regarded all these efforts rather patronizingly as 'unconscious strugglings towards Socialism', which he thought should be made

[1] The League had a membership of 2,500 in June 1892, of whom 300—all financial members—were arsenal labourers. See Quelch's evidence before the Royal Commission on Labour, Third Report of the Commission, *Parl. Pap.*, xxxii, 1893-4.

[2] W. Thorne, *My Life's Battles* (1925), pp. 90-91.

[3] H. Quelch, *Trade Unionism, Co-operation, and Social Democracy* (1892).

conscious by Socialist propaganda among the workers.[1] In spite of this grudging attitude, there was no doubt that the Federation's influence among the unions was rapidly growing. It was significant, for instance, that when the London Trades Council held elections for its executive in October 1891, five of the seven new members belonged to the S.D.F.[2]

2

By 1890 the S.D.F. was again planning its strategy for a General Election, as the end of the existing Parliament gradually came in sight. The decision was made to put forward candidates 'wherever possible at all elections', and a list of nine prospective parliamentary candidates was proposed: it included Hyndman himself for Chelsea, the seat from which Dilke had lately retired. The responsibility for financing this ambitious plan apparently fell on Hyndman, who must have proposed it, but his resources were much depleted by the financial crisis of the same year associated with the collapse of the banking firm of Barings. Being a shareholder of the Buenos Aires Tramway Co., he was able to watch the crisis 'all very close', and he said that it fully revealed the 'imbecility' of British investors who had been attracted to 'the new Eldorado of the South' as he put it.[3] But as he himself had joined in the 'imbecility', the Barings crisis had its impact on the election plans of the Federation. Wise after the event, Hyndman wrote to *The Times* to say that the crisis was due to 'the necessary and unavoidable antagonism between the form of production and the form of appropriation and exchange', and he wrote a book entitled *Commercial Crises of the Nineteenth Century* in which he attacked the 'financial caucus' of the Barings for

[1] *Justice*, 11 Jan. 1890.

[2] Ibid., 17 Oct. 1891. For further evidence of the S.D.F.'s success in permeation of the London Trades Council, see L.T.C., *Annual Report* 1893, 1896.

[3] Hyndman, *Further Reminiscences*, p. 198; Hyndman, *Commercial Crises of the Nineteenth Century* (1892), pp. 154f.

having sacrificed 'the public interests of investors' to their own private ends.[1] The political capital thus gained, however, hardly equalled the loss of hard cash for running the candidatures. Consequently, the Federation had to draw in its horns; and when the election came in July 1892, it put forward only two candidates, W. K. Hall at South Salford and H. R. Taylor at North-East Bethnal Green. Both secured disappointingly small polls.[2] Although Keir Hardie at West Ham and John Burns at Battersea were among the successful candidates, Hyndman's only real consolation came from the return of his Indian friend, Dadabhai Naoroji, who was standing as a Radical at Central Finsbury.

Keir Hardie was the leading representative of a new type of political action—a movement in the North of England and in Scotland to secure independent working-class representation, along the lines originally suggested by Champion. The movement was distinctly Socialist in leadership, partly owing to the propaganda of the Fabians (especially their 'Lancashire Campaign' of 1890) but also because of the influence of S.D.F. agitation and the circulation of its publications. Both these forces helped to develop the Socialist views of the popular journalist Robert Blatchford of Manchester, who in turn made many converts to Socialism through his paper the *Clarion*, founded in 1891. Early in 1892 Hyndman went north and gave a series of lectures at Nelson, Burnley, and Salford; he said that he found 'Nunquam's converts in every direction'. Accepting the idiom already popularized by the Championites and the Fabians, he appealed to the northern workers in an article in the *Clarion* 'to organize a political party for themselves, and to run as Parliamentary candidates men of their own class, or men whom they can rely upon and control'.[3]

The S.D.F.'s own membership in the north was not very

---

[1] *The Times*, 15 Aug. 1891; Hyndman, *Commercial Crises*, p. 158.
[2] Hall received 553 votes and Taylor 106 votes.
[3] *Clarion*, 5 March 1892. 'Nunquam' was Blatchford's pseudonym.

considerable. In the eighties it had managed to win some
support in Lancashire, mostly in the cotton weaving district
of the North-East, but the neighbouring woollen area across
the Pennines owed its introduction to Socialism largely to the
work of members of the Socialist League. As it happened,
the centre of the movement for independent Labour representation was in the woollen area, where the workers'
militancy was largely due to the effect of the McKinley
tariff adopted by the United States in 1890. The movement
thus developed in an area where S.D.F. influence was weak.
The Bradford Labour Union, which had been founded in
April 1891 as a result of a strike by textile workers in the
town, adopted Ben Tillett to contest the 1892 General
Election there; and Tillett, because of his union's rivalry
with the organizations run by Thorne and Quelch, had no
love for the S.D.F. His campaign became a rallying-point
for what Joseph Burgess, the editor of a labour journal called
the *Workman's Times*, already chose to speak of as the
'Independent Labour Party'.

Burgess now transferred his paper from Bradford to
London and sought to establish a nucleus of the 'Independent Labour Party' in the metropolis. This was a serious
challenge to the S.D.F.: and Hyndman was concerned about
'a certain sense of exclusion' which the title 'labour party'
would carry with it. It is true that the S.D.F. co-operated
with the London Independent Labour Party (as yet a somewhat shadowy organization) and other Socialist and Radical
bodies in reasserting the right of free speech in Trafalgar
Square on the fifth anniversary of 'Black Sunday' in November 1892; and there were other apparent links between the
S.D.F. and the new labour movement. James Macdonald,
for instance, the S.D.F.'s leading representative on the
London Trades Council, joined the Independent Labour
Party as an individual member. But Hyndman and his
colleagues decided that their line towards the new movement
must be one of caution, and the Federation officially

determined to take up no more than 'an attitude of benevolent neutrality'.[1]

The inaugural conference of the national Independent
Labour Party (or I.L.P. as we may now call it) was held at
Bradford in January 1893. There were over 100 delegates,
of whom most came from local labour bodies, but a small
group of five represented the Colne, Nelson, Rochdale,
Heywood, and Padiham branches of the S.D.F. During the
conference, Tillett made a bitter attack on the Social
Democrats, both British and Continental, but the conference
did adopt a resolution proposed by a delegate of the Heywood S.D.F. pledging the party to work for collectivism.
J. J. Terrett, who represented the Colne S.D.F., explained
the policy of 'benevolent neutrality' not, however, to the
satisfaction of many of the delegates. He made it clear that
the S.D.F. branches would be unable to join the new party.[2]

Although the Hyndmanites criticized the new body for
not being sufficiently Socialist, this factor did not worry
Engels very much. He regarded its formation as 'quite a
good thing', partly because it might succeed in 'detaching
the masses' from the S.D.F.[3] The aloofness of the S.D.F.
leaders from the I.L.P. was of course largely due to their
fear that Engels might be correct: they noted the presence of
Engels's protégé Aveling with some of the Championites on
its executive in the first year of its life. Champion himself
emigrated to Australia in 1894, never to return; but Tom
Mann then became the secretary of the I.L.P., and helped
to build up its organization. The S.D.F. thus seemed to be
back in the situation of the middle eighties, when it had to
face the rivalry of the Socialist League. The difference,
however, was that the ramifications of the two bodies now
extended more widely in the provinces, where the I.L.P.
grew much more rapidly than the Federation.

[1] *Justice*, 9 July, 6 Aug. 1892.
[2] Ibid., 21, 28 Jan. 1893; *Workman's Times*, 21, 28 Jan. 1893.
[3] Engels to Sorge, 18 Jan. 1893, *Marx and Engels on Britain*, p. 531.

3

At least, however, the Federation did grow in this period, even if not as quickly as the I.L.P. This was because the two organizations were really complementary rather than directly competitive in their appeal, and the growth of each took place in rather different geographical areas. In Lancashire, the S.D.F. had strengthened its grip before the I.L.P. was founded, and with the aid of two organizers, J. J. Terrett and Dan Irving, its position in the duchy was consolidated. Terrett was in fact a paid organizer of the Federation, at least in 1893. In that year he was reported to have delivered 363 lectures and established twenty-four new branches in the North. This was not done without effort, for in order to save railway fares he often had to trudge across the hills on foot from place to place.[1] But there were also voluntary helpers to join in the work. There were, for instance, several S.D.F. enthusiasts among the members of the Starnthwaite Labour Colony, a farming 'commune' set up by the Rev. H. Mills, a Fabian, at Starnthwaite in Westmorland. Among them was Dan Irving, a Bristol man, who had lost a leg in an accident on the Midland Railway when he had been in the railway service. He retained a sense of grievance against the railway for its failure to give him any compensation, and this was a driving force in his Socialist enthusiasm. With other members of the colony he campaigned in Burnley and Nelson, and in the course of 1893 he accepted an invitation from the Burnley S.D.F. to become that branch's full-time secretary.[2]

All this organizing work resulted in the establishment of a Lancashire District Council of the S.D.F., which comprised twenty-one branches in August 1893. In that month the Federation held its annual conference at Burnley. The

[1] *Social-Democrat*, iii (Aug. 1899), 231.
[2] For the Westmorland 'Commune', see *Clarion*, 4 June 1892, 1, 8, 16 April 1893; *Workman's Times*, 15, 22 April 1893; *Justice*, 24 Sept. 1892, 22 April 1893. For Irving's early career, see *Social-Democrat* iii (Jan. 1899), 3–7.

Burnley branch itself now had 600 members, and this large membership further swelled to 1,100 by the end of the year. The branch had appointed a committee of thirty-six members and this body invited Hyndman to be its prospective parliamentary candidate.[1] Hyndman accepted, impressed as he was by the rapid progress of the branch and the likelihood of success in a constituency so heavily industrialized. 'A beautiful valley has been completely spoiled by one of the most ungainly and smoky manufacturing towns which it is possible to set eyes upon,' Hyndman declared. 'Here, if anywhere, the antagonism between the toilers and the spoilers must surely, I should say, make itself felt.' The whole town of Burnley 'looked like one of the hideous hells of Dante'—its housing abominable, the infant mortality rate terribly high, child labour defended by parents themselves— and Hyndman was determined to unfurl the red flag amidst 'all the elements of a thoroughly degrading form of capitalist wage-slavery'.[2] In October 1893 the *Burnley Socialist and North-Eastern Lancashire Labour News* was founded as the organ of six local branches of the S.D.F., whose aggregate membership had now reached nearly 2,000. Through this organ Hyndman conducted the first phase of his election campaign by writing 'Notes from the Nation-city' and other articles.[3]

Hyndman carried on at the same time with his active propaganda work in London. His prophecy of a social revolution in 1889 had failed of achievement, in spite of the widespread labour unrest of that year; and he now fell back upon a later milleniary date. In January 1891 he predicted that by 1900 England would witness 'the full sweep of that great Social Revolution of which we can already see plainly the beginning'.[4] The most important recruit to the Federation in this period was George Lansbury, formerly a Liberal

---

[1] *Justice*, 12 Aug. 1893, 20 Jan. 1894; *Workman's Times*, 12 Aug. 1893.
[2] Ibid., 19 Aug. 1893; Hyndman, *Further Reminiscences*, pp. 61–62.
[3] *Burnley Socialist*, 7 Oct.–24 Nov. 1893.   [4] *Justice*, 10 Jan. 1891.

election agent, who, having set up a branch of the S.D.F. at Bow, was soon elected a Poor Law Guardian in the area. Hyndman repeatedly reminded Lansbury of the importance of mastering his responsibilities as a Guardian so as to be prepared to take charge of East London when he and others seized the reins of government.[1]

For a man preparing to lead a revolutionary government, Hyndman remained sadly bogged down in petty jealousies arising from the past. Thus, when Burns was quoted in the *Star* as critical of the Federation, Hyndman retorted with a long list of Burns's acts of 'treachery' to Socialism. Burns counter-attacked vigorously; and Lansbury wrote up in defence of Hyndman, saying that Burns had climbed to power 'not by raising men's minds to a high and lofty ideal' but by abusing other Socialist and labour leaders.[2] Lansbury's warm-hearted idealism, however, accorded little with Hyndman's own bitterness, and he cannot have enjoyed the controversy. In May 1895, when Lansbury fought a parliamentary by-election at Walworth, he aroused Hyndman's wrath by the mildness of his election manifesto, which contained a quotation from the American poet James Russell Lowell.[3]

Meanwhile, Hyndman was preparing the ground for his Burnley contest. In January 1894 he had written to the *Manchester Guardian* to declare his firm intention to fight:

Win or lose the first time, I have come to stay. 'J'y suis j'y reste.' We are enthusiasts and fanatics, if you will; but at any rate we mean business, and we fight our own fight. I for one don't believe that you Liberals and Radicals can fight with any hope of success the old enthusiasms aroused by Church, State, monarchy, aristocracy, privilege, empire, domination, unless you can oppose to them a greater and a higher enthusiasm than theirs, fired and stirred by the grand ideal of the social emancipation of mankind.[4]

[1] G. Lansbury, *My Life* (1931), p. 81.   [2] *Star*, 5–27 May 1894.
[3] R. Postgate, *George Lansbury* (1951), p. 47.
[4] *Manchester Guardian*, 17 Jan. 1894.

The prospective candidate was now spending a good deal of his time in or near his constituency. In March 1895 he spoke at the Manchester Free Trade Hall, declaring somewhat aggressively: 'There should be no compromise with privilege; no compromise with plunder.' A week later, to his great satisfaction, William Morris spoke a palinode in the same hall, admitting that Hyndman was right after all in advocating political action for Socialism. In July Hyndman attended three meetings at Burnley and spoke on 'The Practicability of Socialism'. In August he was again in the town, lecturing on 'The First Monday Morning Under Socialism'. During the winter he remained mostly in London, but in April 1895 he was in Burnley once more, and when the election took place in July he delivered more than fifty speeches in the constituency in the course of the two weeks before polling day. An S.D.F. member had just been elected Vice-President of the Burnley Weavers' Association, and Hyndman took this as a good omen for his own contest. But he was at the bottom of the poll, with 1,498 votes against 5,454 for the Liberal victor and 5,133 for the Conservative.[1]

There were three other S.D.F. candidates at the 1895 General Election besides Hyndman; H. W. Hobart at South Salford, F. G. Jones at Northampton, and Lansbury again at Walworth. All were defeated.[2] It was possibly some consolation to them that all the twenty-eight I.L.P. candidates including Keir Hardie met the same fate. *Justice* published a leading article entitled 'Smashed' which, however, referred to 'the extinction of the Liberal Party', which was supposed to give the Socialists 'cause for exultation'.[3] Hyndman attributed his own defeat in large part to the influence of 'the cheap newspaper Press', against which

[1] For Hyndman's Burnley campaign, see *Justice*, 10, 17 March, 14 July, 4 Aug., 1 Sept. 1894, 13 July 1895; *The Times*, 23 July 1895; Hyndman, *Record*, pp. 361–2; Hyndman, *Further Reminiscences*, p. 68.
[2] Jones polled 1,216 votes, Hobart 813, and Lansbury 203.
[3] *Justice*, 20 July 1895.

he had had to fight with the inferior weapons of fly-sheets and propaganda leaflets.[1]

The General Election of 1895 marked the climax of the growth of organized Socialism in Britain in the nineteenth century. Something like a decade was to pass before either the S.D.F. or the I.L.P. was to flourish as much as in the years 1893-5. The failure of both bodies in the General Election led to no little heartsearching, and there were prominent members of both who came to the conclusion that the divisions among the Socialists themselves had had much to do with their defeat. It seemed more than possible that the trouble lay, not in the failure of the S.D.F. to resemble the I.L.P., or *vice versa*, but in their joint failure to unite their forces in support of a common cause.

4

A certain sentiment in favour of 'Socialist Unity' had already appeared before the 1895 election. Hyndman, Morris, and Shaw had got together to draft a 'Manifesto of English Socialists' for May Day of 1893, which seemed to indicate a certain willingness of different groups to work together. Shaw, however, took a cynical view of the affair; the manifesto was, he said, 'a string of platitudes hiding a disagreement as to methods at a time when the whole concern of the Socialist movement was with methods'.[2] Consequently the Fabian Society, feeling it was getting nowhere, soon withdrew from collaboration. As for the I.L.P., however, Hyndman regarded it as more worthy of consideration than the Fabian Society in spite of what he privately described as 'the queer jumble of Asiatic mysticism and supernatural juggling which we call Christianity put forward by Keir Hardie and Tom Mann as the basis of a

---

[1] *The Times*, 31 July, 13 Aug. 1895.
[2] Comment by Shaw on his own copy of the manifesto, now in the library of the University of California (Los Angeles).

social and economic propaganda'.[1] He hoped, however, that the S.D.F. which was then still growing would detach the 'genuine' Socialists from the I.L.P.; and so he saw no immediate necessity for attempts to secure the unity of the two bodies. The official attitude of the S.D.F. to the I.L.P. as expressed at the former body's 1894 conference was to be 'dignified neutrality'—a slightly more aloof attitude than the 'benevolent neutrality' declared in 1893.[2]

On the side of the I.L.P., Tom Mann at least was keen to arrive at some understanding with his former colleagues. In 1894, shortly after having become secretary of the I.L.P., he wrote a pamphlet entitled *What the I.L.P. is Driving At*, in which he declared that the objects of the two Socialist bodies were identical. But while both the I.L.P. and the S.D.F. were still rapidly growing and increasing their membership, there was little effective pressure for negotiations for a merger of the two bodies.

In 1895, however, the situation changed. First of all, there was the setback of the election results, which was followed by a decline in membership, especially of the rapidly-developed I.L.P. No longer led by a Member of Parliament after Keir Hardie's defeat, and seeing their membership in the local branches dwindling, the I.L.P. leaders were much more amenable to negotiation on equal terms. Then shortly after the election the death of Engels removed an important obstacle to negotiation, for his influence on the I.L.P. through the Avelings had been one of Hyndman's main objections to any attempt at collaboration.

On the initiative of James Macdonald, now the secretary of the London Trades Council, unity negotiations were begun and soon made progress. Indeed, at one point the only problem that seemed to remain was the name of the new united party. The S.D.F. was anxious to retain the words 'Social Democratic' and urged the clumsy title of 'the

---

[1] Hyndman to Ely, 28 Sept. 1894, Richard T. Ely Papers.
[2] S.D.F. *Conference Report*, 1894, pp. 25–26.

Independent Social Democratic Labour Party'. The I.L.P. preferred the simple name of 'the Socialist Party'. Hyndman sought to define the difference between a Social-Democrat and a Socialist; the former, he said, would recognize the class war and would concentrate upon political action so as to 'prepare, as far as possible, peacefully for the social revolution'. Socialism, on the other hand, might embrace any type of aspiration for social betterment, from Christian Socialism to the utopian colonization projects of Paraguay, or even anarchism.[1] On this issue, the negotiations came to a deadlock. Not until July 1897, by which time two years had passed since the election, was it decided to submit the issue of unification to a vote of the membership of the two parties. The members were to vote, first, on whether the parties should amalgamate, and secondly, if this was agreed to, on the name for the new body. The result of the first vote was 5,158 for the amalgamation and 886 against it. Thereupon the S.D.F. pressed for the opening of formal negotiations to secure unity, but the I.L.P. executive, which was now anxious to escape its commitments, refused to accept the result on the ground that only one-third of the party's membership had voted on the question.[2]

The reason for the I.L.P. leaders' change of heart probably lay in their growing expectations of winning the support of the organized trade unions. Most union officials, at least in the provinces, looked askance at the S.D.F., but they were often willing to associate with the more moderate representatives of the I.L.P. Tom Mann, the keenest advocate of 'Socialist unity' on the I.L.P. executive, gradually lost influence to Keir Hardie and his leading supporters, Bruce Glasier and Ramsay MacDonald, who had no affection for the S.D.F. These men realized only too well how much the thorough-going Marxism of Hyndman and

[1] Hyndman in *Social-Democrat*, i (Aug. 1897), 231.
[2] S.D.F., *Conference Report*, 1898, pp. 11–15; I.L.P., *Conference Report*, 1898, pp. 5–6.

his colleagues was disliked by the average trade union leader and indeed by the electorate. At the I.L.P. conference in April 1898, the party executive submitted a report criticizing the Federation's sectarianism; and Bruce Glasier read a paper which eloquently if speciously stated the case against unity:

> The cry and craving for unity is often a cry and confession of lack of faith, of lack of bigness of heart. . . . Unity has evermore been the pretext of the tyrant and the inquisition. It is on the plea of unity of nations and unity of churches that the swords of war and persecution have been sharpened all down the years.[1]

The I.L.P. conference accepted these arguments, and it was only a tiny minority of branches that decided to reject the decision and seceded to join the S.D.F.[2] As for Tom Mann, he dropped out of political activity altogether in 1898 and shortly emigrated to New Zealand.

5

The rapid extension of unionism in the late eighties and early nineties had alarmed employers of labour throughout the country, and after a few years many of them seemed deliberately to take up a counter-offensive against the unions. The growth of employers' organizations, the systematization of the supply of 'blacklegs' by the National Free Labour Association, the increasing threats to the position of the unions by fresh legal decisions apparently infringing their established rights—all these elements in the political situation were observed and commented on by Hyndman. And interested as he was in developments abroad, particularly in America, he could not but feel that the phenomenal growth of trusts there and the fierce treatment to which the nascent American trade unions were subjected was something of a portent for the future development of Britain.

[1] I.L.P., *Conference Report*, 1898, pp. 25–28.   [2] *Justice*, 2 July 1898.

Hh

Hyndman had not revisited America since 1880. He had planned to go in 1886, at the time of the great growth and strikes of the Knights of Labor, but he was apparently held back by his financial worries.[1] He retained many American contacts, however, and corresponded regularly with leading Socialists across the Atlantic. One of these was H. Gaylord Wilshire, a Californian of considerable wealth, who was then active in New York politics. Wilshire had visited England in 1892, had joined the S.D.F., and had served on the financial committee of the party. In the later 1890's Wilshire contributed several articles to *Justice*, drawing attention to the growth of the trust in America and its implications for Socialism. In the last few years of the century, this development was further accelerated, and Hyndman spoke of it as the 'most remarkable phenomenon of the century', promising a 'tyranny' which the workers would have to resist.[2]

By this time many trade union leaders were already much concerned about their own difficulties, especially after the defeat of the Amalgamated Society of Engineers in their great conflict with the Engineering Employers' Federation in 1897–8. Socialists of all complexions seized upon these events as confirming their predictions and making even more urgent a definite movement for independent political action. If trade union funds could be harnessed for Socialist objectives, it was obvious that Socialism would begin to make some impact on the electorate. The S.D.F. had this object in mind almost as much as the I.L.P., as was shown by their conference decision of 1897 to urge their members 'to become members of their respective trade unions, and to work harmoniously with trade unionists and co-operators' in order to gain their political support.

When the Trades Union Congress met at Plymouth in September 1899, the S.D.F. organized a mass demonstration

[1] Champion to T. Davidson, 11 June 1886 and 6 July 1887, Davidson Correspondence.

[2] *Justice*, 18 Feb. 1899. See also *Burnley Socialist*, 13 Oct. 1893; Hyndman, 'Socialism', *Johnson's Universal Cyclopoedia*, vii (New York, 1895), 594–9.

there. At this meeting Hyndman displayed his usual impatience with the slowness in securing labour representation in Parliament; Ben Tillett and James O'Grady assured him that they were prepared to fight for it; Pete Curran of the I.L.P. declared that their aim was to 'direct the trade union movement into the Socialist channel'; and finally, the meeting unanimously adopted a resolution moved by Will Thorne to the effect that trade unionism should be regarded as an important factor in the task of overthrowing capitalism by parliamentary action. Meanwhile, however, it was the I.L.P. which had managed to put into action the policy which the leaders of the Federation were demanding. Through the Amalgamated Society of Railway Servants, its members had placed on the T.U.C. agenda a resolution in favour of the summoning of a conference of Socialist Societies and trade unions, to find ways and means of collaborating for political purposes. This resolution was carried, principally with the support of the new unions and by the abstention of some of the older societies.

What was to be the S.D.F.'s attitude to the labour representation conference that would result? Hyndman wrote in *Justice*: 'The mere fact that we shall be in a minority as avowed revolutionary Social-Democrats ought not to deter us . . . from participating.' He advised his fellow Social-Democrats to 'refrain from any attempt to dictate' to the other delegates. 'Of course, we cannot expect to convert the trade union delegates to our opinions all at once,' he said, 'but every time we meet them in conference we gain ground against the old school and hearten up the new.'[1] If the S.D.F. had followed Hyndman's advice in this respect, the history of the Labour Representation Committee, and the Labour Party into which it developed, might have been somewhat different from what it was. But he did not personally attend the conference, which met in February 1900 at the Memorial Hall, Farringdon Street—

[1] *Justice*, 16 Sept., 28 Oct. 1899.

the scene, nineteen years earlier, of the formation of the Federation. He thought 'perhaps foolishly', as he later wrote, that not being himself a manual worker he was not entitled to appear at such a conference.[1] In any case he was at the time deeply disappointed by the decline of the Federation's fortunes after so many years of Socialist propaganda, and he was about to retire from active political work for some time. Consequently, he took little part in the early discussions within the S.D.F. about the attitude to be adopted towards the nascent Labour Party.

The S.D.F. sent four delegates to the Memorial Hall conference, among them James Macdonald and Harry Quelch. They moved a resolution to get the new party committed to 'a recognition of the class war'—hardly a tactful move if the object was to obtain as much support as possible for political action. The more opportunist I.L.P. delegates felt this to be too strong a pill to be swallowed as yet by the trade unionists, and so Keir Hardie put forward an amendment with no such binding clause, but merely declaring in favour of establishing 'a distinct Labour group' in Parliament which would co-operate with any other party 'in the direct interest of Labour'. This proposal was carried. The I.L.P. also succeeded in having Ramsay MacDonald chosen as secretary of the new organization.

The views of the S.D.F. leaders on being thus out-manœuvred were published in the following issue of *Justice*. They described the I.L.P.'s attitude as 'treachery' to Socialism, and they suggested that Ramsay MacDonald's election as secretary had been due to misapprehension on the part of many of the delegates, who mixed him up with their own James Macdonald, now secretary of the London Trades Council.[2] The prospects for future S.D.F. participation in the work of the new body—the Labour Representation Committee as it came to be called—did not seem very bright.

[1] Hyndman, *Further Reminiscences*, p. 268.   [2] *Justice*, 3 and 10 March, 1900.

6

The relations of Hyndman with his colleagues at this time naturally suggest the question: how democratic was the control system of the Social-Democratic Federation? Shortly after the 1895 General Election, it seems that steps were taken to strengthen further the executive power, which had remained somewhat decentralized since the criticism of Hyndman's dictatorial tendencies in the eighties. By the time of the Birmingham conference in August 1895, the old delegate council had largely ceased to function as an executive body, and a new executive council consisting of twelve London and twelve provincial members was set up. On the executive there were a number of men who had long been prominent in the Federation's activities—not only Hyndman and Quelch, but also Herbert Burrows, Jack Williams, Hunter Watts, Jonathan Taylor of Sheffield, and Nairn of Glasgow. In addition, George Lansbury and H. W. Hobart of the London Society of Compositors both joined this group in 1895. Two years later, they were joined in turn by Dan Irving, the Burnley organizer, and by John Spargo, a Cornish stone-mason who later emigrated to America and became prominent in the American Socialist Party. But the London members of the executive exerted a far greater influence than their provincial colleagues did, owing to the fact that the meetings were usually held in the metropolis.

The executive was the supreme governing body of the Federation, but it did not directly control the official organ, *Justice*. This was owned by the Twentieth Century Press which had been established in October 1891, as a limited liability company with a nominal capital of £1,000. The press not only printed *Justice* but also ran a general printing business mainly for Socialist and trade union organizations. It was, of course, controlled directly by its directors, who were elected by its shareholders—most of them being the older members of the party, colleagues and friends of Hyndman himself. The company's general business was used to subsidize *Justice*, the sales of which were no more than 2,500 in 1891 and 4,000 in 1893. By 1900 the press's contribution to the paper had reached a total of £500. Under the circumstances, the directors could not afford to be very generous to their staff. 'We have no lofty ideas of putting Socialism in practice . . . or of inaugurating a microscopic millennium for the compositors and other workmen employed in our Press', they declared.[1] Nor indeed, it may be added, were they willing to enforce changes in the control of policy of *Justice* at the whim of a temporary majority of the executive.

The size of the Federation increased rapidly in the middle 1890's, and was reported as 10,536 to the London Congress of the Second International in 1896. At the party conference in Nottingham in 1897, however, a fear was expressed that a period of 'slump' was beginning, although the number of branches seems to have increased at least until 1898, when a total of 137 branches, 'the highest on record', was reported. In 1900 the total of branches mentioned in *Justice* seemed to be a little less than 100, and the official figure of party membership reported to the L.R.C. conference in the same year was 9,000. The dues-paying membership, however, must have been far smaller.[2] The rapid growth of the Federation in 1893–6 was bound to be followed by a reaction, but this was accentuated by the electoral failure, by the national recovery of trade, and by the growth of imperialism culminating in the South African War.

It was in any case only a limited number of workers who could stomach the anti-religious tone of the S.D.F. propaganda. Doubtless the working classes as a whole were little interested in church-going; they nevertheless did not

---

[1] *Social-Democrat*, iv (May 1900), 13; *Justice*, 14 Nov. 1891, 20 May 1893.
[2] See Appendix B, p. 284.

care for anti-clericalism, and given the choice between this
and the nonconformist enthusiasm of the I.L.P. leaders,
most of them probably preferred the latter. Hyndman had
no patience with this outlook. 'Protestantism must go
down,' he declared, 'with the overthrow of the competitive
struggle for respectability here, and the keen bidding for a
snug billet hereafter.'[1]

Hyndman never concealed his contempt for the individualist type of religious faith which, he believed, would
decline as soon as its real basis—economic individualism—
was undermined. But he took Catholicism more seriously,
for he saw in it a well-organized international rival to
Socialism. He had written to Cardinal Manning: 'That the
fight of the future will be between Catholics and ourselves
both sides recognize, but that is surely no reason why each
should not recognize the economic truths taught by the
eminent men of the opposite camps.'[2] In 1891, when Pope
Leo XIII issued his famous Encyclical on Labour, Hyndman
regarded it as a declaration of war by Catholics on Socialists.
'So much the better', he wrote, 'we declare war against
them.'[3] Hyndman's periodical attacks on the 'Catholic
International' probably cost him a good deal of support
among Irish working men which his sympathy for Home
Rule might otherwise have secured for him.

While the I.L.P. had a certain temperamental affinity
for Liberalism, the S.D.F., by contrast, had an equally
temperamental dislike of it. At the S.D.F. conference of
1898, Harry Quelch went so far as to propose a policy of
'smashing' the Liberal Party by casting the Socialist vote
'steadily on the Tory side up to and through the General
Election'. Hyndman supported the proposal, but it was
defeated. Quelch, however, carried on a campaign in its
favour in *Justice*, and a year later he and Hyndman again

[1] *Justice*, 22 April 1893.
[2] Hyndman to Cardinal Manning, 26 Nov. 1886, S. Leslie, *Henry Edward
Manning* (1921), p. 367.
[3] *Justice*, 22 April 1893.

urged the conference to adopt it.[1] The idea was, as Hyndman explained, to force the Liberal Party to withdraw its candidates from certain constituencies where 'we are entitled by our work, our numbers, and our enthusiasm to be left a fair field to contest the seat'.[2] Not anxious to offend its leaders, the conference cautiously adopted the proposal, but decided to suspend its operation until the Federation's own voting strength became more clearly known.

With the outbreak of the South African War and the formation of the Labour Representation Committee, the Federation in any case had to adopt a new electoral policy. As we shall see in the next chapter, Hyndman and his colleagues, however positive in their attitude to imperial responsibilities, could not approve of the way that the war had come about. The Federation's 1900 conference therefore decided to concentrate on Socialist candidatures and to support those Liberals who were opposed to the war.

Three members of the S.D.F. fought the 1900 General Election—Lansbury at Bow and Bromley; Will Thorne, the official candidate of his union, the Gasworkers, at West Ham South; and A. Clarke, the nominee of the local I.L.P. and S.D.F. branches, at Rochdale. All of them were also given the endorsement of the L.R.C. None was successful, though Lansbury and Thorne, having straight fights, secured the Liberal vote and polled well.[3] Elsewhere, however, two L.R.C. candidates were returned to Parliament— Keir Hardie of the I.L.P. at Merthyr Tydfil and Richard Bell of the Railway Servants at Derby. These successes were contrary to the general trend of the voting, which confirmed the government in favour and put the stamp of popular approval on the South African War.

The misfortune of most of the Socialist and Labour candidates was that the South African War had become so

---

[1] S.D.F. *Conference Report*, 1898, pp. 23–24 and 1899, pp. 22–25.

[2] Hyndman, *Social-Democrat*, ii (April 1898), 108–19.

[3] Lansbury 2,558 (Unionist 4,403); Thorne 4,419 (Unionist 5,615); Clarke 901 (Unionist 5,204, Liberal 5,185).

much the primary political issue of the day, and that on this issue their views ran counter to popular feeling. Even in slum districts the streets were decorated with flags at every British victory, and anti-war meetings held by Radicals or Socialists were broken up by hooligans. In London, the S.D.F. branches suffered from what they called 'jingo persecution', and in Lancashire, where the *Clarion* was most widely read, Blatchford's support of the war encouraged the existence of 'jingo Socialists' in S.D.F. branches in opposition to the leadership. The Federation's organization suffered: a note in *Justice* spoke of 'apathy in Manchester', and a report from Scotland said that the branches were 'lying low'.[1]

Hyndman had hoped that the end of the century would bring, if not the social revolution, then at least some tangible results of his many years of propaganda. But the S.D.F. entered the new century with its membership declining and its branches in disruption. Hyndman felt the situation most keenly when he met the leaders of the Continental Socialist parties, with their hundreds of thousands, even millions, of supporters. Whereas the leaders of German and French Socialism were by now of national importance, Hyndman could speak only for a tiny sect. This was all the more embarrassing as Hyndman himself always aspired to play a significant role in the councils of international Socialism. But this is a subject which deserves a chapter of its own.

[1] *Justice*, 22 Sept., 13 Oct., 3 Nov. 1900.

VI ∿ IMPERIALISM AND THE SECOND INTERNATIONAL

I

WHEN Hyndman wrote his *England for All* for the inaugural conference of the Democratic Federation, he devoted nearly two-fifths of its pages to a review of foreign and colonial affairs. Like many other British Radicals, he saw in the issues of Continental politics a struggle between 'tyranny and freedom'. He advocated active intervention in the interests of the 'democracies of Europe' and against the expansion of 'militarism' and 'barbarism'—by which he obviously meant Bismarck's Germany and Czarist Russia. He was firmly convinced that Britain's strength must always be on the sea, but at the same time he hoped that international action on the part of the working classes might lead to progress everywhere.

Yet, as Hyndman himself admitted at the time, the prospects of international co-operation among the European Socialists remained doubtful. The First International which had been founded by Marx in 1864 had been rent by conflict between the Marxists and the anarchists, and had died quietly in America in 1876. The French Socialists had been disrupted by the failure of the Commune, and the German Social-Democratic Party was driven underground by Bismarck's anti-Socialist laws. In the 1880's, the initiative in reviving the International came from the French, but they were still weak and seriously divided among themselves.

Meanwhile, the anarchists held an international conference in London in 1881 and were said to have established a secret International of their own. Hyndman was worried by this development, and thought he should do something to counter it by organizing a rival International. In 1883 he wrote to Henry George:

> We should decide as soon as possible upon a definite international action which shall be clear enough, strong enough, and noble enough to give an outlet to enthusiasts who otherwise may rush into dynamite. . . . Davitt for instance would do much to bridge over the gap between Irish and Englishmen: you have done much to unite Englishmen and Americans: Hirsch can greatly help us in Germany: Lafargue and Guesde would assist in France. I will look up others. . . . The determination to stop the wholesale exploitation of labour must of necessity take an international range.[1]

George, who, after all, was not a Socialist, showed no sign of enthusiasm about Hyndman's proposal, and nothing came of the correspondence.

After this, Hyndman temporarily lost hope of organizing an international organization. But he still believed in the concept of international action. Always a Francophile, the prospect of a fresh German attack on France alarmed him in the mid-eighties. 'In a war of Germany against France', he wrote, 'who can feel sympathy with an Empire where nearly a million of men of our opinions are practically deprived of almost all the rights of citizenship?' But, he said, 'if war does break out it is for us to watch our opportunity carefully' and to take 'simultaneous, international action by the workers against the plundering classes throughout the civilized world'.[2] Apparently he thought that world revolution would emerge from any new war, just as the Paris Commune had emerged in 1871 as a result of the Franco-Prussian War.

---

[1] Hyndman to George, 6 April 1883, Henry George Papers.
[2] *Justice*, 11 Dec. 1886.

In the later 1880's, however, serious efforts began to be made to re-establish the International. The main difficulty was that different Socialist groups were in competition to secure the initiative. At the end of 1888 both the French Possibilists, or reformist Socialists, and their revolutionary Marxist rivals, were planning separate inaugural conferences for the following year in Paris. The Socialists of other countries, even if they were Marxists, could not decently ignore the Possibilist proposal, which had secured the support of many trade union leaders. The German Socialists, and especially Wilhelm Liebknecht, whose 'mania for unity' was deplored by Engels,[1] sought to heal the breach, and they managed to arrange a preliminary discussion at The Hague in February 1889. At this meeting it was resolved to invite the Possibilists to act as organizers of a united international congress on one condition—that the congress itself should be the final authority for the verification of delegates' credentials. The Possibilists, however, were reluctant to accept this condition as they regarded it as a threat to the autonomy of each national group. Reckoning that their own numerical strength would overcome that of their domestic Marxist rivals, they insisted that the verification for each country should be done by its own nationals and not by the conference as a whole.

Hyndman was affronted by the fact that the S.D.F. was not invited to send representatives to the meeting at The Hague. This was of course because of the influence of the Marx-Engels family group. He therefore denounced the revival of intrigues that had broken up the old International. He declared that each nation was the best judge of the tactics to be followed by its own Socialists in winning power, and that the S.D.F. and the Possibilists would 'not allow foreigners to interfere in their own internal and national affairs'.[2]

---

[1] Engels to Laura Lafargue, 28 June 1889, *Correspondance Engels-Lafargue*, ii, p. 293. The word was 'Vereinigungswut'.

[2] *Justice*, 9, 16, 23 March 1889.

His views were at once attacked by Eduard Bernstein, the German Socialist leader who was then living in London. Bernstein wrote a pamphlet in reply to Hyndman in which he said that Socialism in Europe and America owed much of its strength to the movement among German refugees and immigrants. Hyndman retorted with a reference to 'a certain inherent Teutonism which leads them [the German Socialists] to force German methods on all countries and to use their own language for purposes of propaganda even where another would be more useful'.[1] His attitude, however, was not entirely hostile, and it must have been about this time that Bernstein and Eleanor Marx called upon him personally and persuaded him to urge the French Possibilists to comply with the Marxist terms. Hyndman accordingly wrote as follows:

They [the German party] will, I still hope, come to the Congress, but they insist upon it that they shall have the right to spit on the carpet. That, I admit, is a very nasty habit. . . . But, remember, you are the hosts on this occasion. Don't, therefore, annoy our German comrades with spittoons or sawdust. Spread for them a new carpet of beautiful texture, and say to them in the spirit of the truest fraternity, 'Friends and Fellow Citizens, Spit away!'[2]

Justice published a new circular issued by the Possibilists in which certain concessions were made to the German and other parties suffering from 'a political régime of despotism', but formal agreement was not reached on the question of the verification of credentials, and so by the beginning of May the Marxists had finally decided not to abandon their plans for a separate conference of their own.

In Britain, the supporters of the Marxist conference consisted of a curious mixture of elements hostile to the Federation. They included William Morris and the fast-disintegrating Socialists League; Cunninghame Graham;

[1] E. Bernstein, *The International Working Men's Congress of 1889. A Reply to 'Justice'* (1889); *Justice*, 6 April 1889.
[2] Quoted in *Justice*, 15 June 1889.

Champion and his working-class supporters, including Tom Mann and Keir Hardie; and also John Burns, who though elected by his union, the Amalgamated Society of Engineers, to attend the Possibilist congress, was confidently expected by Engels to 'act in accordance with our opinion'.[1]

Engels now thought that the Marxists were 'victorious' in the battle for control of the new international. He saw in the conflict a repetition of the old split in the First International, aligning on one side 'the disciples of Bakunin, with a different flag, but with all the old equipment and tactics' and on the other side 'the real working-class movement'.[2] Whatever the 'real' movement might have been, Engels had good reason to fear the consequences of a congress that he could not control. For the dispute between the two sections of European Socialists represented a fundamental difference of opinion as to the role of an International. Hyndman supported the Possibilists, for he saw in their efforts an attempt to assert national autonomy and to resist the domineering influence of what A. S. Headingley once called the 'family clique' in the International. He chose to be associated with reformists and trade unionists rather than to work with revolutionary Marxists, if the latter course involved the subordination of the British movement to control by foreigners.

2

On 15 July 1889, the two rival congresses met in Paris, their meeting places being about a mile apart. Nearly 400 delegates from twenty countries (including some rather unreal 'countries' such as Alsace-Lorraine) attended the Marxist congress, and they spent three whole days listening

[1] Engels to Paul Lafargue, 25 May 1889, Paul Lafargue to Engels, 30 May 1889, *Correspondance Engels-Lafargue*, ii, pp. 273, 277; *Justice*, 25 May, 15 June 1889.

[2] Engels to Laura Lafargue, 11 June 1889, Engels to Paul Lafargue, 16 June 1889; Engels to Laura Lafargue, 28 June 1889, *Correspondance Engels-Lafargue*, ii, pp. 286, 289-90, 293.

to long orations from their leaders. The real business of the congress was crammed into the last few hours of the proceedings when resolutions on the eight-hour day, war and peace, universal suffrage, and international May Day celebrations were hastily passed without much discussion. This congress, according to Hyndman, was looked upon in Paris as the 'German congress', as opposed to the 'French, English, and International congress' which he himself attended.[1]

The Possibilist congress was the larger of the two, with over 600 delegates present. The British, who were the second largest national group after the French, consisted of thirty-nine delegates claiming to represent a combined membership of 139,272. Of this total, the fifteen S.D.F. delegates claimed only to represent 1,926—a surprisingly honest admission of their own numerical weakness.[2] The meetings were conducted in a more orderly and businesslike manner than those of the rival congress. A series of resolutions on 'palliatives' such as the eight-hour day and the abolition of child labour were discussed and carried, as was an S.D.F. motion urging the workers to prepare for the day when they could take over industrial monopolies. Hyndman emphasized the importance of national autonomy and the employment of a variety of tactics inside the International. 'Each country knows its own needs and must decide on its own action,' he emphasized.

As we have seen, the Possibilist congress was dominated by reformists and trade unionists, and Hyndman showed that he was quite capable of wooing them with almost Fabian tactics. 'We were rather surprised at his coquetting with the trade unionists, and patting them on the back', wrote Burns.

[1] *International Review*, Aug. 1889; J. Joll, *The Second International* (1955), pp. 33f.

[2] There were also delegates from fifteen trade unions and five political and working men's clubs including the Metropolitan Radical Federation and the Fabian Society. For English accounts of the Possibilist congress see *P.M.G.* 16–22 July 1889 (Annie Besant); *Justice*, 20, 27 July; *Labour Elector*, 3 Aug. (John Burns); and *International Review*, Aug. (Hyndman).

Hyndman proposed the establishment of two committees for international communication, one for the trade unions and the other for Socialist bodies, and this he did apparently as a concession to the trade unionists who were reluctant to accept Socialism. Even the 'Lib-Lab' M.P., Charles Fenwick, who was present as a miners' delegate, thought that this was going too far and would accentuate the existing differences. It was finally decided to set up one international bureau of correspondence only for both Socialists and trade unionists. Hyndman himself was impressed by the friendly feeling which he felt existed between the Socialists and the non-Socialists throughout the congress.

Furthermore, the basis for an understanding between the Possibilists and the Marxists did emerge before the sessions concluded. Both congresses appointed the Belgian Labour Party to act as the convener of the next meeting. Consequently, it was a united international which met at Brussels two years later, in 1891. This agreement, it must be said, was not much to Hyndman's liking, as he knew that he would continue to be ostracized so far as possible by Engels and his friends.

The Marxist congress also passed a special resolution calling for simultaneous demonstrations in every country on 1st May 1890. As the Possibilist congress had taken no part in the decision, the S.D.F. at first held aloof from the arrangements for what it called 'the First of May folly'. Later, however, its policy changed, and it decided to support a trade union rally to be held on the first Sunday of May. This rally, which was held in Hyde Park, turned out to be a tremendous success. A *Times* reporter declared that the demonstration was 'the greatest one of modern times', and that the 'unexpected crowd of people' made it seem as if 'all London working men were in favour of an eight hours day'.[1] Engels, who watched it all from a wagon which was used as a speakers' platform, was positively ecstatic. 'It was tremen-

[1] *The Times*, 5 May 1890.

dous. England at last is stirring, and no mistake', he wrote.[1]
The success of the demonstration was largely due to its link
with the eight-hour day campaign; and Hyndman joined in
this heartily, himself preparing a draft bill and also holding
a public debate on the subject with Charles Bradlaugh.

Although their immediate objects were so similar, the
feud beyween Hyndman and Engels persisted. In 1890, the
Bismarckian anti-Socialist legislation was sufficiently re-
laxed for the German Social-Democrats to secure a resound-
ing electoral success; but Hyndman deplored their readiness
to go on following the personal leadership of the *émigré*
Engels. Because of Engels's exclusive attitude, Hyndman
nicknamed him 'the Grand Llama of the Regent's Park
Road' and suggested that he had become 'far more Marxist
than Marx himself'. Hyndman appealed to the German
Socialists to 'eschew dictation' and to throw in their lot with
the British Social-Democrats.[2] Coming from the leader of
such a tiny organization, however, it is not surprising that the
appeal fell on deaf ears; and Bax countered with the suggestion that the British Social-Democrats should now look for
their own leadership to Germany instead of to France. This
naturally annoyed Hyndman, who roundly declared:

> We have not the slightest confidence ourselves in the com-
> petence of the German Social-Democrats to lead the international
> revolutionary party. Neither the economical nor geographical
> position of their country nor their national characteristics qualify
> them for this post.[3]

When the International held its second and formally united
congress at Brussels in 1891, Hyndman was deliberately
absent. He sensed that the German influence would be much
too persuasive for his own liking. Although nine delegates
of the Federation were present, there was little that Hyndman could find to say in favour of the decisions of the

---

[1] Engels to Laura Lafargue, 10 May 1890, *Correspondance Engels-Lafargue*, ii,
pp. 395–6.
[2] *Justice*, 10 Jan., 28 Feb., 7 March 1891.　　　[3] Ibid., 24 Oct. 1891.

congress. 'It was all very well', he wrote, 'that Liebknecht and Vaillant had both denounced the growth of militarism in Europe and had taken care not to mention the question of Alsace-Lorraine; nevertheless, it is not the few well-organized and thoughtful Socialists of France or of Germany that govern in these questions, but the mass which is still stirred when the patriotic chord is touched.'[1] Hyndman's realism on this point contrasted strongly with the optimism of other Socialist leaders, but time was to justify his attitude.

3

One of the problems of the early Socialist bodies was to avoid identification with the anarchists, who formulated and put into practice a drastic policy of violence in order to disrupt society. The political Socialists did not like being associated with assassins such as the French anarchist Ravachol, who was executed in 1892 after committing several murders. In Britain, the trial in the same year of the Walsall anarchists (including David Nicoll of the Socialist League), on charges of manufacturing bombs, caused Hyndman to emphasize the differences between them and the Social-Democrats, although he expressed sympathy with the plight of the defendants. 'We Social-Democrats abjure and protest against individual violence', wrote Hyndman, 'but compared with the infamous creatures who dominate our present system Ravachol himself is respectable and Nicoll is assuredly a hero.'[2]

It was especially important for the Socialists, however, to prevent the anarchists from dominating the International. At the third congress, held at Zurich in 1893 (again in Hyndman's absence) the parliamentary Socialists, including representatives of the S.D.F, secured the exclusion of anarchist representatives. This was not, however, the end of the

[1] *Justice*, 5 Sept. 1891.   [2] Ibid., 14 May 1892.

matter; the anarchists showed a persistent enthusiasm for participating in Socialist congresses; and when plans were laid for a congress of the International in London in 1896, they set about the task of securing entry to the proceedings.

One reason why the anarchists had a chance of re-asserting themselves was that some of the parliamentary Socialists had a certain sympathy, or at least tolerance, for their views. This was particularly the case in England, where the I.L.P. leaders were inclined to feel that the issue had been pre-judged by their rivals of the S.D.F. and by the Continental Socialists. Eleanor Marx wrote just before the congress that Keir Hardie and 'his henchman' Tom Mann were doing all they could 'to get the anarchists in on the usual ground of "fair play" '.[1]

The London congress was held at St. Martin's Hall and lasted for a week from 27th July. Hyndman was present, and was soon involved in the debate which took place at the outset on whether to admit the anarchists. He expressed his own opposition in no uncertain terms: 'I yield to no man in toleration . . . but I denounce anarchy. I denounce disorder, and I stand up for order and organization of International Social-Democracy.' After 'a scene of indescribable confusion and tumult' the resolution to expel the anarchists was carried, and the proceedings somewhat quietened down. It was not, however, a very successful congress. The discussion of delegates' credentials went on until the third day; and the debates on such topics as the Socialist attitude to war, the general strike, and the establishment of a permanent seat for the International—this last being introduced by an S.D.F. delegate—were all very indecisive.[2] Future congresses of the International, however, were no longer to be concerned with the problem of anarchism, and this at least was an advantage from the point of view of securing a

[1] E. Marx to Liebknecht, 11 July 1896. E. Marx Correspondence.
[2] *Conference Record*, 26 July–2 August 1896; *Justice*, 28 July–1 August 1896. *Justice* was published daily during the congress.

common basis for the discussions and of conducting the proceedings with more discipline and dignity.

With the death of Engels in August 1895, the main obstacle to co-operation between the S.D.F. and the orthodox Marxists disappeared. The supporters of the Engels group in the Socialist League had already been returning to membership of the Federation, for lack of any alternative; and in 1896 even Aveling, who had been expelled from the I.L.P., secured re-admission to the ranks which he had quitted with Morris in 1884. According to Bernstein, the unreliable Aveling was re-admitted 'only with reluctance', and 'because it was thought that in entering their organization he had said farewell to his old life'. In March 1898, however, Eleanor Marx, committed suicide—an event for which Aveling was given much of the blame, especially when her private letters was published in *Neue Zeit* and later in *Justice*.[1] Aveling himself, however, only survived the unhappy Eleanor by a few months. Thus within three years the Marx-Engels family group in London had disappeared.

These events encouraged the growth of a more friendly feeling between the S.D.F. and the German Socialists. Liebknecht had found himself working together with Hyndman on various questions—especially that of anarchism—at the London congress of 1896; and thereafter the two leaders remained in friendly contact. Theoretical differences remained, however, and the Germans naturally did not like Hyndman's tendency to criticize themselves and their country. The leading Marxist theoretician and protector of orthodoxy was Karl Kautsky, and his views of the S.D.F. at this time were somewhat contemptuous. Already he was linking Bax and Hyndman together, although Bax had sided with Engels against Hyndman:

> Though I have little in common with the Fabians theoretically, they are yet more attractive to me than Bax and Hyndman with their utopianism concealed behind Marxian phraseology. The

[1] Bernstein in *Neue Zeit*, xvi (1897–8), Nr. 42; *Justice*, 30 July 1898.

Fabians have damaged our movement in England much less by their criticism of superficial Marxism than Bax and Hyndman have by having compromised Marxism.[1]

In fact, Bax was at the time engaged in a controversy with Kautsky on the materialist conception of history. Bax, who as Bernstein said was prepared to put forward the most heretical views by the side of his Marxist orthodoxy, held that ethical as well as material factors were at work in shaping events, and on this issue he was later supported by Hyndman himself.[2] At the same time, the British Marxists strongly condemned the views of Bernstein himself, who partly under Fabian influence began to put forward criticisms of the revolutionary aspects of Marxist theory. An article in *Justice* suggested that Bernstein was trying to 'show Marx in the light of the Fabian ass in the lion's skin of Social-Democracy';[3] and Bax demanded his expulsion from the Socialist movement in an article entitled 'Treacherous Toleration and Faddist Fanaticism'.[4] Facing as they were the competition of Fabian ideas and a modified Socialist faith propounded by the I.L.P., Hyndman and his colleagues feared that toleration of 'revisionist' doctrine would leave them without a leg to stand on. For this reason, they were more hostile to Bernstein than were the orthodox members of his own party, the German Social-Democrats.

Orthodox Marxism was also under constant challenge in France, where the issues of the Dreyfus case had now arisen to divide Socialist leaders on questions of tactics. Here, however, the Federation tended to side with the opportunists rather than with the strictest Marxists. Jean Jaurès, a former radical deputy, who had made his debut on the stage of international Socialism at the London congress, joined the 'Dreyfusards' or 'Revisionists' in demanding a retrial of the

[1] Kautsky to Adler, 12 Nov. 1896, Adler, *Briefwechsel* (Vienna, 1954), p. 221.

[2] *Neue Zeit* in 1896-7, translated in *Social-Democrat*, Aug. 1902-Feb. 1903; Hyndman in *Social-Democrat*, x (Feb. 1906).

[3] *Justice*, 15 May 1897.　　　　[4] Bax in *Social-Democrat*, iv (Jan. 1900).

Dreyfus case; but Guesde and the other 'Marxists' regarded the whole affair as an irrelevant crisis of bourgeois society. From across the Channel, however, Hyndman supported Jaurès in his fight against 'the whole clerico-military-chauvinist-anti-Jew combination'. Another bitter controversy was stirred up when Alexander Millerand, an independent Socialist deputy, entered the Waldeck-Rousseau cabinet, a coalition ministry of the Republicans and other parliamentary groups. In July 1899, the Guesdists and Blanquists issued a joint manifesto condemning the action taken by Millerand as having compromised the Socialist principle of the class war. Hyndman, who always professed to follow French politics very closely, declared that the publication of the manifesto was motivated by 'personal jealousy'; and *Justice* expressed approval of Millerand's action, although with some reservations. 'It is possible', the paper said:

that a crisis so menacing to popular liberty may arise as to justify the temporary participation of a Socialist in a bourgeois Ministry, but such part should only, in our opinion, be taken upon the advice of the national party, and the position be resigned as soon as the crisis is over. We held it to be the duty of French Socialists to support the Waldeck-Rousseau Ministry against the clerico-military reaction.[1]

When the fifth congress of the Socialist International was held in Paris in September 1900, the French delegates, now divided between the Ministerial and Anti-Ministerial factions, exhibited what Hyndman dryly called 'Gallic fraternity, which could scarcely be distinguished from a keen disposition for mutual slaughter'.[2] The congress, however, managed to accept a compromise which was framed in a resolution by Kautsky. This resolution expressed hostility in principle to the idea of a Socialist entering a bourgeois government, but admitted that in cases of emergency it might be justifiable. The British delegation, of which the

---

[1] *Justice*, 2 Sept. 1899.   [2] Hyndman, *Further Reminiscences*, p. 116.

S.D.F. representatives formed a majority, cast its two votes in favour of the resolution, but its compromise character and ambiguity were such that it provided no real guide for future action by Socialists. In the event, therefore, the French Socialists went on quarrelling as fiercely as before.

One practical result of the Paris congress was the establishment of an International Bureau or council with a permanent headquarters at Brussels. Hyndman had been a keen advocate of such a body, and he and Quelch were elected to the Bureau as the British representatives. But Hyndman, whose hostility to the Germans had increased again after the recent death of Liebknecht, cannot have felt comfortable in membership of an organization in which German influence and ideas bulked so large. This was particularly the case as the international scene darkened and national rivalries in Europe and the rest of the world increasingly focussed the attention of all.

4

The growth of imperialism as an element in British policy in the 1890's presented the S.D.F. with food for thought. Could it approve of such a development as 'the opening up of the dark continent to commercialism', especially as it meant, as H. W. Lee put it, 'a fresh lease of life to the capitalist system?'[1] It was perhaps not surprising that the S.D.F. felt obliged to condemn the Jameson Raid on the Transvaal, for William Morris, a genuine 'little Englander' if ever there was one, had lately rejoined its ranks, and at the Federation's New Year gathering of 1896 (just after the news of the raid arrived) he delivered one of his last public speeches, saying that the Transvaal situation was 'a case of a pack of thieves quarrelling about their booty'. But Hyndman took the same view, turning his customary tendency towards chauvinism into an attack upon the cosmopolitan

[1] *Justice*, 12 Dec. 1892.

character of the people who had precipitated the raid. The Transvaal, he maintained, had originally been 'stolen from the natives' by the Boers, but the Boers were less criminal than 'the most loathsome set of Jew capitalists and Christian financiers' who had financed the 'piratical expedition' and who had made a popular hero of Jameson. The situation made Hyndman feel 'almost ashamed of his country'.[1]

At the same time, Hyndman naturally did not forget that other persons were also to blame, and he was not in favour of any concessions by Britain to the imperialism of other countries—not even to France. At the time of the Fashoda incident he chided the French public for its attitude, and in an article in the *Petite République*, the organ of the French Independent Socialists, he bluntly contended that France would be unwise to maintain a big fleet: 'Such a fleet is a luxury for France; for us it is a necessity.'[2] Hyndman later applied the same argument to Germany, and indeed when German warships appeared at Delagoa Bay shortly after the Jameson Raid, the S.D.F. issued a manifesto in favour of an 'adequate increase of our navy'.[3]

Although Hyndman was in favour of Britain defending her empire against all comers, he still maintained that imperial reform was an urgent necessity. In particular, he remained a critic of British policy in India and actually spoke of 'British-made famine' there. At a meeting at the Mansion House in January 1897 to discuss famine relief, he sought to move a resolution criticizing the government for diverting Indian famine relief funds to pay for military operations. The Lord Mayor who was presiding ruled him out of order, but he persisted, and finally had to be ejected from the meeting by 'the City Marshal and an inspector and sergeant of police'.[4] Addressing a Socialist demonstration shortly

---

[1] *Justice*, 6 Jan. 1894, 11 Jan., 4, 25 April 1896.
[2] *Petite République*, 17 Dec. 1898. The phrase was almost identical with that used by Winston Churchill in February 1912, but in relation to Germany. E. L. Woodward, *Great Britain and the German Navy* (Oxford, 1935), p. 370 n.
[3] *Justice*, 23 Jan. 1897.   [4] *The Times*, 18 Jan. 1897.

afterwards, he declared that the Queen's diamond jubilee should be celebrated as the jubilee of 'the Empress of Famine and the Queen of Black Death'.[1] With his friend Dadabhai Naoroji, he then started an 'Anti-Famine' agitation throughout the country. Indians themselves, he felt, were far too slow in taking up their own cause. 'I cannot help feeling contempt', he wrote to Naoroji:

for the Indians here and in India who . . . pass such a silly resolution of congratulation to the Queen as was passed at the Indian National Congress the other day. Congratulation for what? For having ruined India for two or three generations to come? It is pitiful. . . . It is time to be up and stirring, if any good is to be done. I will help, and so will our organization and *Justice*, as much as possible; but 'Providence helps those who help themselves'.[2]

Yet at no time was Hyndman in favour of the severance of Indian ties with Britain. What he wanted from the Indians was 'vigorous attacks and the use of strong language' against British rule, so as to lead to a fairer partnership between the two countries.[3]

The most important external issue of the time, however, from the point of view of the Federation's domestic popularity, was that posed by the situation in South Africa. Even before war broke out Hyndman, who continued to deplore the attitude of the government, had personal cause to realize the disadvantages of going against the tide of public opinion. On 24th September 1899, shortly before the outbreak of hostilities, he participated in an anti-war demonstration in Trafalgar Square organized by the Radical *Daily Chronicle*. A concerted attempt was made to break up the meeting and knives and other missiles were thrown at speakers on the plinth. Hyndman himself was particularly victimized. 'It was solely due to the admirable and courageous behaviour of the police that I have the honour of addressing you with only

1 *The Times*, 20 Feb. 1897.
2 Hyndman to Naoroji, n.d., quoted in Masani, *Naoroji*, pp. 398–9.
3 Hyndman to Naoroji, 25 Jan., 23 July 1900, ibid., pp. 410, 412.

sore ribs, a bruised leg and a battered hat to complain of',
he wrote afterwards to the editor of the *Daily Chronicle*.[1]

Here again, however, as in his attitude to the Jameson
Raid, Hyndman found an opportunity for somewhat
chauvinistic utterances in the very act of opposing his
country's policy. He spoke of the war as 'the Jews' war', and
declared that it was 'worse than the Dreyfus case'. More
explicitly he described it as an 'abominable war on behalf of
German-Jew mineowners and other international inter-
lopers'. Even at a time when anti-semitism was not un-
common in left-wing political circles, Hyndman gave much
offence. At a London meeting of the Federation in March
1900, he attached such emphasis to the 'Jewish International'
that a motion of censure was tabled for the party conference
in August.[2]

Although most of the British Socialists opposed the war,
their ranks were not entirely united. Blatchford, for instance,
the editor of the *Clarion*, had been a regular soldier, and he
felt that he must support the Army in action. The Fabian
Society, for more abstract reasons, also took an opportunistic
attitude and maintained that a British victory in South
Africa would benefit that country. All this provided some
reason for the Continental Socialists to criticize their British
comrades at the 1900 congress of the International in Paris.
Hyndman, who was present, largely agreed with them at the
time: 'As an English Socialist and therefore as one of those
who belong to the greatest colonial empire in the world', he
expressed his full sympathy with their criticism.[3] But it was
not long before he began to change his mind on the question.

By 1901 the bulk of the fighting was over, and only a bitter
guerilla campaign remained. Hyndman had been reflecting

---

[1] *Daily Chronicle*, 26 Sept. 1899; F. W. Soutter, *Fights for Freedom* (1925),
pp. 212–16; *Justice*, 30 Sept. 1899.

[2] *Justice*, 7 Oct. 1899, 10 March, 11 Aug. 1900; Hyndman, *Further Reminiscences*, p. 165.

[3] *Internationaler Sozialisten-Kongress zu Paris, Verhandlungen* (Berlin, 1900),
pp. 4–26.

on the relationship between the Boer settlers and the African natives, and sympathizing as usual with the latter. By the summer he had decided that under the circumstances the best thing for the Africans was a British victory. He explained his new attitude in a letter to *Justice*:

I hold, with our friend Cunninghame Graham, that this is a struggle between two burglars. . . . The country belongs neither to Boer nor to Briton. . . . The Zulu would be glad, I take it, if this war between the kites and the crows ended in the disappearance of both. The future of South Africa is, I believe, to the black man; and, if I am going to agitate for the independence of anybody, it is for the independence of the splendid native tribes who are being crushed by the Boers and ourselves together that I propose to go to work.[1]

His influence was sufficient to carry the S.D.F. executive, which forthwith passed a resolution to the effect that further anti-war agitation was 'a waste of time and money'. At a time when the appalling conditions in the South African concentration camps drew a number of humanitarians, Liberal or otherwise, into the pro-Boer cause, this attitude was severely criticized by a minority, prominent among whom were Bax and also a new and vigorous member of the executive, Theodore Rothstein, a Jewish refugee from Tsarism.[2]

Although Hyndman had signed a manifesto against the war put out by the International Socialist Bureau, he now began to complain against 'the strong Continental prejudice against England' which had emerged as a consequence. In October 1901 Joseph Chamberlain, the Colonial Secretary, defended the action of the British troops in South Africa by comparing their behaviour favourably with that of the German and other Continental armies. This point was taken up by Hyndman who wrote in *Justice* that the atrocities committed by Russia in Manchuria, by Germany and France in China, and by France and Belgium in Central

[1] *Justice*, 20 July 1901.   [2] Ibid., 20, 27 July, 17 Aug. 1901.

Africa had, each of them, 'far surpassed anything of which England has been guilty in South Africa'.[1]

Thus Hyndman's national feelings, always lurking in the back of his mind, came to the fore as usual. But it would be wrong to describe his change of attitude as having been motivated by this alone. His sympathy with the Africans in South Africa was not merely an excuse for his decision not to go on opposing the war. It was rather a natural consequence of his general sympathy with subject peoples, already manifested for other parts of the world. It would, therefore, be difficult to describe the conflict between himself and the other S.D.F. leaders as one simply of chauvinism versus internationalism, although his opponents naturally often saw it in this light.

5

By the turn of the century, Hyndman had devoted twenty years to the active work of Socialist propaganda. At a dinner given to him by *Reynolds's Newspaper* in May 1898, he was acclaimed by many of his colleagues in the Socialist movement, both young and old; several with whom he had often differed, such as Tom Mann and Bernstein, made flattering speeches. Hyndman spoke with nostalgia of the time when he had begun his public agitation for Socialism, 'under the pump on Clerkenwell Green'.[2] In these early days, as we have seen, he had convinced himself that England was almost ripe for social revolution. He had set the date of its advent in 1889 and, when that was not realized, he had moved it to 1900. But as the nineteenth century drew to its end with the S.D.F. in decline, he was obliged to discard his sanguine expectations of the immediate success of Socialism in England. 'It is manifestly not true', he now declared:

that the earlier development of capitalism of necessity entails, in the community which has led the way in this respect, the

[1] *Justice*, 23 Nov. 1901.   [2] Ibid., 21 May 1898.

earlier development of organized Socialism. On the contrary, the complete capitalist predominance in industrial England has been the main cause of the reactionary attitude of the workers at the present time.[1]

Hyndman had repeatedly pointed to various obstacles to Socialism: the exclusion of the working class from full educational opportunities, the influence of 'bourgeois' political economy, the existence of 'reactionary' leaders in the old trade unions, the quietist doctrines of religion, the semblance of political democracy, the 'astute' behaviour of the aristocracy, and the power of the capitalist press. He was now able to see these difficulties in the perspective of twenty years of unsuccessful agitation. 'Things are moving very slowly here', he wrote to Richard T. Ely, the American economist, 'and I despair, as I have long despaired, of any great change being wrought until there comes some severe shock from without, or some complete economic collapse within.'[2] It was a situation which also worried his remaining colleagues, and caused further dissensions within the Federation itself.

[1] Hyndman, 'Socialism and the Future of England', *Cosmopolis*, ix (1898), 34.
[2] Hyndman to Ely, 4 March 1898, Ely Papers.

VII ～ LOW SPIRITS,
HIGH FINANCE

I

THE dawn of the new century had now come, but with it, no relief to Hyndman's gloom about the prospect of the Federation. He was irritated by the attitude of the membership which, while so largely dependent in the past upon his efforts, now failed to provide him with an opportunity for fighting the 1900 General Election. By far the best prospect of a straight fight without Liberal opposition was at Northampton, where the Radical Henry Labouchere would have welcomed him as a colleague in the representation of the two-member constituency. But unfortunately, the Northampton S.D.F. branch was far too slow in removing its existing candidate, who was something of a 'Jingo' on the South African War, and inviting Hyndman in his place. 'I am angry I confess', Hyndman wrote privately, 'that the workers have shut me finally out of the H. of C. Next time I shall be too old. But the workers always prefer mediocrities. . . .'[1]

It was also a matter of concern to him that the 1900 elections for the Federation's executive resulted in the return of Theodore Rothstein, the Russian *émigré*, at the top of the poll. Rothstein, apart from being a Jew—an offence in itself to Hyndman—had ventured to speak of past S.D.F.

[1] Hyndman to Wilshire, 8 Sept. 1900, Wilshire Papers; Hyndman, *Further Reminiscences*, pp. 421f.

policy as 'fossilized academism'.[1] Rothstein was much more consistently 'internationalist' in his outlook than Hyndman, but it could not have been merely the cosmopolitan element in the party which had given him so large a vote.

The fact was that there was a new generation of members who felt that Hyndman, who was now almost sixty, and most of his immediate colleagues were too old a leadership for a revolutionary party. These youngsters, most of them either in London or in Scotland, got much of their knowledge of Marxism, not from the profusion of Hyndman's pamphlets and the limited selection of works of Marx and Engels published by the Twentieth Century Press in London, but from the American Socialist publishers, the Labor News Company of New York and Charles Kerr's press in Chicago.

American publications could easily enter Britain, of course, and there was no language problem. But the link of the young S.D.F. members with American Socialism was largely forged in the first place at the meetings of the International. It was especially significant that at the 1900 Paris Congress an S.D.F. delegate from Scotland, S. G. Yates of the Leith branch, identified himself with the delegates of the American Socialist Labor Party (S.L.P.) in supporting a resolution to condemn Millerand's tactic of joining a bourgeois government. This was contrary to the official policy of the Federation which, as we have seen, had committed itself to Kautsky's compromise resolution.

Hyndman had not formed any favourable impression of the S.L.P. 'S.L.P. men seem quite impossible', he wrote to Wilshire. '. . . Oddly enough our difficulty here is with the trimming leaders of the I.L.P. and not with our fanatics at all.'[2] He spoke too soon; for thanks to their contacts with the American organization, its weekly and daily journal the

---

[1] *Social-Democrat* iv (1900), 167, 174; Hyndman to Wilshire, 19 Aug. 1901, quoted *Challenge* (Los Angeles) 11 Sept. 1901.
[2] Hyndman to Wilshire, 11 Dec. 1900, Wilshire Papers.

People and the pamphlets by its leader Daniel De Leon, the British 'fanatics' gradually developed strength in the Federation, especially in the Scottish branches. They derived much support from the Irish Socialist James Connolly, who had been at odds with Hyndman at the Paris congress. Hyndman had tried to prevent Connolly from winning recognition for his Irish Socialist Republican Party at the congress, on the grounds that Ireland was not an independent unit: but Connolly had been successful in the upshot. During the summer of 1901 he visited Scotland on lecture tours and was enthusiastically received by the younger Socialists there.[1] These so-called 'impossibilists' soon became an active force which could not be ignored by the official leadership.[2]

It was at this point that Hyndman, challenged from so many sides, worried about his financial situation, anxious to alter the Federation's 'line' towards the South African War, and distressed in general by the failure of so many years of Socialist agitation, took a definite decision to withdraw from political activity. He wrote out a letter of explanation to H. W. Lee, the Federation's rather colourless secretary, which was to be read at the annual conference in August 1901. It was a curious mixture of his usual arrogance and a strong sense of disillusion and frustration.[3]

Dear Lee,—In withdrawing from the Executive of the Social-Democratic Federation, after more than twenty years of continuous service, during which I have placed myself unreservedly at the disposal of the organization which I helped to establish, I think I owe it to myself and my old comrades to lay before the Twenty-first Conference of our body a few of the reasons that had led me to take this step.

1. After so long a period of work on the Executive, I wish to look at matters from the outside.

[1] R. M. Fox, *James Connolly* (Tralee, 1946), p. 51; *Justice*, 4 May, 22 June, 13 July 1901.
[2] For a fuller study of the impossibilists, see my article, 'The Impossibilist Revolt in Britain', in the *International Review of Social History*, i (1956), 377–97.
[3] *Justice*, 10 Aug. 1901.

2. I fail to detect among the English workers that class consciousness and class antagonism without which no good whatever can be done. Even the members of the S.D.F. leave very much to be desired in this respect. As one of the highly-educated well-to-do class myself, I am quite astounded at the ignorance and apathy of my countrymen, and I am deeply discouraged at the result of our long-continued propaganda.

3. Under existing conditions our only hope lies in successful political action. Yet the majority of our organization seems wholly destitute of political aptitude. Constituencies are worked up to a certain point and then no steps whatever are taken to secure permanent advantage for revolutionary Social-Democracy from the time, trouble, and money expended on them, while suggestion and interference by the Executive have not infrequently been resented. Burnley, Blackburn, South Stratford, Aberdeen, Reading, Bow and Bromley, Northampton, South West Ham, Walworth are all examples of this. The canvassing, which is an indispensable preliminary to success, is persistently neglected.

4. I feel I have done all the good I can do in the detail work of the organization. When the workers at large or the members of the Social-Democratic Federation rouse themselves in earnest, and show a determination to deal effectively with the dangerous situation around us and ahead of us, I shall be glad to make common cause with them in a vigorous attempt to relieve our country from the corrupt and incapable government by gang which now oppresses and degrades us, and to help to the best of my ability in the establishment of a co-operative commonwealth of organized Socialism. Till then, I remain,—yours fraternally, H. M. Hyndman.

2

Bereft of its one outstanding leader, the Federation more and more degenerated into a cockpit of small disputing factions, among whom for purposes of analysis we can distinguish a 'left', a 'centre', and a 'right'. The 'right' was constituted by the Lancashire members, many of whom were unionists in the weaving towns, anxious to maintain the S.D.F. link with the trade unions through the Labour Representation Committee. Quelch and his colleagues—

Hyndman's old associates—constituted the 'centre' and were not so much interested in the Labour Representation Committee as in 'Socialist Unity' with the I.L.P. They aimed at the formation of a powerful Socialist Party under S.D.F. leadership. On the 'left' were the 'impossibilists' in Scotland and London, who opposed not only affiliation to the Labour Representation Committee but also the concept of 'Socialist unity' if it meant any compromise with the reformist I.L.P. The Scottish 'impossibilists', at a meeting of the Scottish S.D.F. District Council in March 1901, had in fact already forced the issue of withdrawal from the Scottish Workers' Parliamentary Committee, an organization parallel to the English Labour Representation Committee.

When the annual conference of the S.D.F. met at Birmingham in August 1901, it was not surprising that withdrawal from the Labour Representation Committee was agreed upon. It was in fact proposed by Quelch himself, who had failed to carry a resolution endorsing the 'class war' at the second L.R.C. conference in February.[1] The Lancashire branches apparently opposed withdrawal, and an Accrington delegate called the proposal 'foolish', saying that it was the Federation's task to 'permeate and capture trade unions'.[2]

On certain other issues, however, Quelch and his colleagues found themselves at odds with the 'impossibilists', and then the sessions became very stormy. Quelch himself was in fact to the 'left' of Hyndman, but he was still not 'left' enough for the impatient young men of the Federation. He tried to defend the official attitude of the S.D.F. delegates over the Millerand affair at the Paris congress:

We are not impossibilists, and circumstances must determine our policy. We must defend any and every means . . . from the ballot-box to the bomb, from political action to assassination. (Cheers.) Oh, yes, the movers of the resolution cheer assassination, but they will not allow a Socialist to enter a Ministry.[3]

[1] L.R.C. *Conference Report*, 1901, p. 21.   [2] *Justice*, 10 Aug. 1901.   [3] Ibid.

The 'impossibilist' resolution was lost by thirty-seven votes to eight.

Undeterred by this defeat, the 'left' in the Federation—the 'unholy Scotch current' as Rothstein called it—continued its agitation. 'Economic classes' were organized to spread the knowledge of Marxism along S.L.P. lines, and James Connolly lectured to many of the branches.[1] In August 1902 there appeared the first number of the *Socialist*, described as the organ of the Scottish District Council: Connolly was largely instrumental in founding it, and to start with it was printed in Dublin. The Socialist alliance between Scotland and Ireland naturally brought republicanism to the fore, and the *Socialist* bitterly attacked the S.D.F.'s 'Open Letter to the King' in which the party leaders sought to give advice to the new King, Edward VII, so that he could secure for himself 'a name in history which mankind will look back to'.[2] There were, however, two schools of thought among the 'impossibilists' as to their future tactics. The Scotsmen, who had 'captured' the District Council, were for turning that body into the nucleus of the new party: but the Londoners still entertained the hope that their representatives on the executive could do something to reform the S.D.F.

At a meeting of the Scottish District Council held in February 1903, it was reported that 'some very important business' had been transacted. In the following month the printing of the *Socialist* was transferred from Dublin to Edinburgh; and soon afterwards Connolly's own *Workers' Republic* ceased publication and was incorporated in the Scottish paper. Connolly had just paid a brief visit to America where he had heard Daniel De Leon, the S.L.P. leader, declare that 'the historic mission of America' was to liberate Ireland, Finland, Poland, and all the subject nations

[1] T. A. Jackson, *Solo Trumpet* (1953), p. 56; T. Bell, *Pioneering Days* (1941), pp. 35–38; *Justice*, 19 Oct. 1901.
[2] *Justice*, 21 June 1902; *Socialist*, Aug. 1902.

of the world. He was now determined to emigrate to America and to work for American Socialism. It may have been his decision which persuaded the Scottish 'impossibilists' to establish themselves as an independent body to carry on Connolly's work in Britain. At any rate, in the March number of the *Socialist*, Yates issued an ultimatum to the Federation leadership, and indicated that the Scotsmen were on the verge of secession.[1]

The London 'impossibilists', however, had been ignored in the consultation which had been going on between Edinburgh, Dublin, and New York, and even in the conduct of the *Socialist*, the 'impossibilist' organ. According to Jack Fitzgerald, the leader of the Londoners:

> During the whole time they [sc. the Scottish members] were supposed to be working with the London section for the re-organization of the S.D.F., they were playing a double game by forming a new organization in secret . . . The London section were no more ready to blindly follow would-be geniuses from Scotland than 'highly educated' leaders from Queen Anne's Gate.[2]

They naturally resented the way in which the Scots had abandoned them, leaving them as an even smaller minority in what was left of the Federation.

At the London conference of the Federation in April 1903, Yates was duly expelled; and in the following month he and his friends in Scotland announced the formation of the 'Socialist Labour Party'—the same title as that of the American organization—which would strive for 'the political overthrow of capitalism'. The new party, however, seemed very like the S.D.F. in its programme, which included several immediate demands such as the legal eight-hour day and full enfranchisement of the people. In the autumn of the same year it fought municipal elections in Leith and

---

[1] *Socialist*, Jan., March, Aug. 1903, Sept. 1906.
[2] *Socialist Standard*, Aug. 1906. Since 1893 Hyndman had been living at Queen Anne's Gate, St. James's Park.

Glasgow and polled 796 votes. Its total membership at this time cannot have been more than 200 at the most.[1]

Meanwhile Quelch and his colleagues—who had been reinforced once again by Hyndman—were anxious to clear all the remaining 'impossibilists' out of the Federation. At the annual conference held at Burnley in April 1904, Fitzgerald and another London leader were expelled, and Hyndman wrote to Wilshire: 'We are troubled here just now by a crew of impossibilists, whose faculty of lying, slander, and vilification is only equalled by the De Leon crowd. We have turned the whole pack of them out at last.'[2] The followers of Fitzgerald held a meeting of their own in June, at which they formally announced the formation of yet another body—the Socialist Party of Great Britain (S.P.G.B.). In September they began to issue their own journal, the *Socialist Standard*, with the declared purpose of raising the standard of Socialism which had in their view been lowered by the Federation. The S.P.G.B. was even smaller than the Scottish body and its membership appears to have been about 100. It refused to accept any programme of 'palliatives' and was thus in the strictest sense 'impossibilist' —as indeed it remains today.[3] The Socialist Labour Party on the other hand was more important though less long-lived: it became absorbed in the problems of industrial unionism, gained some strength on Clydeside in the following decade, and after the war became a major component of the Communist Party.

3

The revolt of the 'impossibilists' was primarily directed against Hyndman, whose chauvinism and parliamentary ambition appeared to them to have diverted the S.D.F. from

[1] *Socialist*, May, Nov. 1903, Sept. 1904; *Platform of the Socialist Labour Party* (?1903).
[2] Hyndman to Wilshire, 27 May 1904, Wilshire Papers.
[3] *Socialist Standard*, Sept., Oct. 1904, May 1905; *Socialist*, June 1904; S.P.G.B., *Question of the Day* (n.d.), p. 120.

the straight path of Marxism. But Hyndman, as we have seen, had side-stepped most of the controversy, leaving Quelch to bear the brunt of the attack. At the peak of his disappointment and irritation in 1900 he reflected wryly on the possibility that if he had kept clear of Socialism he 'could have been Secretary of State on the Tory side'.[1] But he had no real desire to abandon the Socialist movement, and was only anxious to repair his financial position, which had suffered so much from his political activities. He therefore plunged back into the City, and resumed the activities in company promotion which he had originally developed in the 1870's.

In 1902 his name appeared for the first time in the *Directory of Directors*. He was then director of at least six companies with a combined nominal capital of £635,000. One of them, the Komati Exploration Co. Ltd., had been formed in March 1896—just after the Jameson Raid—with the object of acquiring 'certain mines in South Africa'. It had had a nominal capital of £300,000, but apparently issued only ten £1 shares and must have been a failure.[2] At the turn of the century, however, Hyndman's interest turned to the Gold Coast, where there was a mining boom as a result of the Ashanti war. 'I am busy indeed with my money grabbing', he wrote to Wilshire in that year:

It is quite essential I should be. I have started three Ashanti Syndicates & got the money for them, and am now about to go into a much bigger thing than either. . . . There are prospects that . . . I may be a rich man & do something for the movement yet.[3]

Hyndman's three syndicates—the Upper Wassau Gold Mines (founded in December 1900), the Ashanti Gold Reefs Syndicate, and the Ashanti Gold Mines Selection Syndicate (both set up in March 1901), each of them with a nominal

[1] Hyndman to Wilshire, 8 Sept. 1900, Wilshire Papers.
[2] *Directory of Directors* (1902), p. 432; *Mining Year Book* (1902), pp. 497, 851, 907, 1103; (1906), pp. 474, 480.
[3] Hyndman to Wilshire, 25 Oct. 1900, Wilshire Papers.

capital of £10,000—did succeed in obtaining land concessions in the area, and for a time his hopes were high. It was
not long, however, before most of the expectations of a Gold
Coast boom were disappointed, although it is not clear
whether Hyndman succeeded in selling his companies or his
concessions in time.

The sensational Yukon boom which followed the Klondyke gold discovery of 1896 had also attracted Hyndman's
attention. A wild rush to the 'mountain of gold ore' took
place, and the output of gold rapidly increased to a climax
in 1900. 'I am now interested in this Yukon region & am
brought into contact with the men . . . who at least have
lived more than one winter in the country', he wrote to
Wilshire at the time.[1] He had just formed a Stewart & Indian
Rivers Gold Hydraulic Syndicate with the nominal capital
of £5,000. In March 1901 he started a 'much bigger thing',
the Klondyke Consolidated Goldfields with a nominal
capital of £300,000. 'My Klondyke venture is coming to
fruition, I think', he wrote to Wilshire: 'Happily also my
West African Syndicates—I am chairman of three—are
doing very well. When I can clear up reasonably, if ever I
can, I shall cut business & devote the rest of my life to
literature & Socialism.'[2]

The Klondyke company, however, required fresh sources
of capital; and Hyndman, who was always interested in
France, decided to tap the Paris money market for his
project. The company, therefore, set up a Paris office, which
Hyndman frequently visited, though its headquarters remained at his London home in Queen Anne's Gate, St. James's
Park. Hyndman had other French interests, and sought to
buy up a French company which was making a net profit of
£280,000 a year; he was also associated with a 'big group"
which was planning to construct 'a superb hotel' in Paris.[3]

[1] Hyndman to Wilshire, 4 Sept. 1900, Wilshire Papers.
[2] Ibid., 21 Feb. 1901.
[3] Ibid., 21 Feb. 1901, 27 Oct. 1903, 26 March 1904; *Mining Year Book* (1902),
p. 497; (1907), pp. 463-4.

These activities were by no means the sum total of Hyndman's interests. By arrangement with his cousins in Barbados, he was also trading in West Indian properties. He
was impressed by the merits of the Colt Gun, 'admittedly by
far the first weapon of its class' as he put it, and became a
director of the Colt Gun and Carriage Company. And he
was always on the look-out for new possibilities. 'Klondyke
is not doing badly. Colt Gun is working up. I have a new
tyre which we guarantee against puncture for 12,000 miles
& is as fast as Dunlop!' he wrote to Wilshire in 1903 with
the same energy and enthusiasm as if he were speaking of a
campaign to found or develop branches of the S.D.F.[1]

In spite of his retirement from political office Hyndman
did not stop writing for *Justice* on various topics of home and
foreign affairs, and he also gave four lectures at the South
Place Institute, London, in February 1902. 'I never spoke so
well in my life', he wrote to Wilshire: 'I am beginning to
think I get stronger as I get older . . . I go on speaking and
writing, and writing and speaking much after the fashion of
a circus horse, and to much the same effect. I suppose something will come of it some day.'[2] He also considered undertaking the translation of the second and third volumes of
Das Kapital—a formidable task by itself. He believed at the
same time that he could do plenty of valuable work without
participating in the activities of the Federation, and he even
expressed regret that he had tied himself 'to such an extent
to the S.D.F.'[3]

His business activities although not uniformly successful
appear to have brought some return, and to have provided
him with a degree of financial security once more. In April
1902 he felt able to take occupancy of Brasted House, near
Westerham in Kent, 'a charming old village house with
plenty of room and a beautiful garden', which had belonged

[1] Hyndman to Wilshire, 4 July 1902, 20 March 1903, 22 Oct. 1903; *Directory
of Directors* (1906), p. 453.
[2] Hyndman to Wilshire, 13 Feb. 1902.
[3] Ibid., 13 Feb. 1902, 23 April 1902.

to his great-uncle, J. P. Mayers, and had since been in his cousins' hands. His object was in large part to provide a restful home for his wife, who had been ill for some time. In August while staying at Brasted, Hyndman himself had severe attacks of rheumatism and took to his bed for some time. 'Five weeks in bed . . . *very seriously* ill, with much pain, with [little] or no sleep, & great depression, complete breakdown of nerves', he wrote despondently to Wilshire in September. He had an easy explanation for this unaccustomed breakdown of his health: 'All the doctors' fault. I wonder I did not die.'[1]

But Hyndman at least enjoyed his own convalescence at what he called 'Yesterday House, Longago Lane, Backbeyond Kent', surrounded by 'a lawn of all lawns, stretching down to the brooklet at the bottom'. The peaceful village with its cottages, inns, and general air of comfort, pleased him, and if it too had its social problem, this had the advantage of confirming him in his own well-established views. 'You can study here the economics of class rule in the country very nicely,' he said. 'Yesterday House' had two pews in the parish church, one for the family and the other for the servants, to show how carefully class distinctions were maintained in the presence of the Deity. Mrs. Hyndman discovered that she could not get servants unless she herself attended services and so she 'reverently' took her place in the family pew.[2]

Early in 1903 Hyndman resumed much of his political work; but he was still spending a good deal of his time on business activities. In May he went to Budapest on business, though he found himself travelling from Paris to Vienna with his old friend the Irish labour leader Michael Davitt, who was on his way to Odessa to investigate the Russian pogroms. The two veterans seem to have enjoyed each other's company, although Hyndman could not share

[1] Hyndman to Wilshire, 23 Sept., 14 Oct. 1902.
[2] *Wilshire's Magazine*, Dec. 1902; Hyndman, *Further Reminiscences*, p. 481.

Davitt's admiration of the independent peasantry of Bavaria
and Austria.[1] In the following year, business was not so
satisfactory, for the Russo-Japanese war 'knocked off the
supplies of working capital from Paris'. 'A succession of
disasters' followed, and Hyndman had to give up Brasted
House, which he had wanted to occupy permanently. 'I do
wish I could clear myself finally of business', he wrote in
March 1905, although he admitted 'I make enough to keep
myself going'. So his business had to continue, and ranged
from Canadian oil shale to a new type of American pencil
called the 'Arc Lamp Pencil'.[2] In 1905 he began to feel the
burden of his incessant work; he wanted a holiday, and
dreamed of a trip around the world with his wife. 'If we do
go', he wrote to Wilshire, '. . . we shall probably go south
first, to Egypt & then to Australia; then to Japan & on home
by America. India I scarcely dare hope to visit. Probably
they would put me in gaol. But I should get a reception if I
did go.'[3] Nothing of this materialized, however; his own
renewed political work, combined with his continued business activities, seem to have tied him to his native land.

4

Hyndman's return to Socialist politics was formally
marked by a celebration in March 1903 at the Queen's
Hall, London. A. E. Fletcher, a Radical journalist and
former editor of the *Daily Chronicle*, took the chair and in his
speech presented a list of a Socialist Cabinet with Hyndman
as first President of a British Co-operative Commonwealth.
Hyndman was immensely flattered by this, and by the whole
occasion. He now plunged into a fresh campaign against the
movement for tariff reform which had just been initiated

[1] Hyndman to Wilshire, 14 May 1903, Wilshire Papers; Hyndman, *Further
Reminiscences*, pp. 51–53.
[2] Hyndman to Wilshire, 27 May 1904, 16 March 1905, 7 Oct. 1905, 2 Nov.
1905, 25 Oct. 1911.
[3] Ibid., 4 June 1905.

by Joseph Chamberlain. Chamberlain's proposals appeared
to many to be an effective and attractive remedy for trade
depression and unemployment. In Hyndman's view, however, protection was a more formidable enemy than Liberalism, for it would tend to strengthen capitalism with its
horrors and miseries. 'Old as I am,' he said, 'I have some go
still left in me, and I cannot spend what remains to me of
life better than in endeavouring once more to rouse the
people of England and Scotland to the dangers and the
opportunities ahead of them.'[1]

Hyndman followed Chamberlain on the latter's speaking
tour through the country and held a number of meetings in
opposition to tariff reform. He started his campaign at
Manchester, the citadel of Free Trade. After another
meeting at Northampton, he appeared in Glasgow on
9 October and was 'received with loud and prolonged
applause' by '5,000 Socialists and Socialist sympathizers' at
a meeting held in St. Andrew's Hall, where Chamberlain
had held his own meeting only a few days before. Hyndman
spoke on 'Free Trade, the Colonies, and India': 'It was as
big a meeting as he [Chamberlain] had and quite as enthusiastic', he wrote afterwards, 'I don't know what these
extraordinary meetings mean. Can we have taken a turn in
this stick-in-the-mud old country?' A meeting at Bradford
appeared equally successful, and from there he wrote to
Justice: 'I had a packed meeting here last night (Sunday), in
the halls of the Labour Church Institute, which I should say
held some 1,500 people. . . . The great towns of Yorkshire
are getting far beyond mere "Labourism", I rejoice to say.'
He was elated and exuberant: 'What do these meetings of
mine in Great Britain mean? They amaze me. People get
wildly enthusiastic', he wrote to Wilshire.[2]

On 14th November, Hyndman addressed a meeting at the

---

[1] *Justice*, 4 April, 11 July 1903.
[2] Ibid., 17, 24 Oct. 1903; Hyndman to Wilshire, 15, 22 Oct. 1903, Wilshire
Papers.

Queen's Hall, London, at which a resolution was carried to the effect that the present fiscal controversy should be treated as 'a quarrel between two sections of the capitalist classes as to the best method of securing the fruits of the exploitation of labour'. He even carried his campaign across the Channel, and declared in Paris that Chamberlain, who linked his tariff proposals with a plan for imperial preference, had no right to speak of an imperial policy so long as he ignored India's claim to self-government.[1]

Hyndman's campaign against tariff reform was carried out with such vigour and zeal that it gave the impression that he was supporting the cause of Free Trade, and thus identifying himself with Liberalism. At the end of his campaign, therefore, the S.D.F. issued a manifesto declaring:

> International Social-Democracy will know no tariff walls and require no import duties. . . . But it is because we are Free Traders in the best and fullest sense that we oppose the capitalist Free Traders no less than their Protectionist opponents. They profess to look after your interests by securing for you cheap food, whereas they are really concerned only with the cheapness of the supply of labour.[2]

Reynold's Newspaper, the old champion of Radicalism, which was publishing a symposium on 'Liberalism and Labour', invited Hyndman, Bax, and Quelch among others to state their views in its columns. All of them bitterly criticized the Liberal Party and especially the 'Lib-Labs' for their 're-actionary' cry of 'Free Trade for ever'.[3] Thus Hyndman and the S.D.F. made it clear that they were as much opposed to the old Liberalism as to the new Imperialism on the question of fiscal policy.

Meanwhile, trade depression had returned; Lancashire, in particular, began to suffer from the loss of some of its export markets. In 'the cotton distress and capitalist anarchy' Hyndman was only too glad to find another sign of capitalist

[1] *Justice*, 7, 21 Nov. 1903.   [2] Ibid., 2 Jan. 1904.
[3] *Reynolds's Newspaper*, 28 June, 19 July, 2 Aug. 1903.

crisis: 'A state of things is arising in Lancashire wholly un-
paralleled since the Civil War in the United States.'[1] Trade
depression directed attention once more to the question of
unemployment; and S.D.F. branches especially in East and
South London were busy again organizing demonstrations
of the workless, though they were much more orderly than
twenty years before. In 1904 the figures of unemployment
reached their highest point since 1893. In Poplar, where
there were several S.D.F. members on the Board of Guardians, an investigation of unemployment in the borough was
made, and the result showed that one out of every four
workers was unemployed.[2]

Mass meetings were also being held in Manchester and
Salford where distress had considerably increased. Hyndman
himself went up to Manchester at the invitation of a local
unemployed committee. He spoke at a meeting presided
over by the Lord Mayor and caused a sensation by declaring
that 'the men of my own class . . . always looked upon the
workers either as "food for powder or food for plunder" '.[3]
A member of the Federation also invented a new form of
propaganda at this time—the long-distance protest march.
The army boot-makers of Northampton, who were on strike,
marched to London under the leadership of one James
Gribble, an S.D.F. member. In the same year Parliament
passed an Unemployed Workmen Act which authorized
the establishment of local relief committees to assist emigration and to provide work for the unemployed. This Act did
not go very far, however, for private charity was expected to
supply the necessary funds. 'Curse their charity and socialize
the means of production' was the S.D.F. reaction, as its
leaders co-operated with other Socialist bodies to form a
'Right to Work' Committee, to demand public provision
of work for the unemployed.[4]

[1] *Justice*, 19 March 1904.   [2] Ibid., 19 Nov. 1904.
[3] Hyndman, *Further Reminiscences*, p. 279; *Justice*, 26 Nov., 17, 24 Dec. 1904.
[4] *Justice*, 18 Nov., 9 Dec. 1905; S.D.F., *Conference Report*, 1906, p. 16.

During the course of this agitation the S.D.F. held a number of meetings to press for the free maintenance of schoolchildren. Hyndman had meanwhile been advocating free meals for children in letters to the Conservative *Morning Post*. His arguments were based on national policy and not on humanitarian sentiment. 'Lack of good food, good clothes, and good air in children,' he maintained, 'is the main reason why some 50 per cent. of our urban working-class population is unfit to bear arms. Even from the new "Imperialist" point of view this is a serious matter.'[1] H. W. Lee, the party secretary, looked upon the problem from the trade union angle: 'In strikes,' he said, 'it is always the children that are the weak links in the chains of resistance.' This proposal, at once the most practical and the most humane of the S.D.F.'s palliatives, differentiated the Federation clearly from the 'impossibilists' or what Hunter Watts called 'the "let the pot boil over" school of revolutionists'.[2]

In January 1905 Hyndman represented the S.D.F. at the Guildhall conference on state maintenance and met with a reception 'from all the trade unionists there' which, he said, 'more than repaid me for many a day of weariness and depression'.[3] He had by now recovered from the effects of his disillusionment with the working class, but he was not at all sure about the future fulfilment of his own political ambitions. 'Sometimes, I think my turn may come. Then again I feel depressed', he wrote to Wilshire in 1905. 'I have been up & down since 1874, like a jack-in-the-box,' he said. 'For the moment the lid is half-open & I am poking my nose out.'[4] By now, however, the S.D.F. had overcome the setback it experienced during the South African War

[1] *Morning Post*, 29 Oct. 1900.

[2] J. H. Watts, *State Maintenance for School Children* (1904); H. W. Lee in *Justice*, 3 Dec. 1904.

[3] *Justice*, 28 Jan. 1905.

[4] Hyndman to Wilshire, 19 May, 18 Nov. 1905, Wilshire Papers. 1874 was the year in which he entered business.

and had also retaken the ground lost as a result of the 'impossibilist' revolt. Its vicissitudes had served to strengthen the *esprit de corps* of its leadership, and it was ready for a fresh campaign.

5

The Federation also received an unexpected boost at this time from the adhesion of a wealthy and colourful member of the aristocracy. This was the Countess of Warwick, the wife of the fifth Earl, who was born in 1861 and had settled upon her an inheritance which gave her an income of £30,000 a year. She was a celebrated society beauty of the late Victorian period and for some time lived a gay social life. In 1895 she held a fancy-dress ball at Warwick Castle, the extravagance of which was bitterly criticized by Blatchford in the *Clarion*. Acting on an impulse, she hurried to London to visit the *Clarion* office and demand an explanation from the editor; Blatchford in reply pointed out to her 'the difference between productive and unproductive labour'. The Countess thereupon began to see the light, and next day, as she wrote in her memoirs, 'I sent for ten pounds' worth of books on Socialism.'[1] Finally she decided that she must identify herself with the political cause, and so she joined up with the S.D.F.

Hyndman made the acquaintance of the Countess some time in 1903. Early in the following year, he confided to Wilshire:

I am just off to lunch *tête-à-tête* with Lady Warwick with whom I have at the present time a great deal to confer upon. . . . When in Paris I asked Clemenceau and Jaurès to meet her at lunch at Merguery's. . . . They were both quite swept off their legs by her beauty (tho' 42, as she constantly tells people, she looks 26). . . . As the world is today she is a most valuable recruit & I am very glad we have got her.[2]

[1] Frances, Countess of Warwick, *Life's Ebb and Flow* (1929), pp. 90–92.
[2] Hyndman to Wilshire, 7 Jan. 1904, Wilshire Papers.

In August 1904 the Countess attended the Amsterdam congress of the Socialist International and this gave her another opportunity to talk with Hyndman. She wrote at the time to Lady Dorothy Nevill, the well-known London hostess, that Socialism was 'the *one* religion that unites the human race all over the world, in the Common Cause of Humanity, and it is very, very wonderful, and it is *growing* as mushrooms grow, and nothing can stem the tide'.[1]

Lady Warwick's relations with Hyndman were friendly enough, though according to Hyndman they were 'a little afraid of one another'. She was soon busy conducting a speaking tour throughout the country to advocate the free maintenance of schoolchildren. 'We are having fine meetings with the Countess as a speaker or in the chair', Hyndman wrote to Wilshire. 'People come to see and hear her who would never come to see or hear you or me.' And again he wrote: 'You know how rank counts in this country . . . and we became quite respectable(!) in consequence.'[2] The Countess's speeches assumed a tone that bore a striking resemblance to Hyndman's. At the opening meeting of the S.D.F. conference in Northampton in April 1905, she declared:

> I am one of the land-owning class of Northamptonshire. . . . I am very sorry I own 3,000 acres! Until you do away with a thing called the law of entail I do not see how I am to avoid possessing 3,000 acres in Northamptonshire.[3]

Hyndman thought that the Countess spoke well, but when in her usual extravagant fashion she ordered a special train to take her on her way from Northampton he thought it 'foolish'.

The Countess appears to have taken the view that Hyndman would soon be the first Socialist Prime Minister.

[1] R. H. Nevill, *Life & Letters of Lady Dorothy Nevill* (1919), pp. 169f.
[2] Hyndman to Wilshire, 4 Jan., 16 March, 4 April, 25 April 1905, Wilshire Papers.
[3] Countess of Warwick, op. cit., pp. 262-3.

Hyndman did not entirely discount the possibility himself. 'Her idea is', he wrote:

that, within two years, I, *moi qui vous parle*, shall 'have the ball at my feet'. That seems to me incredible. But things are moving, & Lady W. would not have joined the S.D.F., the most advanced & irreconcilable body in Great Britain, without careful consideration of possibilities.[1]

In return for this generous view of his own future, Hyndman formed the belief that the Countess for her part would become 'a considerable historic figure' as a result of her activities on behalf of the cause. Buoyed up by mutual encouragement, these two devoted yet ambitious Socialists looked forward with optimism to the political future.

[1] Hyndman to Wilshire, 25 April 1905, Wilshire Papers.

VIII ～ LABOUR ALLIANCE
OR SOCIALIST UNITY?

I

AFTER its withdrawal from the Labour Representation Committee in 1901, the Federation maintained a constant criticism of the new organization for its failure to adopt Socialist principles. At the same time, however, it sought to influence the individual trade unions in the same direction. S.D.F. members continued to appear at conferences of the Labour Representation Committee whenever they were appointed as delegates by any of the unions, and in 1905 they actually moved and carried a resolution in favour of public ownership of 'all the means of production, distribution, and exchange'.[1] This was agreed to without discussion, however, and it clearly did not bind all the unions or candidates of the party to a Socialist policy. The Federation also made renewed efforts to secure 'Socialist unity' with the I.L.P., and in conjunction with the Kelmscott Club, the successor of William Morris's Hammersmith Socialist Society, held several meetings with this object. Quelch's candidature at the Dewsbury by-election in January 1902 had demonstrated the success which local co-operation of the two major Socialist bodies could achieve. E. R. Hartley, a well-known local I.L.P. member, who had been nominated by the local Trades Council and the I.L.P., refused to stand against Quelch and wrote a letter to the *Clarion* urging all

[1] L.R.C., *Conference Report*, 1905, p. 52.

sections of the movement to unite to help him. The national
executive of the I.L.P. refused to endorse this attitude, and
Keir Hardie wrote to Bruce Glasier predicting a crushing
defeat for Quelch and 'the disruption, or at least the total
eclipse, of S.D.F.-ism'.[1] But Quelch, though he did not win
the seat, received 1,597 votes, and the whole campaign was
regarded by the S.D.F. as a victory for its policy.[2]

The Amsterdam congress of the International held in
August 1904 was also interested in achieving Socialist unity,
and passed a resolution which pointed out that there was 'but
one proletariat in each country'. The British section compromised by electing both Hyndman and Keir Hardie to the
International Bureau, but Hardie did not attend a meeting
of the Bureau held in January 1905 at which the French
delegates formally announced the formation of a united
party in France. Hyndman took this opportunity to plead
for a similar unity in Britain.[3] Towards the end of 1905,
however, an International Socialist Council for Great Britain
was set up combining various sections of the movement.
'Out of this a consolidation of forces may come', wrote
Hyndman. 'Hardie took the chair on Thursday last. I proposed he should. I am getting quite diplomatic in my old
age!'[4] But Hyndman's diplomacy (if such it was) could not
conceal the serious differences of opinion which remained
between the leaders of the two British parties on the question
of Socialist tactics.

Shortly after the Amsterdam congress Hardie wrote an
article entitled 'An Indictment of the Class War', which
gave rise to a fierce controversy among the British Socialists.
He ridiculed the 'quaint spectacle' of 'a top-hatted, frock-
coated member of the prosperous middle class sweating on
a platform to prove his "class-consciousness" with the poor

[1] Hardie to Glasier, 26 Dec. 1901, quoted F. Bealey and H. Pelling, *Labour
and Politics, 1900–06* (1958), p. 165.
[2] *Clarion*, 13 Dec. 1901; *Justice*, 11, 18 Jan. 1902.
[3] *Justice*, 27 Aug., 3 Sept. 1904, 21 Jan. 1905.
[4] Hyndman to Wilshire, 18 Nov. 1905, Wilshire Papers.

worker'. Capitalism, he said, was 'the product of selfishness' and Socialism would make 'war upon a system, not upon a class'.[1] To this Bax replied that Socialism needed men of 'enlightened selfishness' rather than 'unselfish saints', and Hyndman objected to what he regarded as the 'snobbery' against 'the highest and richest people in the realm' which, he said, was just as bad as refusing to admit an unemployed worker into the movement.[2]

The dominating personality in this 'class war' controversy, however, was Bernard Shaw, who launched a merciless attack on the S.D.F. If the international resolutions on the class war were to be taken as real indications of the actual views of the working class, he maintained, England would by now have been in the throes of a violent revolution; Hyndman would have been Prime Minister, Blatchford generalissimo of the revolutionary army, and Shaw himself President of the British Co-operative Commonwealth. But the real conflict among social classes, he said, was the one between the buyer and seller of labour—the antagonism which would explain 'the success of trade unionism in class organization, as compared with the failure of Socialism'. 'What of the Social Democratic Federation?' he asked. 'Failure and futility unspeakable, in spite of Hyndmanic brilliancy, Baxterous subtlety and philosophy, Quelchful conviction and pertinacity, enthusiasm and fanaticism galore. . . . Still no nearer to the Co-operative Common-wealth!'[3]

In 1905 there appeared a book by Ramsay MacDonald entitled *Socialism and Society*, in which the secretary of the L.R.C. adopted the theory of 'biological evolution' and declared that Socialism was 'the legitimate heir of Liberal-ism'.[4] As the German Socialist Max Beer pointed out at the time, the aim of the book was to 'conclude an *entente*

---

[1] *Labour Leader*, 2, 9 Sept. 1904.   [2] *Justice*, 31 Dec. 1904, 11 March, 1905.
[3] *Clarion*, 30 Sept., 4 Nov. 1904.
[4] J. R. MacDonald, *Socialism and Society* (1905), pp. 164–5.

cordiale with the Liberal Party',[1] which was in fact what
MacDonald had achieved in a series of secret negotiations
with Herbert Gladstone, the Liberal chief whip.[2] Even if
the S.D.F. leaders had known far more about the existence
of this *'entente'*, they were not in a strong position to criticize
MacDonald, for neither Hyndman nor even, as we shall see,
Quelch was averse to the idea of establishing some kind of
understanding with the Liberals, each for his own electoral
campaign.

After the expulsion of the 'impossibilists', the S.D.F.
appeared united at least on the question of Socialist unity,
but the northern branches which had on many occasions
actually co-operated with local I.L.P.s favoured the union
of all Socialist forces inside the Labour Representation
Committee and were opposed to the London leaders who
were anxious to achieve unity outside the framework of the
labour alliance. The foremost advocate of the official policy
was Quelch who, as the editor of *Justice*, exerted quite as
much influence as Hyndman, and perhaps even more. It
was Quelch who at the party conference held in Northampton in 1905 most vehemently opposed a resolution from the
Rochdale branch demanding reaffiliation of the S.D.F. to
the Labour Representation Committee. Hyndman's attitude
on the question was ambiguous, partly perhaps because of his
sanguine expectation that soon or later he would lead a
Socialist Party in Parliament. He had advocated the S.D.F.'s
affiliation to the Labour Representation Committee prior to
its formation, and when he visited the industrial North in 1904
he thought that the policy advocated by Dan Irving and
others in Lancashire had been 'successful all along the line'.[3]
At the Northampton conference, however, he declared that
the Labour Representation Committee had changed for the
worse, and he would not allow himself to be bound by its
constitution to support its non-Socialist leaders.[4] Shortly

[1] *Justice*, 16 Sept. 1905.   [2] See Bealey and Pelling, op. cit., ch. vi.
[3] *Justice*, 2 April 1903.   [4] S.D.F., *Conference Report*, 1905, p. 14.

before the 1906 General Election he predicted that after the campaign it would be

> forced . . . to come down from the fence either on the side of out-and-out Class-War Socialism, or on the side of Liberal-Labour trade unionism. Then will be the time to advocate the unification and consolidation of Socialist fractions, with far greater prospects of success than exist today.[1]

The prospect of Socialist unity now appeared to Hyndman to depend entirely upon whether the Labour M.P.s elected to Parliament would accept Hyndman's leadership or continue to follow the evolutionary tactics of MacDonald. There was, therefore, all the more reason for Hyndman to do his utmost to capture Burnley at the General Election.

2

Burnley, a traditionally Radical constituency, had been won by the Conservatives at the 'khaki' election of 1900. According to Hyndman, the Burnley Liberals had been demoralized by the set-back. They were 'unable to obtain a candidate', he said:

> Several wealthy Liberals were applied to, and one in particular was pressed to contest the seat three times. They were all good enough to say that on my general knowledge and reputation, I ought to be in the House of Commons if I wished to go there. . . . At last the Imperialist Liberals who ousted Mr. Stanhope bethought them of Mr. Fred Maddison as exactly the man for their money.[2]

Stanhope, a genuine Radical, had fought Burnley as a Liberal in 1900, but had been defeated. Maddison, a 'Lib-Lab' compositor and journalist, was adopted as candidate in September 1903, and shortly afterwards Hyndman started his own campaign. The cotton crisis of the time seemed to Hyndman to favour his own chance of success;

---

[1] *Clarion*, 17 Nov. 1905.   [2] Ibid., 26 Jan. 1906.

in October he wrote to Wilshire: 'Lancashire is in a *frightful* state. . . . People living on potato-puddings! . . . In Burnley in particular and all round there it is nothing short of actual famine. I believe our time is coming & coming soon.'[1]

As usual, Hyndman set about his campaign with plenty of energy. *Reynolds's* was friendly to his cause, and in its issue of 30th August 1903 it announced an essay competition with a prize of two guineas for the person who would supply the most satisfactory answers to twenty-six questions set by Hyndman, 'the leading exponent of Social Democracy in this country, and the Socialist, Labour, and Democratic candidate for Burnley'. Another competition followed when one John Dent of Scotland offered a guinea for the essay giving 'the twelve best reasons why Mr. Hyndman should receive the votes of the Burnley electors'. One of the reasons given by the prize-winner was that 'his return to Parliament would strike terror into the hearts of royal paupers, landlords, sweaters, and exploiters of labour generally.'[2]

Early in December 1905 the Conservative Government resigned; a Liberal Government was formed by Campbell-Bannerman, who brought in the ex-Socialist John Burns as President of the Local Government Board; and a General Election was announced to take place in the following month. Hyndman at once resumed his Burnley campaign; though a resourceful propagandist, he was not a thoughtful strategist, and was soon dragged into a religious controversy in Burnley from which he emerged with the ominous remark that Christianity was 'played out'. Michael Davitt came to his support, but his personal influence was weakened by the manifesto of the United Irish League which advised the Irish voters to vote Liberal; and the Irish electors, who were also disturbed by Hyndman's secularism, probably mostly decided to vote for Maddison, the 'Lib-Lab' candidate. Meanwhile, the Burnley Labour Representation Committee,

[1] Hyndman to Wilshire, 27 Oct. 1903, Wilshire Papers.
[2] *Reynolds's Newspaper*, 30 Aug. 1903, 31 Jan. 1904.

took up a rather unenthusiastic attitude; it passed a resolution in favour of Hyndman's candidature but refrained from committing its associated bodies to this decision. The Burnley Weavers' Committee and the Overlookers' Association in fact declared their political neutrality.[1]

Yet it was as a moderate that Hyndman fought Burnley, and his election address contained nothing that would suggest revolutionary Socialism; there was no reference to the class war and no attack on Free Trade as a purely capitalist device. He declared himself in favour of four main objects— Free Trade, secular education, the suppression of indentured Chinese labour in South Africa, and Home Rule for Ireland. He advocated a series of parliamentary reforms, the S.D.F. 'palliatives', and the Socialist programme of nationalization. But his special recommendation was his knowledge of foreign affairs. 'As delegate of Great Britain on the International Socialist Bureau side by side with Bebel, Jaurès, Ferri, Adler, Vandervelde, Hillquit, and others,' he said, 'I have opportunities for obtaining information of world-wide importance to the popular cause here and elsewhere.' He concluded his election address with a reference to the ruin of both India and Lancashire under capitalist imperialism.[2]

The local Socialists, both S.D.F. and I.L.P., gave great assistance to Hyndman's campaign; Lady Warwick and Bernard Shaw both came to lend a hand; Keir Hardie sent his warm good wishes; and the candidate himself worked unceasingly. But in spite of all efforts, the verdict went against the veteran Socialist, albeit by a narrow margin. Hyndman polled 4,932 votes as against Maddison's 5,288 and 4,964 for the Conservative candidate. After the announcement of the fateful figures, Hyndman spoke to his supporters from a window of the Empress Hotel where he had stayed during the campaign. He expressed regret that

1 *Burnley Gazette*, 6, 16 Dec. 1905, 3, 6, 10, 13 Jan. 1906.
2 *Justice*, 13 Jan. 1906.

he had been defeated, solely, as he maintained, by failure to win the Irish vote. 'It was . . . simply a statement of fact,' he said:

that the eyes of the world were upon Burnley. He was fairly be-sieged by letters from distinguished men in Germany, America, and all over the world, and particularly from the dumb millions of India, speaking through one or two of their spokesmen, asking them to send the message that Burnley had returned the first Socialist representing the Social Democratic Federation to the House of Commons. It was a bitter disappointment to the whole on-looking world of democracy to find that England was still apparently to keep back the world movement.[1]

Deep personal frustration, however, only added to his usual presumptuousness. 'If I had been in Parliament', he wrote to Wilshire, 'there would be an organized and vigorous Socialist Party within three months. As it is with Keir Hardie, Ramsay MacDonald & Snowden as leaders, nobody can say what will occur.'[2] At any rate the small majority of less than 400 votes cast in favour of Hyndman's 'Lib-Lab' opponent had prevented the Federation from securing a parliamentary spokesman of its own.

There were, however, nine other candidates of the S.D.F. at this election—among them Quelch at Southampton, Jack Williams and James Gribble at Northampton, and Dan Irving at Accrington. There was also Will Thorne, an S.D.F. member, standing at West Ham South as the candidate of the Gasworkers, and endorsed by the Labour Representation Committee. Several of these candidates were assisted by the Countess of Warwick, who for a fortnight during the election spoke from Socialist platforms up and down the country. She sold some of her jewels in order to contribute to the S.D.F. election funds a donation of £500.[3]

With the exception of Thorne and Irving, all the Federation candidates were opposed by both the major parties and all

[1] *Burnley Gazette*, 17 Jan. 1906.
[2] Hyndman to Wilshire, 17 Jan. 1906, Wilshire Papers.
[3] *Labour Leader*, 27 April 1906.

were defeated.[1] In later years they were to make a virtue
out of this demonstration of their intransigence: but it was
not a situation which they deliberately chose, as was indicated very clearly by the behaviour of Quelch. Now the
chairman of the London Trades Council as well as editor
of *Justice*, Quelch stood as 'Socialist and Trade Unionist'
candidate at Southampton, a two-member constituency,
where he hoped to fight the election in conjunction with a
single Liberal candidate. To his chagrin, the local Liberals
did not like his look and put forward two candidates of their
own, blaming the Labour group for its 'gigantic mistake of
choosing a Socialist'.[2]

As for Will Thorne, he finally succumbed to persistent
pressure from Ramsay MacDonald, the secretary of the
Labour Representation Committee, and agreed to stand
under the title of 'Labour' candidate. Although in his
election manifesto he boldly emphasized the doctrine of the
'class war', it was evident that endorsement by the Labour
Representation Committee made his situation entirely
different from that in other constituencies fought by the
S.D.F. There was no Liberal standing against him; the
Canning Town branch of the United Irish League decided
to back him; and the Free Church Council and the Temperance Party gave full support. On polling day, six motor-cars
were placed at his disposal, four by the Countess. It was a
great victory: Thorne polled 10,210 votes as against 4,973
for his Conservative opponent, Sir J. Nutting, whom he had
loudly denounced as 'a rich man and a—huntsman' and
'an insult' to a working-class constituency.[3]

[1] The results of the other S.D.F. candidatures were: Southampton: Quelch
2,146, 2 Libs. 7,032 and 6,255, 2 Cons. 5,754 and 5,535; Northampton:
Williams 2,544, Gribble 2,366, 2 Libs. 4,479 and 4,244, 2 Cons. 4,078 and 4,000;
East Bradford: Hartley 3,090, Lib. 6,185, Con. 4,277; Rochdale: Hobson
2,506, Lib. 5,912, Con. 4,449; Accrington: Irving 4,852, Lib. 7,209, Ind. 619;
North Aberdeen: Kennedy 1,935, Lib. 4,852, Con. 931; Camborne: Jones 109,
Lib. 4,614, Con. 2,384.
[2] *Southampton Daily Echo*, 12 Jan. 1906; *Justice*, 17 Oct. 1903, 21 Jan. 1905.
[3] *Reynolds's Newspaper*, 31 July 1904; *West Ham Mail*, 6, 13, 20 Jan. 1906.

The 1906 General Election turned out to be a great victory for the Liberals and for the Free Trade cause. The Federation was not slow to point this out, and to maintain that the new Labour M.P.s were largely dependent on Liberal support. Yet it is not so easy in fact to draw a distinction between the behaviour of Hyndman and Quelch on the one hand and that of Ramsay MacDonald and Keir Hardie on the other, for they all tried to avoid having to face Liberal candidates. It was just that the Labour Representation Committee was stronger and more skilful in deploying its strength to force concessions from the Liberal Party. It did not make much difference what the candidates said: so long as they had the endorsement of the Labour Representation Committee they could talk about the 'class war' as much as they liked— as indeed Will Thorne did—and still be triumphantly elected under the special agreement that MacDonald had made with Herbert Gladstone, the Liberal Chief Whip.

3

At first, therefore, the emergence of a considerable Labour group in the House of Commons impressed even Hyndman. He spoke of the boundless opportunities now open to the Labour Party to 'give a lead to Great Britain, to Europe, and to the world' by carrying into effect the S.D.F. 'palliatives'. While predicting that the Labour M.P.s would have difficulty in keeping their independence in the traditional 'House of the well-educated and well-to-do', he promised that the Federation would provide them with 'any assistance we can do outside the House of Commons'.[1] He attended a great meeting of congratulation and jubilation held at the Horticultural Society's Hall, Westminster, in February. 'If there lurked in the back of my mind just a touch of genial cynicism as I recalled the past and speculated on the future', he wrote:

[1] *Justice*, 17 Feb. 1906.

any such untimely investigation into the hard realities of life
and the soft sentimentalities of these robust-looking legislators
was swept aside as I looked round the crowded hall, surveyed the
blaze of scarlet decorations, and read the telling mottoes in-
scribed all over the walls in praise of Socialism as 'The Only
Hope of the Workers', 'Workers of the World Unite' for the
Social Revolution, and so on. A wave of enthusiasm temporarily
swamped my critical faculty. It was good for me to be there. I
shook hands with everybody; I told all the world what splendid
fellows they all were; . . . I even delivered a speech of such
abounding effusiveness that I look back upon it with pride to
this day.[1]

He was so much encouraged by 'the most enthusiastic
reception' accorded to him at the hall that he almost mistook
the success of the Labour Party for that of his own organization. In a letter to Morris Hillquit, the American Socialist,
he said: 'We are really beginning to make great way here.
Our electoral successes give no idea of the extent to which
our Revolutionary Social Democratic propaganda has made
way among the people.'[2]

At the same time Hyndman saw danger from the opportunists within the Labour Party. He was annoyed that Hardie
was elected chairman of the parliamentary party by only
one vote. 'Hardie . . . has just the qualities needed for the
present juncture', he wrote to Wilshire. 'That J. R. M.
should intrigue against him is not only personally most dis-
graceful . . . but an outrage upon the Movement.' And he
added that Hardie and himself were 'on very good terms
now'.[3] In his view David Shackleton, Hardie's rival for the
chairmanship, who was 'not a Socialist at all', presented a
further danger to the party. 'The chief bond which holds the
Labour Party together,' he wrote 'is its determination not
to be handled by any other party. . . . But can they keep

---

[1] Hyndman, *Further Reminiscences*, p. 273.
[2] Hyndman to Hillquit, 28 March 1906, Hillquit Papers.
[3] Hyndman to Wilshire, 31 March 1906, Wilshire Papers. J.R.M. is Ramsay
MacDonald, for whose role in this election see Bealey and Pelling, op. cit.,
pp. 278f.

solid without some clearly formulated programme for action?'[1] He thought that the S.D.F. should do something to help the Labour Party find a 'programme for action'. Hoping again to play an important role of leadership, he sought re-election to the S.D.F. executive, which he had not attempted since 1901. The first opportunity for this was at the Federation's conference at Bradford in April 1906, and on this occasion he was duly re-elected.

It was noteworthy, however, that Hyndman did not take part in the debate on the Labour Party that took place at this 1906 conference. Instead he moved a resolution to congratulate Hardie on his independent position in the House of Commons, but the motion was ruled out of order. A Lancashire resolution in favour of reaffiliation to the Labour Party was hotly opposed by two of Hyndman's old colleagues, Quelch and Hunter Watts, and it was defeated by 55 votes to 29.[2] Shortly afterwards Hyndman wrote in *Justice* that if the Labour Party would adopt the attitude even of the Lassalleans 'with all their "nationalism" ', the S.D.F. would 'affiliate tomorrow'.[3] Clearly, therefore, he was already more flexible on this question than some of his colleagues.

At first the Labour Party in Parliament gave the impression of having some influence: it secured a Trade Disputes Act to protect trade union funds from the effects of the Taff Vale Decision, and it initiated the Education (Provision of Meals) Act—a permissive act still far short of achieving in full the S.D.F. 'palliative' of state maintenance of schoolchildren. But these limited successes failed to satisfy Hyndman, who declared towards the end of 1906: 'Not a single Socialist speech has been delivered in the English Popular Assembly.'[4] The official policy of the Federation was to carry on its own Socialist agitation outside the Labour Party until the Labour Party was forced to declare for Socialism.

---

[1] *The Times*, 23 April 1906.   [2] S.D.F., *Conference Report*, 1906, p. 13.
[3] *Justice*, 30 June 1906.   [4] Ibid., 15 Dec. 1906.

The organization was expanding at the time: it had a new hall for meetings in London, the Chandos Hall in the Strand, which was opened in May 1906; and *Justice* was enlarged at the beginning of 1907 from eight pages to twelve. The Twentieth Century Press published many propaganda pamphlets, and the number of branches increased from 187 in December 1906 to 211 in the same month one year later. In October 1907 this progress and the desire to emulate the Labour Party encouraged the executive to change the name of the Federation to the Social-Democratic Party (S.D.P.).

Meanwhile, Hyndman and his colleagues took advantage of the Labour Party's willingness to join the Socialist International in order to bring pressure on it to accept all the principles of Socialism. Hyndman, with Bruce Glasier of the I.L.P., attended a meeting of the International Bureau held in Brussels in June 1907 in order to make arrangements for the Stuttgart congress in that year. Glasier's mission was to place on the congress agenda an I.L.P. resolution to the effect that 'a bona-fide Trade Union or combination of unions' should be entitled to membership of the congress, which had previously recognized only those who accepted the 'class war' principle. Hyndman translated Glasier's speech, but he was 'in too good-natured a mood to draw forth the sword of controversy'; and he even protested against the 'seeming indifference' of the continental Socialists to Glasier's case.[1]

When the congress met at Stuttgart in August, the British section was the largest foreign contingent, containing 115 delegates: 61 S.D.F., 30 I.L.P., 15 Fabians, 9 from the Labour Party and trade unions. Glasier complained of the 'disparity of representation', for, he maintained, the S.D.F. had a 'paying membership' of only 6,000, whereas the I.L.P. had 25,000 and the Labour Party nearly a million. The 'disparity' was no doubt due in part to the greater interest

[1] *Labour Leader*, 14, 21 June 1907.

of S.D.F. members in Continental affairs and perhaps also to their greater capacity to afford a trip to the Continent. After all, most of the I.L.P. members lived in the North of England or in Scotland. Hyndman was re-elected to the chairmanship of the British section, and this honour, said Glasier, was 'more than deserved by [his] admirable tact and absolute fairness'. But the S.D.F. was determined to oppose the I.L.P. resolution on the admission of trade union organizations, and Quelch spoke 'strongly, and, to the Continental ear, effectively' against Ramsay MacDonald, the I.L.P. spokesman.[1] It appeared to Hyndman, however, that MacDonald was treated unfairly by 'the cast-iron German method of applying the closure'. 'I put his case, though I did not agree with him, most strongly to the president,' he said, 'but, as it turned out, to no purpose.'[2] This was only the beginning of a series of protests by Hyndman against what he took to be the air of superiority assumed by the Continental Socialists. When a delegate of the Dockers' Union was debarred from speaking on the question of 'blackleg' labour at Hamburg, 'the British section rose *en masse* in their seats to protest, Hyndman . . . acting as protestant-in-chief':

Hyndman, with his locks, flowing beard, and waving arms, hurled unparliamentary imprecations at the chair. He shouted out that he and his fellow-British delegates had been supremely self-effacing at the congress, that the German and French speakers had, by their long-winded orations . . . monopolised and dissipated the time of the congress. Cries of 'Order, order! Chair, chair!' in a dozen different languages rose simultaneously in the hall. But Hyndman stood like Casabianca on the burning deck, amidst the flames of Continental wrath, and would not sit down. He was flatly and transparently out of order; he was wildly and shamelessly anarchistic; but the British delegates abetted him in his 'manifestation'.[3]

This episode must have been an almost unique incident of

[1] *Labour Leader*, 23, 30 Aug. 1907.   [2] *The Times*, 28 Aug. 1907.
[3] *Labour Leader*, 30 Aug. 1907.

collaboration between Hyndman and the national leaders of the I.L.P.

It is true that Hyndman, as the chairman of the British section at Stuttgart, felt it necessary to take a more conciliatory attitude to the Labour Party than did Quelch on whom fell the responsibility of acting as the S.D.F. spokesman. Yet his mellower standpoint was obvious afterwards as well. When at its 1908 conference the Labour Party passed a new resolution in favour of Socialism, Hyndman was highly encouraged and declared that Labour 'could not rub the red paint off the face'. At the S.D.P. conference in the same year, he went so far as to support a Burnley resolution in favour of reaffiliation to the Labour Party, though the resolution was again defeated after unfavourable comments from Quelch on the prospects of a Socialist-Labour alliance.[1]

Later in the year, when the problem of the Labour Party and its relation to International Socialism was again discussed at a Bureau meeting held at Brussels in October, Hyndman spoke 'with great moderation'. 'He explained frankly,' said Glasier, the I.L.P. delegate, 'that he himself had urged the Social Democrats at their last conference to join the Labour Party, but had been defeated by two to one. Nevertheless he was bound to present the view of his organization.' But the meeting adopted a resolution moved by Kautsky to accept the Labour Party's affiliation on the ground that in practice it waged the class struggle though it did not recognize it.[2]

Meanwhile, the I.L.P. began to develop an interest in Socialist theory, and in 1908 started to publish a monthly journal, the *Socialist Review*. The first issue contained a translation of correspondence between Marx, Engels, and F. A. Sorge, the last secretary of the First International.[3] This contained some bitter criticism of the S.D.F. and

[1] S.D.P., *Conference Report*, 1908, pp. 10–12; *Social-Democrat*, xii (April 1908), 158–63.
[2] *Labour Leader*, 23 Oct. 1908; *Lenin on Britain* (1934), p. 94.
[3] *Socialist Review*, i (March 1908), 24–32.

Hyndman, and appeared to provide justification in Marxist orthodoxy for the I.L.P. policy of the 'Labour Alliance'. Max Beer, the German Socialist who acted as the London correspondent of *Vorwärts*, interpreted it in this way. He described the Labour Party as the true development expected by Marx and spoke of Hardie as the leader who 'grasped the essence of modern Socialism—aye, of Marxism —better than' any other British Socialist.[1] But this view appealed neither to the S.D.F. nor to the growing number of British Marxists (not all of whom were in the S.D.F.); and as the years went on, the failure of the Labour Party to secure distinctive parliamentary legislation, and its tendency to merge with the Liberals and to pursue a very cautious by-election policy, led to an increasing popular impatience of which the S.D.F., or S.D.P. as it now was, sought to take advantage.

4

The growth of local Socialist societies independent of the S.D.F. and I.L.P., and often under the influence of Blatch-ford's *Clarion*, was a feature of the first decade of the twentieth century. In 1904 the Federation decided for the first time since 1885 to accept the 'affiliation' of local Socialist bodies in the hope of promoting the cause of 'Socialist unity'. One instance of the benefit accruing from this arrangement was provided by the Bury Socialist Society. This organization, which had been set up by local S.D.F. and I.L.P. branches, decided to join the national S.D.F. when the I.L.P. failed to act in conformity with a resolution of the 1904 congress of the International calling for 'Socialist unity'.[2]

The 'unity' movement was given a further impetus by the 1906 General Election. 'The Labour movement is only just beginning. The Socialist movement is hardly begun. Wait a while, and you will see', wrote Blatchford in his comment

[1] *Labour Leader*, 27 Nov. 1908; *Socialist Review*, iii (April 1909), 148–57.
[2] S.D.F., *Conference Report*, 1904, pp. 18–20; *Justice*, 9 Dec. 1905.

on the election results.[1] E. R. Hartley, who had fought the election as a 'Socialist unity' candidate, now revived the Clarion Van campaigns for Socialism that had first taken place in the 1890's, and by the summer of 1907 seven vans were on the road preaching the gospel of Socialism. In the following year the S.D.F. introduced two 'Red Vans' of its own to reinforce the Clarion campaign. But the converts of the Clarion campaign and many of the members of the local Socialist societies were largely indifferent to the divisions between the S.D.F. and the I.L.P., and their affiliation to one or other of these national bodies was often quite accidental.

In the meantime, the I.L.P. leadership was stubbornly resisting persistent demands from a minority of its members for unity with the S.D.F. The I.L.P. leaders realized that this would put an end to the 'Labour alliance' with the trade unions which they had made the corner-stone of their policy. The hostile minority, however, grew rapidly and found a leader in the young Victor Grayson, who in June 1907 was elected as a 'Socialist' at a parliamentary by-election at the Colne Valley. The result of this by-election—a three-cornered contest for a former Liberal seat—caused a great sensation. Grayson acted in Parliament as if he were indeed 'the first Socialist M.P.' as Blatchford chose to call him. He refused to accept the Labour Party whip, regarding it as a sign of submission to Liberalism. In October 1908 he was suspended from the House after having refused to obey the order of the Speaker to stop speaking and sit down. He had been demanding the attention of the House for the distress of the unemployed, but he got little sympathy from the members of the Labour Party, who were much embarrassed by the affair.[2]

Hyndman, as we have seen, had come out openly for the

---

[1] *Clarion*, 26 Jan. 1906.
[2] Ibid., 26 July 1907; *The Times*, 17 Oct. 1908; W. Thorne, *My Life's Battles*, pp. 173–6.

idea of the 'Labour alliance' and for the reaffiliation of the
S.D.F. to the Labour Party. But the widespread support
now being gained by the 'Socialist unity' movement led him
to hope once more for the establishment of a powerful
Socialist party outside the Labour Party. Together with
Blatchford and Grayson he launched a campaign for
Socialist representation in Parliament, and determined to
put this in practice by again standing for Burnley. 'Hyndman
on the floor of the House of Commons,' said Grayson at a
Burnley meeting, 'would be Gulliver among the Lillipu-
tians.'[1] Grayson, however, was an unreliable ally: in some
mysterious way he missed a debate at the Labour Party
conference held in January 1909, at which he was expected
to defend his action in the House and to formulate a policy
for the critics of the I.L.P. leadership. His behaviour was
increasingly erratic, probably owing to irregular habits
including heavy drinking. Soon his reputation was in
decline; and Hyndman, who had envied his meteoric
career, lamented the great opportunities that he had missed.[2]

But in spite of Grayson, the movement for 'Socialist
unity' continued to grow. The tacit parliamentary alliance
between the Liberal and Labour Parties had placed a considerable restraint on the latter, and this loss of militancy
in turn weakened the defenders of the policy of the 'Labour
alliance' inside the I.L.P. In 1908 the S.D.P. fought three
by-elections, which the Labour Party refused to attempt:
Manchester North-West, Haggerston, and Newcastle-on-
Tyne.[3] The Labour Party was not even willing to fight
Newcastle, a two-member constituency where it had already
gained one seat at the General Election. The S.D.P. executive, in their 1909 report, condemned the official attitude
of the Labour Party towards two-member constituencies,

[1] *Justice*, 7 March 1908.   [2] Hyndman, *Further Reminiscences*, pp. 281–2.
[3] The results of the three elections were: Manchester North-West: Irving
276, Con. 5,417, Lib. 4,988; Haggerston: Burrows 986, Con. 2,867, Lib.
1,724; Newcastle-on-Tyne: Hartley 2,971, Con. 13,863, Lib. 11,720. Winston
Churchill was the defeated Liberal at Manchester.

which, it said, was 'striking at the very roots of political independence'. The question also gave rise to much dissatisfaction inside the I.L.P., and was raised at the I.L.P. conference of the same year.[1]

The decline in Grayson's popularity did little to retard the growth of criticism within the I.L.P. of its own established leadership. There were many who resented the fact that Hardie, MacDonald, Glasier, and Snowden had virtually controlled the party executive for over a decade. They denounced 'the inner ring' of the National Council as 'an aristocracy' and urged the branches to strive for the 'democratic' reorganization of the party leadership.[2] At the I.L.P.'s 1909 conference a band of critics demanded the reference back of the whole section in the executive report dealing with the question of 'Politics and the Labour Party'. This was carried, but great confusion followed when the four veteran leaders resorted to the tactic of resigning from the Council in a body. The Conference then had second thoughts and rallied to their support.[3] The controversy inside the I.L.P., however, did not end with the end of the conference: it dragged on through the national constitutional crisis and the General Elections of 1910.

5

The first General Election of 1910 took place in January, and was fought on the issue of Lloyd George's radical budget proposals, which the Lords had rejected. The S.D.P. issued an election manifesto attacking both the Lords and the budget. It supported seven candidates from its national fund or 'War Chest', including Hyndman at Burnley again, and each of them had to fight a three-cornered campaign. Refusing as they did to take a clear stand on the main issue

---

[1] S.D.P., *Conference Report*, 1909, pp. 9–10; I.L.P., *Conference Report*, 1909, p. 66.
[2] *Labour Leader*, 15, 22 May 1908.   [3] See I.L.P., *Conference Report*, 1909.

of the election, they all found themselves at the bottom of the poll.[1] This was true even of Hyndman although in a poll of over 16,000 he was less than 900 votes short of victory. Forty Labour M.P.s were returned, each and all without official Liberal opposition. But the Liberal majority was wiped out at this election, and it now became clear that independent action in Parliament on the part of the Labour Party would mean the destruction of the Liberal Government. Ramsay MacDonald, who became the leader of the parliamentary party, was quite willing to give support to the Liberals, especially as the Osborne Judgment had seriously endangered the party's source of election funds.[2]

The January election resulted in the passing of the budget, but it did not solve the constitutional problem presented by the conflict between 'Peers and People'. In Hyndman's opinion continued existence of the Lords' veto power should now have been turned into a fight between 'Capitalist Parliament and People'. He advocated a 'Constituent Assembly' of Democracy, which was somehow to be more representative than the existing House of Commons.[3] But no notice was taken of this, and the dispute of the two Houses led to a second General Election in December 1910. Owing to lack of funds, the S.D.P. could afford to run only one official candidate, and this was naturally Hyndman at Burnley. But he was again at the bottom of the poll, and his vote dropped by more than 1,000, while both his opponents did better than before. 'I had a very bad defeat at Burnley', he wrote in *Justice*:

[1] The polls of the seven candidates were: Burnley, Hyndman 4,948, Con. 5,776, Lib. 5,681; Northampton: Gribble 1,792, Quelch 1,612, 2 Libs. 5,398 and 5,289, 2 Con. 4,569 and 4,464; East Bradford: Hartley 1,740, Lib. 7,709, Con. 5,014; Haggerston: Burrows 701, Lib. 3,041, Con. 2,585; North Aberdeen: Kennedy 1,344, Lib. 4,297, Con. 2,314; Carlisle: A. C. Bannington 777, Lib. 3,270, Con. 2,815. In addition, Dan Irving contested Rochdale with local funds only and polled 1,755 as against Lib. 6,809 and Con. 5,381. Thorne, as a Labour candidate, was re-elected for South West Ham.

[2] For the Osborne Judgment, see below, p. 180.

[3] *Socialist Annual*, 1910, pp. 17–23; *Justice*, 19 March 1910; *Church Socialist Quarterly*, April 1910.

I believe I was beaten by ignorance, poverty and weight of money. . . . Taking a calm survey of the contest, I can only come to the conclusion that I have fared precisely as the great Chartist leaders did in Lancashire sixty years ago or more.[1]

Hyndman had started the Democratic Federation with a view to succeeding where the Chartists had failed, and now at the age of sixty-nine he seemed to have missed his last chance of getting into Parliament.

For some time now Hyndman had been engaged in writing his memoirs. He published the first volume with Messrs. Macmillan in 1911 under the title of *Record of an Adventurous Life*—a title well justified by his career. This entertaining volume only deals with events up to about 1890, but its reception encouraged him to write a second volume entitled *Further Reminiscences*, which came out in the following year. This time he developed themes of current politics, and spoke of the 'Dependent Labour Party' with the philosophic reflection of the Irish peasant who took a pig to market, and afterwards remarked: 'That pig doesn't weigh as much as I thought it did, but then I never thought it would.'[2] The failure of his Burnley campaigns certainly damped his hopes of the 'Labour alliance'. But it was not only Hyndman and his S.D.P. colleagues who were disillusioned by the 'sad subservience' of the Labour Party to 'Capitalist Liberalism'. Even Hardie had to admit at the 1910 conference of the I.L.P. that the Labour Party had 'almost ceased to count';[3] and Blatchford went so far as to declare that the Labour Party had 'sold the movement'.[4] While Hyndman was in semi-retirement, preparing the volumes of his autobiography, the Socialist critics of the Labour Party were making yet another effort to consolidate their strength and transform the character of politics on the Left.

---

[1] *Justice*, 17 Dec. 1910. The result was: Hyndman, 3,810; Lib. 6,177; Con. 6,004. At Rochdale: Irving, 1,901; Lib., 5,850; Con., 5,373.

[2] Hyndman, *Further Reminiscences*, p. 259.

[3] I.L.P., *Conference Report*, 1910, p. 58.   [4] *Clarion*, 7 Jan. 1910.

6

In the summer of 1910, four dissenting members of the
I.L.P. National Council issued an appeal to the members of
the party. Their statement, generally known from its appearance as the 'Green Manifesto', but actually entitled 'Let Us
Reform the Labour Party', was an indication of the wide-
spread discontent among the Socialists, which had already
taken the form of the growth of many local societies for
'Socialist unity'. The *Clarion* had been encouraging the
formation of these local bodies of so-called 'unattached'
Socialists, and Grayson, who had lost his seat at the General
Election of January 1910, gave the signal for a further stage
of the movement by disaffiliating his Colne Valley Socialist
League from the national I.L.P. Socialist Representation
Committees had now come into existence in three important
centres—Manchester, Liverpool, and Birmingham. Leonard
Hall, one of the signatories of the 'Green Manifesto', also
set up the Birmingham Socialist Party with the object of
promoting both the political and the industrial unity of
Socialist forces. In London, a Provisional Committee for
the Promotion of Common Action among Socialists was
formed by members of the S.D.P., the I.L.P., the Clarion
group, and the Church Socialist League. The S.D.P. adapted
itself to take advantage of the movement: by the end of
1909 its branches in the industrial North and Midlands were
largely grouped into district councils, so as to encourage the
affiliation of local Socialist bodies.[1] An attempt to re-open
negotiations with the official I.L.P. was abruptly terminated
after what Lee called 'an abusive letter' from Ramsay
MacDonald,[2] and the party now made a final bid to bring
about 'Socialist unity' with its own organization as the
nucleus.

At the Coventry conference of the S.D.P. held in April

[1] *Clarion*, Dec. 1909–June 1910, *passim*; *Justice*, 16 July 1910.
[2] H. W. Lee, *The Social-Democratic Party (S.D.F.) and Socialist Unity* (1910).

1911, a resolution was passed calling for the establishment of a 'United British Socialist Party'. Early in August, the party executive in conjunction with twelve local Socialist bodies issued a circular asking all Socialist groups in the country whether they were ready to participate in a unity conference.[1] The S.D.P. leaders were probably not worried by the refusal of the I.L.P. and the Fabian Society to have anything to do with it. Even so, the task of uniting the remaining Socialist groups did not appear easy. Victor Grayson, who was writing stirring articles on the 'new enthusiasm and new hope' in the pages of the *Clarion*, was seeking to set up an entirely new party, the 'Clarion British Socialist Party', whilst the S.D.P. was anxious to maintain its own traditions as the nucleus of the new organization. A further embarrassment was provided by Leonard Hall and his followers in Birmingham, who were attracted by the industrial unrest of the time and began to move in the direction of Industrial Unionism and Syndicalism. The 'Manifesto of the Birmingham Section of the British Socialist Party' issued in September was a declaration of this new industrial gospel. Socialist representation in Parliament, it said, was subsidiary to the 'first and vital business', which was 'the machine-gun action of vast armies of Labour organized as a national union of all workers in all industries'.[2] These conflicting tendencies inside the movement indicated the difficulty of forming a new party.

[1] Apart from the S.D.P., the circular was signed by the following bodies: Essex Socialist Federation, South-Eastern Counties Federation, National Clarion Cycling Club, Hyde Socialist Church, Manchester Socialist Representation Committee, Liverpool Socialist Representation Committee, Birmingham Socialist Representation Committee, Bolton Socialist Party, Derby Socialist Society, St. Helens Socialist Society, Walton Socialist Society, Mid-Devon Socialist League.

In addition, the Church Socialist League, Glasgow Clarion Scouts, Birmingham Clarion Scouts, Huddersfield Socialist Society, Bury Socialist Society, Openshaw Socialist Society and Colne Valley Socialist League encouraged the S.D.P. executive to take action on the unity resolution passed at Coventry.

[2] *Clarion*, 22 Sept. 1911. For the Birmingham B.S.P. and its tendency towards Industrial Unionism, see the B.S.P. (Birmingham Section) Papers.

At first, however, all seemed to be going well, and Hynd-man was asked to take the chair at the inaugural conference of the British Socialist Party (or B.S.P. for short). The conference was held at Caxton Hall, Salford, on 30th September and 1st October 1911, and was attended by 200 delegates representing 85 S.D.P. and 41 I.L.P. branches, 32 Clarion Clubs and Fellowships, 12 newly-organized B.S.P. branches, and 50 local Socialist Societies and Representation Committees with a total claimed membership of 35,000. It was indicative of the seriousness of the industrial struggles of the time that A. A. Purcell, president of the Manchester Trades Council, who had been expected to preside over the conference, was prevented from coming to Salford by a trade dispute in Liverpool. Hyndman, the chairman, however, speaking, as he said, 'not as a Social-Democrat, but simply as a common or garden Socialist', welcomed with his usual optimism 'the dropping of sectional differences and the consolidation of a genuine Socialist party'.[1] Indeed, the spirit of the conference did seem to combine something of the jovial good nature of the Clarion cyclists and the grim earnestness of the class-war revolutionaries. Hyndman agreed to act as chairman of the new executive, on which the old S.D.P., the Clarion group, the I.L.P. rebels, and the Industrial Unionists all had representatives.

Although the Clarion group wanted the new party to 'do away . . . with all heresy hunting', the conference carried a 'class war' resolution, which was strongly favoured both by the S.D.P. and by the Industrial Unionists. On other issues, however, the alignment of forces was different. The I.L.P. rebels in alliance with the Industrial Unionists launched an attack on the S.D.P.'s 'long list of absurd palliatives' and succeeded in rescinding all such 'reformist' suggestions. On the question of Industrial Unionism, Grayson made common cause with Leonard Hall, but a Birmingham motion in favour of 'revolutionary industrial

[1] B.S.P., *Unity Conference Report*, 1911, p. 1.

tactics' was finally overcome by the onset of the S.D.P.
delegates.[1] Unfortunately, those whose views had been
defeated at the conference had no intention of abandoning
them for the sake of the common cause. It was thus a very
divided new party which had been brought into existence
by the movement for 'Socialist unity'.

7

The industrial group, as we shall see in the next chapter,
did not long stay inside the new party. Within the first two
years both Leonard Hall and George Simpson, its principal
leaders, had withdrawn, and with them the party lost a
number of strong branches. This considerably reduced the
total membership, and soon the B.S.P. found itself to be
little more than 'the S.D.F. in disguise'. The idea of con-
solidating the Socialist forces outside the Labour Party had
thus turned out to be a chimera. Indeed, the Socialist movement could not escape the effects of its internal differences
on tactics, and it now appeared practically impossible to
achieve unity without entering the main stream of the working-class movement, and forming an association with the
trade unions or rather their political expression, the Labour
Party. Events now served to induce the B.S.P. to accept a
solution of the question along these lines.

In 1912, shortly after its formation, the B.S.P. had applied
for independent membership of the International Socialist
Bureau, for it was not prepared to join in the British section
of the Bureau which was then composed of delegates from
the Labour Party, the I.L.P., and the Fabian Society. The
Bureau, however, was interested in effecting a consolidation
of all the Socialist elements in Britain, so as to form a strong
organization capable of meeting the critical international
situation. It therefore turned down the B.S.P. application
and urged the B.S.P., the I.L.P., and the Fabian Society to

[1] B.S.P., *Unity Conference Report*, 1911, *passim*.

unite in one party. This led to a series of negotiations between these three bodies, and at a joint meeting held in
July 1913 it was decided to adopt the two proposals for
collaboration put forward by Keir Hardie: the establishment of a United Socialist Council and the affiliation of the
B.S.P. to the Labour Party.[1]

The B.S.P. had moved a long way in accepting these
proposals, though Quelch was still fighting—practically
alone among its leaders—for the 'independence' of Social-
Democracy. 'Shall we haul down our flag?' he asked:
'It is our duty to lead, not to follow the main army of the
working class.'[2] But he was a sick man at the time, and his
illness had already cost him the control of *Justice*, which was
now publishing more articles in favour of the 'Labour
alliance' than against it. He died in September 1913, and
three months later the main elements of Hardie's proposals
were accepted at an impressive conference attended by all
the members of the International Socialist Bureau, which
now represented twenty countries.[3]

Hardie's attitude to a complete merger of the Socialist
groups remained lukewarm. His organization, the I.L.P.,
had already set up a committee with the Fabian Society
for joint propaganda work, but its leaders were not keen on
expanding the committee's scope to include the B.S.P., for
they thought that the adhesion of the B.S.P. would weaken
their influence with the trade unions. Glasier went so far as
to declare at one of the preliminary meetings: 'I understand
the tactics of the Bureau very well. They want unity in Great
Britain not for the advancement of Socialism here, but for
the benefit of the Continentals.'[4] In other ways, too, Hardie
and his colleagues showed reluctance to make concessions.
Although they decided to support the B.S.P.'s application

---

[1] British Section of the International Socialist Bureau, *Memorandum on the
Application of the British Socialist Party for Separate Affiliation to the International
Bureau* (1912); *Justice*, 26 July 1913.

[2] *Justice*, 26 July 1913.   [3] B.S.P., *Conference Report*, 1914, p. 39.

[4] *Justice*, 9 Aug, 1913.

for affiliation to the Labour Party, they opposed the demand that B.S.P. parliamentary candidates should be allowed to call themselves 'Labour and Socialist'.[1] On the other hand, there was always a good deal of enthusiasm for some sort of 'Socialist unity' inside the I.L.P., especially among the younger members. Fenner Brockway, for instance, who had succeeded Glasier as the editor of the *Labour Leader*, the I.L.P. organ, was a vigorous supporter of unity. A series of meetings to demonstrate the growing solidarity of the Socialists was held in major cities, and addresses were given by Hyndman, Shaw, Hardie, and Webb. The B.S.P. and the I.L.P. also exchanged fraternal delegates at their Easter conferences in 1914. At the B.S.P. conference Hyndman spoke of the weakness of his party and the bright prospects of collaboration. Now that Quelch, his principal opponent on this issue, had died, he could say that he was 'sorry' that the S.D.F. had ever left the Labour Representation Committee:

Had we remained that party would have had a different history. The present conference did not show that the thirty-three or thirty-four years of Socialist propaganda had produced a satisfactory result, and the reason was that we had never got near enough to those we wanted to convert. To a large extent they even looked upon us as enemies. If we went in we should do so with the red flag flying, in order to take Socialism to them and help them to victory.[2]

In May a ballot of the B.S.P. membership confirmed the decision to seek affiliation to the Labour Party, and in June the formal application was made. The Labour Party's national executive decided to refer the matter to its next annual conference, due to be held in January 1915. But the war intervened, and the conference was cancelled. It was not until January 1916 that the application from the B.S.P. was considered and accepted by the Labour Party. Hyndman's organization thus at last entered the 'Labour alliance' which he and his colleagues had so often criticized in the past.

---

[1] I.L.P., *Conference Report*, 1914.   [2] B.S.P., *Conference Report*, 1914, pp. 15–16.

IX ❧ SYNDICALISTS AND SUFFRAGETTES

I

HYNDMAN had almost invariably hoped for 'a peaceful revolution', and the Socialists with whom he associated had long settled down to constitutional methods. It is true that he was never satisfied with piecemeal social change; that he showed contempt for the series of social reforms effected under the Liberal Government; and that at times he hinted at militant action on the part of the organized workers as an alternative policy. Social-Democracy in his definition, however, stood for an orderly change of society, and when the advocates of 'direct action' made their appearance, whether in the trade unions, or in the women's suffrage movement, or in the campaigns for and against Irish Home Rule—Hyndman and his followers rather awkwardly held back and disassociated themselves from the politics of violence. In fact, Hyndman found himself in some embarrassment because of his objections both to gradual reform and to 'direct action'. He had no sympathy for reforms which in his view did not go far enough, but he did not dare to support any really militant activity.

2

The usual lag of wages behind rising prices played its part in the growth of the militant trade union movement in this period. Hyndman at first supported and even encouraged the new ferment of unrest: in 1907 when the railway workers pressed their all grades movement almost to the point of a national strike, he declared that as political action which was 'far better and far less costly' had been rendered 'impossible' by the 'huge repressive Liberal majority' in Parliament, they had no alternative but to 'make their power felt by a hold-up of national trade'.[1] At this stage Hyndman still took a favourable view of Industrial Unionism. He wrote in a letter to Wilshire: 'My confidence in parliamentary action, never great, is getting small by degrees. . . . Some form of Consolidated Organization which will hold up the entire industrial system, without actually starving the workers first, is I think coming everywhere.'[2] But he soon had second thoughts. Although he welcomed what he called 'the revival of the cataclysmic view' he found himself unable to support a general strike which 'leads direct to civil war'. 'Are we ready to provoke a civil war?' he asked. 'I am not ashamed to confess that I have not yet thought out the complete plan that I should like to submit to the Committee of Public Safety which would take charge of such a business, and I doubt if anyone else has.'[3]

Meanwhile, one W. V. Osborne, a member of the Amalgamated Society of Railway Servants, had started a legal action against the political use of trade union funds, which resulted in the famous Osborne Judgment of 1909. The immediate reaction of the S.D.P. to this new juridical limitation of trade union rights was what Rothstein called 'Schadenfreude'.[4] Clearly it was the Labour Party and the I.L.P. that received the heaviest blow by this decision: but the S.D.P. was also to suffer from it, for it encouraged the unions to turn to a policy of direct action, which was embarrassing for all political Socialists of whatever complexion.

The gospel of Industrial Unionism—which involved the

[1] *Justice*, 10 Aug. 1907.
[2] Hyndman to Wilshire, 23 May 1908, quoted in a letter from Wilshire to Hyndman, 8 Oct. 1913, Wilshire Papers.
[3] *Justice*, 23 Jan., 27 March 1909.   [4] Ibid., 7 July 1912.

aspiration of workers' control of industry—found its leading
exponents among those Socialists who had broken away from
the S.D.F., whether for its suppression of the 'cataclysmic
view' of revolution or for its comparative neglect of trade
unionism. This may be illustrated by an examination of the
process by which the American Industrial Workers of the
World (I.W.W.) and the French syndicalist movement came
to influence British labour politics.

When the I.W.W. was formed in Chicago in 1905, the
British reaction to this new industrial movement was
largely unfavourable. The ill-informed *Labour Leader* welcomed it as 'an American I.L.P.', but was soon frightened
into silence when it discovered that the American body was
even more revolutionary than the S.D.F. *Justice* ignored it
and printed only derogatory comments from across the
Atlantic.[1] Only the S.L.P. (the Scottish 'impossibilists' who
had seceded from the S.D.F.) responded favourably to it,
and in 1907 set up a 'British Advocates of Industrial Unionism' as an adjunct to its own organization.[2] This body soon
developed into the 'Industrial Workers of Great Britain',
with the declared aim of substituting an industrial administration for the political parliament.[3] The Industrial Unionists
followed Daniel De Leon's tactics of 'dual unionism' and
urged their members to leave the craft unions. Their propaganda, aided by innumerable American pamphlets,
rapidly influenced the young trade unionists who went to
study economics at Ruskin College, the workers' college at
Oxford. In 1909 'rebel' students at Ruskin, with the support
of their Principal, Dennis Hird, went on strike against the
governing body of the college, and finally seceded to form
the Central Labour College. This new educational body for
the workers, which was strongly Marxian in tone, secured
financial assistance from the South Wales Miners' Federation and from the Amalgamated Society of Railway Servants,

[1] *Labour Leader*, 10 March 1905; *Justice*, 21 Oct. 1905.
[2] *Socialist*, Oct. 1907.   [3] *Industrial Unionist*, March 1909.

and was able to exert some influence upon the industrial struggles of the time as well as upon the ideological background of generations of union leaders.

Meanwhile, Tom Mann, who had been away in Australasia, returned to throw himself into a propaganda campaign for Syndicalism. The passing of the years had softened his earlier bitterness against Hyndman, and he urged Ben Tillett, his colleague in the London dock strike of 1889, to join the S.D.P.[1] Tillett himself had visited Australia in 1907–8; on his return to England he started an active campaign against the parliamentary Labour Party in the pages of *Justice*. Tom Mann landed in England in May 1910 and received an enthusiastic welcome from the S.D.P. Among those who welcomed him on his return was Guy Bowman, then a director of the Twentieth Century Press. Bowman had come under the influence of Gustave Hervé, the French advocate of the general strike; and towards the end of May he took Mann to Paris to see at first hand the work of the revolutionary French Confederation of Labour (C.G.T.).[2] Mann also joined the S.D.P., but in July together with Bowman he started the publication of an independent journal called the *Industrial Syndicalist*. Four months later they organized a Syndicalist conference in Manchester at which it was decided to set up a 'Syndicalist Educational League' to propagate the principles of Syndicalism 'with a view to merging all existing unions into one compact organization'.[3]

The S.D.P. had tried to ignore the movement for Industrial Unionism, but when the Ruskin dispute led to the establishment of the Central Labour College, it denounced the move as 'a manœuvre of Industrial Disunionists', and the delegates at the S.D.P. conference in 1910 refused to hear

[1] See letters from Mann to Hyndman published in *Justice*, 9 March, 3 Aug. 1907, and a letter from Mann to Tillett in *Justice*, 15 May 1909.
[2] G. Bowman, Introduction to Tom Mann, *From Single Tax to Syndicalism* (1913), p. x.
[3] *Industrial Syndicalist*, Dec. 1910.

George Sims, the secretary of the new Labour College, who had been trying to win their support.[1] Meanwhile, Mann was asked by the S.D.P. to contest the parliamentary division of North Aberdeen; but he declined the invitation and resigned altogether from the party in May 1911. Though his paper had declared that it was not opposed to political action by Socialists, the hostility of the S.D.P. to the new industrial movement led him to believe that parliamentary action was an obstacle in the development of trade unionism. He declared himself to be an anti-parliamentarian and concentrated all his efforts on the organization of the Transport Workers.[2]

In the early stages of the 'labour unrest' Hyndman was not unfriendly to the movement. Speaking at a reception in 1910 for William Haywood of the American I.W.W., who was then on a visit to Britain, Hyndman declared that 'the conception of insurrection would never die'.[3] Shortly after the first series of strikes had broken out in the summer of that year, he wrote an article in the *English Review* in which he made a careful analysis of the unrest. He attributed the growing discontent among the rank and file of the trade unions to four factors—first, the failure of the Labour Party as an independent working-class party; secondly, the 'yearning' of union leaders for industrial peace; thirdly, the rise in prices, which had an adverse effect on those workers who were bound by long-term wage arrangements; and fourthly, the Osborne Judgment which had 'finally shaken the confidence of the mass of the workers in the fairness of our judges where class questions are involved'. Though he was critical of direct action, he still believed that 'Socialism will gain ground in consequence of this more or less spasmodic unorganized revolt'.[4]

[1] *Justice*, 28 Aug. 1909; S.D.P., *Conference Report*, 1910, pp. 25–26.
[2] *Justice*, 13 May 1911; *Social-Democrat*, xv (Sept. 1911), 420–2; *Industrial Syndicalist*, July 1910.
[3] *Justice*, 8 Oct. 1910.
[4] *English Review*, vi (Oct. 1910), 539–53.

3

In reporting the foundation conference of the B.S.P. Fenner Brockway, writing in *Labour Leader*, expressed his sympathy with the S.D.P. for having to 'disband and join the new party even at the risk of rank impossibilism'.[1] Brockway's analysis of the situation was correct: and the following years saw a competition taking place between the old S.D.F. leaders and their new allies for the control of the new party. One issue between the 'old guard' and the new recruits was that of the former's attitude to the Syndicalist movement. For the most part, Hyndman and Quelch held aloof from the strikes which were precipitated by the Syndicalists, and Quelch declared that the 1911 Transport strike had secured only a slight improvement in the material conditions of the workers and was valuable mainly as a means of education.[2] A similar view was expressed by Hyndman in a comment on the miners' national strike in the following year which resulted in the enactment of the Coal Mines Minimum Wage Act. 'It is surely a very remarkable fact,' he said:

that the entire trade of this commercial country should have been dislocated, and industry and transport virtually held up, by coalminers' interdict, merely in order to return to the system of fixing minimum wages by local tribunal, which was put an end to by the House of Commons in 1814. We have simply gone back a hundred years.[3]

There was thus an obvious discrepancy between the attitude of these leaders and the enthusiasm of many of the rank and file.

Meanwhile, Mann and Bowman were prosecuted and sent to prison for publishing a 'Don't Shoot' manifesto to the soldiers who were sent to intervene in the 1911 transport

---

[1] *Labour Leader*, 6 Oct. 1911.
[2] H. Quelch, Introduction to B. Tillett, *History of the London Transport Workers' Strike, 1911* (n.d.).
[3] *The Times*, 5 April 1912.

strike at Liverpool. This drove the Syndicalists to a more extreme position, and their organ, the *Syndicalist*, launched a relentless attack on political action. The movement gained considerable support among the members of the B.S.P. and became a serious menace to its future as a political organization. While Mann and Bowman were being prosecuted, however, *Justice* remained in the control of the 'S.D.F. Old Guard', and it began to print anti-Syndicalist articles such as A. S. Headingley's 'Syndicalism indigenous to France, inappropriate to England'.[1] This action aggravated the already critical relations between the exponents of Syndicalism and those of parliamentary Social-Democracy.

As we have seen, the formation of the B.S.P. owed something to the industrial unrest as well as to the movement for 'Socialist unity'. Although a resolution in favour of Industrial Unionism was defeated by the S.D.F. delegates at its inaugural conference, it was significant that the new party programme advocated the 'industrial unity of all workers'. Soon an internal struggle developed on this question and endangered the unity of the party. Early in 1912 Leonard Hall published a leaflet on Industrial Unionism which he submitted to the B.S.P. conference of that year. He urged the conference to declare its identity with the industrial revolt. His motion was supported by nearly one-third of the delegates, and he himself was elected to the executive on a poll only less than that of Quelch. Hyndman, the chairman, however, carried the day with a sharp criticism of industrial action:

The worse the Labour Party were in the House of Commons, the greater the need for Socialists to be there to show the work that could be done. Industrial organization without political power was of little use. 'You keep on crying "Don't shoot!" but they shoot you just the same, and you deserve to be shot, because you don't take the means of stopping the shooting.'[2]

[1] *Justice*, 16 March 1912.
[2] B.S.P., *Conference Report*, 1912, pp. 14-19, 31; L. Hall on Industrial Unionism, B.S.P. (Birmingham Section) Papers.

The conference ended, therefore, with a compromise between the Industrial Unionists and the supporters of political action. This was reflected in the party constitution approved by the delegates, which declared that the methods of Socialist progress embraced both 'the advocacy of industrial unity of all workers' and 'the establishment of a militant Socialist Party in Parliament and on Local Bodies'. Although some branches of industrial unionists, dissatisfied with this outcome, threatened to break away, most of them were still trying to capture the party from within, and they were now supported by the Industrial Unionists and Syndicalists outside the party. Tom Mann's *Syndicalist*, for instance, made a direct appeal to the B.S.P. membership:

Most of us who are members of the Industrial Syndicalist Educational League were, and many are now, members of one or other of the bodies that fused together to constitute the B.S.P. . . . It is unfortunate that our worst enemies should be those 'of our own households'. . . . As the idea of Syndicalism spreads among the younger, up-to-date members of the B.S.P. they will realize more and more the necessity for getting rid of the 'Old Guard'. If they don't, the 'Old Guard' will destroy the B.S.P.[1]

Meanwhile the Central Labour College, like the 'impossibilists' of a decade earlier, had been organizing 'economic classes' in conjunction with certain of the branches in Manchester and Birmingham.[2] Syndicalism was described by George Simpson, formerly of the Manchester Socialist Representation Committee, as the only remedy against the evils of the developing 'Servile State'—a phrase coined by Hilaire Belloc at the time of the passing of the National Insurance Act.[3] Hyndman's friend the American Socialist Gaylord Wilshire had also gone over to Syndicalism: during a visit to England he had transferred his little journal *Wilshire's Magazine* from Los Angeles to London and had also edited the March-April issue of the *Syndicalist* when its

[1] *Syndicalist*, Nov. 1912.   [2] *Clarion*, 12 July, 27 Sept. 1912.
[3] *Justice*, 19 Oct. 1912.

editor Bowman was in prison. Hyndman was not afraid to take issue with his old friend: Syndicalism, he said, was 'compounded of ignorance, impatience and hysteria, resulting in an outburst of . . . reactionary rubbish'.[1] In the pages of the *Daily Herald*, a new labour paper which had begun as a strike sheet, Hyndman challenged Wilshire to say if he had altogether abandoned parliamentary action, and the latter, drawing on his American experience, replied that the domination of trusts in politics had rendered it obsolete.[2]

Meanwhile in October 1912 the 'Old Guard' of Hyndmanites, alarmed at the growing influence of Syndicalism, had got together to issue a statement of their official policy:

> Syndicalism is avowedly opposed to Socialism. . . . The tactics of the Levellers and Luddites belong to a lower stage of economic development. . . . These acts of internecine warfare revive the policy of the old 'no politics' trade union leaders who dominated those bodies up to 1890. . . . All workers, whether they like it or not, are consumers as well as producers, citizens as well as wage-earners. . . . Any policy failing to act upon this community of interests must be a disruptive agency, at a time when working-class consolidation is essential.[3]

This appeal for the solidarity of the proletariat as consumers of goods rather than as producers was a remarkable indication of the extent to which the 'Old Guard' had digressed from the orthodox theories of Marxism. It was the last straw for the Industrial Unionists and Syndicalists—mostly militant young Marxists—who now began to withdraw from the B.S.P.

Hyndman's followers did, however, distinguish between Syndicalism, 'a bastard form of anti-political Anarchism' as he put it,[4] and the movement for trade union amalgamation launched by the T.U.C. of which they approved. They welcomed the formation of the National Union of Railwaymen which came into existence in 1913 as a result of the

[1] Hyndman to Wilshire, 4 April 1912, Wilshire Papers.
[2] *Daily Herald*, 25 Sept.–30 Oct. 1913.   [3] Ibid., 31 Oct. 1912.
[4] Hyndman, *Further Reminiscences*, p. 457.

amalgamation of three railway workers' unions. The B.S.P. conference in 1913 confirmed this attitude and at the same time elected a new executive committee largely free from Syndicalist influence. The 'Syndicalist revolt' inside the B.S.P., which had given Hyndman, as he put it, 'much disagreeable, harassing and anxious work',[1] was now over. It had, however, deprived the party of much of its strength: in 1914 'a reduction of the aggregate number of branches' was reported at the party conference, and although no figures were given, the party had apparently lost about a fifth of its membership.[2]

4

By the summer of 1913 the storm-centre of labour unrest had moved from England to Ireland, where a struggle had begun between the Irish Transport Workers and the Dublin employers. Hyndman and his followers stood largely aloof from this struggle, though they made a nominal contribution to the Dublin strike funds; and because of this aloofness Jim Larkin, the leader of the Dublin strike, who made a speaking tour of England under the sponsorship of the Daily Herald League, refused to speak under B.S.P. auspices. *Justice* attributed this, however, to the Catholic influence exerted upon him through the Daily Herald League which, as it pointed out, was then dominated by Catholic intellectuals such as Hilaire Belloc and G. K. Chesterton. Belloc's views were in fact hostile to political Socialism, which he chose to call "Collectivism", and this annoyed Hyndman's followers.[3]

Meanwhile, Protestant Ulster was showing its determination to use force against Dublin control should Home Rule be granted to Ireland; Sir Edward Carson's Ulster Volunteers had begun drilling, and the danger of civil war loomed large. The S.D.F. 'Old Guard' was now taking a totally

[1] B.S.P., *Conference Report*, 1913, p. 28.   [2] Ibid., 1914, p. 30.
[3] *Daily Herald*, 31 Dec. 1913; *Justice*, 8 Jan. 1914.

different view of the issue from that which they had expressed in 1906. Quelch urged support for the Ulstermen on the ground that Socialists should stand up for every small nation;[1] and Hyndman, himself of Ulster stock, welcomed 'the bold front shown by the Ulstermen'. 'It is absolutely certain,' he said, 'that farmers and labourers and artisans constitute fully nine-tenths of the 110,000 men or more of the Ulster Citizen Army.'[2] This was too much for many of the B.S.P. members: it smacked of the current policy of the Unionist Party. The B.S.P. executive issued a manifesto in which it maintained, contrary to Hyndman, that the Ulster crisis had been brought about by 'aristocratic and pluto-cratic leaders'.[3] Thus on this issue Hyndman failed to carry his party with him, though if Quelch had lived it is possible that he could have turned the scales.

5

Hyndman, as we have seen, was reluctant to support the new currents of revolt in the labour movement, and his attitude towards the suffragettes was not much different. In fact, most of the Social-Democrats regarded the agitation for 'Votes for Women' as a middle-class movement and treated it with contempt. Most of them were not actively anti-feminist, except for Belfort Bax, a member of the Men's Anti-Suffrage League, who discoursed upon the 'inferiority' of woman and her 'sex-privileges'.[4] Not unnaturally, how-ever, many of the women members supported the movement for the political emancipation of their sex. Mrs. Dora Montefiore, for instance, who was a keen S.D.F. member, had, in Hyndman's words, 'gone off on the suffrage craze'

---

[1] *British Socialist*, i (Sept. 1912), 385-90; *Social-Democrat*, vi (Nov. 1902), 326-8.

[2] *Daily Herald*, 20 Oct. 1913; *Justice*, 2 April 1912.   [3] *Justice*, 9 April 1914.

[4] S.D.P., *Conference Report*, 1909, pp. 25-26. See also Bax's articles in *Justice*, 14 Dec. 1907, *Social-Democrat*, Jan., April 1901, Dec. 1902, Sept. 1904, and his pamphlet, *The Legal Subjection of Men*.

and was 'as bad or worse than "imps" [impossibilists]'. Hyndman himself was of the opinion that women who advocated their own emancipation as a 'sex question' 'ought to be sent to an island by themselves'.[1]

At the time of the South African war, Mrs. Montefiore had written a pamphlet entitled *Women Uitlanders*, in which she compared the Englishwomen at home to the unenfranchised immigrants on the Rand. She also put into practice the radical slogan 'No taxation without representation' by refusing to pay her income tax.[2] At this stage she was closely associated with the Women's Social and Political Union (W.S.P.U.), the militant organization which, under the leadership of the Pankhurst family, adopted violent tactics to draw attention to its cause. This body, however, soon became willing to accept a women's suffrage act with a property qualification, for it believed that adult suffrage without qualification was a distant aim and that to wait for it would mean the indefinite postponement of the urgent question of women's rights. There were a number of wealthy supporters of the W.S.P.U., and its income increased by leaps and bounds—a feature which aroused suspicion among the Social-Democrats who opposed on principle any limited women's suffrage that might inaugurate 'the open reign of the female capitalist'.[3] In 1906 they tried to start a movement of their own by setting up a Women's Committee of the S.D.F. in rivalry with the W.S.P.U.:[4] but little came of this. Their arguments had some force in the labour movement, however, and it was noteworthy that the Labour Party conference of 1907 adopted an amendment moved by Quelch against women's suffrage based on a property qualification, although this was in defiance of the

---

[1] Hyndman to Wilshire, 27 May 1904, Wilshire Papers.

[2] D. B. Montefiore, *From a Victorian to a Modern* (1927), pp. 41, 72–82.

[3] *Social-Democrat*, viii (April 1904), 217.

[4] In 1910 there were nineteen 'circles' affiliated to the Women's Committee. *Berichte an die zweite Internationale Konferenz Sozialistiche Frauen* (Stuttgart, c. 1910), p. 40.

views of Keir Hardie, then an enthusiastic supporter of the suffragettes.[1]

By this time Mrs. Montefiore had broken off relations with the W.S.P.U., for she could not reconcile herself to the 'physical force' policy and the 'autocratic rulings' and 'Toryism' of the Pankhursts.[2] She began to emphasize the grievances of working women rather than of women in general. 'The working woman is more sweated, more despised, more downtrodden in the last resort,' she said, 'than is the working man, because, though under capitalism the working man is the wage-slave, yet his wife is the slave of the slave.'[3] She joined an 'Adult Suffrage Society' at its formation in 1907, and in the same year attended the International Socialist Women's Conference held at Stuttgart as a delegate of the Society. The conference adopted a resolution in favour of 'Universal Womanhood Suffrage', repudiating any limited measure as 'an adulteration of and a caricature upon the principle of political equality of the female sex'. This was mainly the work of Clara Zetkin of the German Social-Democratic Party, who became secretary of a newly established International Socialist Women's Bureau.[4] A British section of the Bureau was set up by the S.D.F. women in conjunction with the women members of the Fabian Society and Clarion movement, the Adult Suffrage Society, and the Socialist Teachers' Association. But the I.L.P. refused to take part in it and went its own way with a 'Women's Labour League' which had been formed in the previous year under the leadership of Mrs. Ramsay MacDonald. These differences among the women Socialists thus paralleled the differences among the larger organizations which the movement for Socialist unity had been unable to overcome.[5]

[1] Labour Party, *Conference Report*, 1907, p. 61.
[2] Montefiore, op. cit., pp. 108–12.
[3] Montefiore, *The Position of Women in the Socialist Movement* (1909), p. 3.
[4] *Justice*, 31 Aug. 1907; *Labour Leader*, 30 Aug. 1907.
[5] *Berichte*, &c., pp. 36, 41.

Early in 1909, Geoffrey Howard, a Liberal M.P., introduced a Bill to provide adult suffrage for men and women
on a three months' residential qualification. This Bill the
suffragettes criticized as impracticable under existing circumstances. But Mrs. Montefiore, on behalf of the Adult
Suffrage Society, supported it and organized a demonstration which Clara Zetkin was invited to address. At this
meeting a resolution was moved by Lady Warwick calling
upon the Prime Minister to draft a Political Reform Bill
on the lines of a vote for every adult man and woman.
Hyndman, seconding the resolution, declared that the
acceptance of Adult Suffrage was the only remedy for a
situation in which women found themselves as 'a reactionary
force'.[1] Howard's Bill, however, went no further than its
Second Reading in the House. The suffragettes for their part
intensified their militant action by breaking windows and
engaging in other violent acts which led to the imprisonment
of many of their members. They followed this up by system-
atically going on hunger-strike when in prison.

The relative positions of the suffragettes and the adult
suffragists changed when a Conciliation Committee of
Members of Parliament introduced a limited Bill with a
household qualification. The suffragettes of the W.S.P.U.
accepted a truce with the Government; but Mrs. Montefiore
and the Adult Suffrage Society denounced the Bill as a
reactionary measure proposed in the interests of propertied
classes. Quelch declared that the W.S.P.U. was 'anti-pro-
letarian, anti-Socialist and anti-democratic'.[2] A second conciliation Bill was rejected in 1912 to the great satisfaction of
the adult suffragists, but its failure was a signal for the suffragettes to start a fresh and more violent agitation: Christabel
Pankhurst began a yet more extreme campaign, involving
arson, which she conducted from headquarters in Paris.

---

[1] *Justice*, 1 May 1909.
[2] Quelch, 'Social-Democracy and Ladies' Suffrage', *Social-Democrat*, xiv
(July 1910), 293; *Justice*, 23 July 1910.

Although the Syndicalist 'rebels' inside the B.S.P. supported the tactics of the suffragettes, which they regarded as 'comparatively harmless', Hyndman and his followers showed no sympathy for the campaign of arson. In 1913 when Mrs. Pankhurst was sentenced to three years' penal servitude, *Justice* commented that her sentence was 'no more severe, if as severe, as would have been passed on a man convicted on a similar charge'.[1] In 1914, however, the outbreak of war put an end to suffragette militancy, and the Pankhursts were soon demanding compulsory national service for women.

There were thus many forms of serious social unrest in the period immediately preceding the European war. Hyndman disapproved of most of them, and with his senior colleagues did his best to dissociate his organization from them, realizing that they endangered his own programme of political action by their bold challenge to the established order. Much of his own energy, however, was now devoted to other questions of vital importance—the questions of defence and foreign policy, which had always been of great interest to him—and it is to a consideration of these topics, themselves causing much disagreement within the Socialist movement, that we must now turn.

[1] *Justice*, 12 April 1913.

I

Hᴜɴᴅᴍᴀɴ's championship of nationalism—not only that of Britain but of other countries as well—had given distinctive colouring to the S.D.F.'s attitude to international affairs. A statement on foreign policy published by the S.D.F. executive of 1904 criticized undifferentiated inter-nationalism as 'a sort of gigantic steam roller', and it pledged the Federation to 'the old Liberal tradition of the rights of the little peoples'.[1] Hyndman continued to advocate the rights of subject nations, and the S.D.F. was almost unanimous on this question, with the possible exception of Bax, to whom any emphasis on nationality appeared to be contrary to internationalism and therefore anti-Socialist.

Hyndman was a champion of nationalism wherever he saw it asserting itself against foreign domination. Its development in Asia was already attracting his attention. In the Russo-Japanese war of 1904–5 he perceived a sort of Japanese *risorgimento*, and he watched the progress of the war with much of the positive enthusiasm of the young war corres-pondent with the Garibaldians. He attended the Amsterdam congress of the International which took place while the war was being fought, and he witnessed the dramatic hand-shake between George Plekhanov and Sen Katayama, delegates of the two belligerent nations. He rose to point out the significance of the fact that for the first time Asia

[1] 'An Exposition of Socialist Foreign Policy', *Social-Democrat*, viii (April 1904), published also as a pamphlet, *Socialism and Foreign Policy* (1904).

was represented at an International Socialist Congress; and
he concluded his remarks with the words 'Asia for the
Asiatics, and Freedom and Justice for All Mankind!'[1] His
support of Japanese nationalism, however, did not last long:
he soon became critical of Japan's intentions in Asia and
opposed the renewal of the Anglo-Japanese treaty in 1905
because it was to 'put our peace in the Far East wholly at
the mercy of Japan' and especially because it 'proclaims to
the world that we are unable to defend India against
Russian attack without Japanese assistance'.[2]

Nevertheless, Hyndman regarded Japan's victory over
Russia as an event heralding the emancipation of Asia.
He had submitted to the Amsterdam congress a report
criticizing the territorial expansion of the European powers
which he thought would 'prolong capitalist domination'.[3]
He now hoped that the Chinese would 'make a clean sweep
of the Christian preachers and blood-suckers', and he noted
with pleasure 'a most satisfactory and hopeful change' in
the more militant Indian nationalist movement led by
Lokamanya Tilak.[4] At a meeting which was held in the
S.D.F.'s Chandos Hall in May 1907 to protest against the
imprisonment of nationalist leaders in Punjab, he denounced what he described as an 'ugly feature' of the tactics
adopted by the Indian government—an attempt to set the
Mahommedans against the Hindus with a view to weakening
the nationalist movement.[5]

Hyndman's activities on behalf of India were legion. He
wrote on Famine, on Plague, on Despotism, and on Terror-
ism. He opened 'India House', the headquarters of an
Indian Home Rule Society, which was said to be 'the most

[1] *Justice*, 20 Aug. 1904. Hyndman's old Indian friend Naoroji was also
present at the congress.
[2] Ibid., 7 Oct. 1905.
[3] Hyndman, *Report on the Colonies and Dependencies to the International Socialist
Congress at Amsterdam* (1904).
[4] *Justice*, 29 Oct. 1904.
[5] Ibid., 18 May 1907. His speech was published as a pamphlet entitled *The
Indian Unrest* (1907).

dangerous organization outside India'.[1] During the trial of
Tilak for sedition, *Justice* issued a special number dedicated
to the cause of India, in which Hyndman wrote a leading
article entitled 'Bande Mataram'—'Our Dear Motherland'
—and he also sent a letter to *The Times* criticizing the
composition of the jury at the trial.[2] By numerous speeches
and writings as well as by personal contact with Indians in
London, Hyndman exerted considerable influence, direct
and indirect, on the Indian nationalist movement. Yet his
Indian agitation, though it was one of his most serious and
consistent activities, was soon to show signs of flagging as
he became more and more absorbed in the questions of
European politics.

2

Hyndman's attitude to the Russo-Japanese war was
probably just as much anti-Russian as pro-Japanese, for he
was a keen supporter not only of nationalist causes but also
of any 'war against reaction'.[3] When, therefore, the Japanese
war was followed by a revolution in Russia, he was highly
encouraged. 'Warsaw, Moscow, and Baku have already
given forth a fine sulphureous odour. For my part,' he said,

I rejoice in all this movement, in all these forerunnings of upheaval and revolution. I am glad to have lived to see it, and I
hope to see something of the still more serious period which
cannot fail to come after.[4]

Russia had long been regarded as the great citadel of
'reaction' in the world, and the events of the attempted
revolution naturally aroused Hyndman to great enthusiasm
and then to strong words of denunciation of the Czarist
government. Shortly after the suppression of revolt at St.
Petersburg in January 1905, Hyndman spoke at a protest
meeting in London and expressed his 'abhorrence of the

---

[1] V. Chirol, *Indian Unrest* (1910), p. 148; *Justice*, 23 May 1908.
[2] *Justice*, 18 July 1908; *The Times*, 27 July 1908.
[3] *Justice*, 17 June, 22 July 1905.   [4] Ibid., 16 Sept. 1905.

system of butchery and torture pursued throughout Russia at the expense of those who were merely striving for that measure of freedom which the workers of this country had but did not know how to use'.[1]

The Federation did what it could to help the Russian revolutionaries, and one of its workers in Edinburgh, John Leslie, even took part in 'gun-running' to enable their struggle to go on.[2] Most of the help that the S.D.F. could give, however, was in providing hospitality to the Russian Social-Democratic Party in exile. The S.D.F. leaders took little interest, so far as is known, in the internal divisions of this tiny organization, which were later to assume such importance. Although Lenin himself lived in London for a year from April 1902, and edited *Iskra* at the office of the Twentieth Century Press, the S.D.F. on the whole seems to have taken the Menshevik line, as did Rothstein who supported the policy of Socialist-Liberal alliance proposed by Plekhanov.[3] As for Hyndman, his sympathy was not so much with the Social Democrats as with the Social Revolutionaries, the successor body of the Narodniks, which had a wing of direct actionists. He had welcomed the assassination of Grand Duke Sergius, the Czar's uncle, by a Social Revolutionary, and in the conflict between 'divine right and dynamite' he upheld the cause of the latter.[4] He was especially friendly with I. A. Rubanovitch, the Social Revolutionary delegate to the Second International, and always advocated the fair representation of what he called the Russian 'Peasants Revolutionary' party at the International congresses.[5]

Belligerent radicalism, rather than Macchiavellian adaptation of Marxism, was therefore the keynote of Hyndman's

[1] *Justice*, 11 Feb. 1905.
[2] Lee and Archbold, op. cit., pp. 148–9. See also W. S. Adams, 'British Reactions to the 1905 Russian Revolution', *Marxist Quarterly*, ii (1955), 173–86, which, however, ignores this aspect.
[3] *Justice*, 30 March 1907.   [4] Ibid., 25 Feb. 1905.
[5] Hyndman, *Further Reminiscences*, pp. 379–80.

attitude to Russia. At a mass meeting held in Trafalgar Square shortly before the Czar's proposed visit to Britain in 1909, he urged the audience to 'spit in his face'. The police confiscated copies of *Justice* on sale in the Square: they contained a large cartoon entitled 'The Czar's Nightmare', a caricature of the Czar being threatened with dynamite, and also an open letter addressed to 'Nicholas the Bloody'.[1] We shall see, however, that Hyndman's sympathy with the Social Revolutionaries and their policy, combined with his concern for the Allied cause in wartime, was later to place him at odds with the development of the revolutionary movement as it finally emerged from the overthrow of Czarism.

3

More and more, however, Hyndman concentrated on the problems caused by the growth of Germany. This seemed to challenge Britain's position as the premier world power and to threaten the British Empire which, once freed from colonial exploitation, would, in his view, become a stronghold of 'democracy'. The contrast which he drew between 'democracy' and 'despotism' was more important for him than the contrast which other Socialists preferred to draw between international capitalism and the international working class. It is true that at the beginning of the century when the International set up its permanent Bureau, Hyndman for a while entertained hopes for effective united action by the Socialists in the struggle against 'reaction'; and on one occasion he even asserted that 'a "nationalist" Socialist is a contradiction in terms'.[2] But his trust in the International was in inverse proportion to the German influence in that body, and the 'national', if not 'nationalist', aspects of his personal creed reasserted themselves.

Hyndman's dislike of the German Social-Democrats was increased by his contact with them on the International

---

[1] *Justice*, 24, 31 July 1909.   [2] Ibid., 4 June 1902.

Socialist Bureau. As early as January 1902 J. B. Askew, a member of the S.D.F. who had German connexions, wrote to Kautsky: 'Hyndman was very cross with the German party—you are entirely bad and also wholly insignificant and ignorant people who live with the same illusions as William II.'[1] A few days later he again warned Kautsky: 'Hyndman wrote me a long letter to show that the Germans wanted to dominate the International conference . . . [He] also complained that Adler and Singer spoke so much and repeated themselves so often . . . [He] informs me that Jaurès, Bracke, Krichevsky, and other delegates were of his opinion.'[2] As time went on Hyndman became increasingly suspicious and even contemptuous of the largest Socialist party in Europe. 'I am rather sick of the Germans, Kautsky included', he wrote to Wilshire in 1905:

First, what is the good of having a big party if you have no big men and cannot make a big impression? Second, what is the use of pretending that the Germans are completely the leaders in Socialism today when their doctrinaire utterances are falsified constantly? Third, what is the use of talking of internationalism, when the party is becoming more and more national each year since Liebknecht's death, and Bebel himself frequently delivers more or less jingo speeches? But among certain cliques it is as inadmissible to criticize the Germans in Socialism as it is to point out that Jews have their drawbacks.[3]

As Hyndman began to lose hope of the International, his old faith in the 'alliance of democracies' came to the fore. At this time he was making frequent business trips to Paris, and his financial interests there seem to have strengthened his Francophile tendencies. It was indeed an 'unusual experience' for him to find in Sir Charles Dilke an Englishman who took a more favourable view of France than himself.[4]

[1] Askew to Kautsky, 15 Jan. 1902, Kautsky Papers.
[2] Ibid., 19 Jan. 1902.
[3] Hyndman to Wilshire, 9 May 1905, Wilshire Papers.
[4] S. Gwynn and G. M. Tuckwell, *The Life of the Rt. Hon. Sir Charles W. Dilke* (1917), ii, pp. 501–2.

As early as January 1901 he wrote a letter to the *Morning Post*, urging the Conservative Government to take the necessary steps to 'promote cordial relations between the two most civilized nations of Europe.'[1] The Anglo-French agreement was signed in April 1904, but he went further and pleaded for a mutual defence arrangement between England, France, and Italy, running athwart the Triple Alliance.[2]

Hyndman was in the habit of telling Jaurès whenever they met: '*Prenez garde; le plus grand peril qui menace la paix de l'Europe et du monde, c'est l'antagonisme croissant, c'est l'animosité croissante de l'Allemagne et de l'Angleterre.*'[3] Jaurès was of the opinion that France should play the role of a conciliator between England and Germany. Hyndman thought otherwise: he maintained that it was essential to show strength in the face of aggression or the threat of aggression. 'The bourgeois French Republic is progressive, undoubtedly,' he said. 'The bourgeois English Monarchy (Limited) is less progressive. . . . But to permit the people of either France or England to come under the Kaiser's mailed fist would appear to me un-Socialistic as well as unpatriotic.'[4]

The vehemence with which Hyndman attacked Kaiser Wilhelm and his 'detestable' policies[5] during the Moroccan crisis of 1905 aggravated the antagonism between himself and the German Socialists. The crisis was caused by the Kaiser's statement at Tangier to the effect that Morocco should be open to all nations. Hyndman at once wrote an article entitled 'Bombastes Furioso Again' in which he made a bitter attack on the Kaiser as 'an irresponsible firebrand and unmanageable self-idolator'. The Germans, he said, 'must not be surprised if their neighbours, who are aware of the existence of certain powder-magazines here and there in Europe, should make ready an international fire-hose to

[1] *Morning Post*, 7 Jan. 1901.   [2] *Justice*, 12 Nov. 1904.
[3] *L'Humanité*, 17 June 1905, quoted in *Œuvres de Jean Jaurès* (Paris 1931), ii, 220.
[4] *Justice*, 27 May 1905.   [5] *Daily News*, 5 July 1904.

turn on to their Kaiser's sky-rockets, when they come flaring down to earth'.[1] The tone of the article was provocative and even bellicose; and a few months later the German Chancellor Prince Bülow, speaking in the Reichstag in reply to Bebel's criticism of German foreign policy, referred to Hyndman's article as an example of the growing anti-German feeling in England. *Justice* commented that Hyndman's article was 'a mere statement of fact, like Bebel's remark that "England and France together could pave the North Sea with battleships" '.[2]

In the course of the crisis Hyndman wrote to Camille Huysmans, Secretary of the International, calling for a meeting of the Bureau to deal with the critical international situation caused by the Kaiser's statement.[3] Huysmans sent a circular to secretaries of Socialist parties affiliated to the Bureau suggesting an emergency meeting. Bebel's reply, however, written on behalf of the German party and printed in *Le Temps*, was discouraging. It was 'virtually this', said Hyndman:

that we English of today are 'very nervous'; that the Kaiser's proceedings at Tangier were only a nice little diplomatic stroke; that the Bureau had nothing to do with diplomacy generally; that if we meddled in such matters we might sit permanently at Brussels.[4]

The 'picktooth style' of the German reply irritated him, and he went on to criticize the German party for its impotence and timidity. The proposed Bureau meeting was thus never held. But even as it was, Hyndman's attack on the Kaiser had far-reaching consequences, especially for himself: it finally alienated the German Social-Democrats from him, and this alienation in turn confirmed Hyndman's fear that the International would remain powerless as long as it was dominated by the German party.

[1] *Justice*, 1 April 1905.   [2] Ibid., 23 Dec. 1905.
[3] Hyndman to Huysmans, 7 June 1905, Hillquit Papers.
[4] *Justice*, 12 Aug. 1905.

Hyndman had stopped writing to *The Times* because of its
'brutality and blackguardism' about the South African
War.[1] It was, however, necessary for him to have access to
a non-Socialist paper in order to appeal to a wider audience
than the readership of *Justice*, and sometimes even to express
his personal views where they failed to correspond with
official S.D.F. policy. As we have seen, he began to write to
the *Morning Post*, another Conservative paper, and in 1905
when he felt strongly about 'the German menace' he again
favoured *The Times* as a medium for his views. 'Up to the
South African War we were quite friendly', he wrote to
Wilshire on his relations with the paper. 'Then I could stand
them no more. But that was foolish too. What is a newspaper
after all but a newspaper?'[2] It was in these two Conservative
papers as well as in *Justice* that he was to conduct an extended campaign against the German menace.

4

Hyndman and his closest colleagues may have upheld one
Radical tradition in their demands for a new colonial
policy, but they had no faith in that other Radical (or
perhaps Liberal) illusion about the constantly developing
strength of the bonds of international peace. In their view a
defensive war or even a preventive intervention in the
interests of 'democracy', as Hyndman was wont to put it,
was quite justifiable, especially if it involved the protection
of the rights of small nations. They even had a Socialist
policy for building up the armed forces, and in this they
differed widely from the I.L.P. leaders who, true to their
Liberal past and their nonconformist associations, regarded
expenditure on defence as an unfortunate misuse of public
money.

The S.D.F. proposal for defence was summed up in the

1 Hyndman to Wilshire, 11 Jan. 1901, Wilshire Papers.
2 Ibid., 18 Nov. 1905.

phrase 'the armed nation', and as such it had been advocated by Continental Socialist parties and had been endorsed by the Second International. The idea was that all citizens should be trained in the use of arms under civil law. They would then be able to fight their way forward to democracy and Socialism much more effectively than a people without arms who would be 'absolutely at the mercy of organized, combined capital, with its bands of retainers, its police, and its "Pinkertons" '. The revolutionary armies of France, the forces led by George Washington in the War of Independence in America, and Garibaldi's army were all regarded as offering a pattern to follow. Indeed, 'the armed nation' would become 'a guarantee of individual liberty, of social freedom, and of national independence'. These were the views expressed by Harry Quelch in a pamphlet entitled *Social-Democracy and the Armed Nation*, published in 1904 or thereabouts.

In 1907 R. B. Haldane, the Liberal Secretary for War, introduced a comprehensive measure of army reform later known as the Territorial and Reserve Forces Act. Under the act county associations for volunteers were set up, to supplement the Regular Army. The S.D.F. saw in this reform an approach to a type of conscription, to which it was opposed as a matter of principle. Quelch's pamphlet, however, was freely quoted by supporters of conscription and, as Glasier said, was 'earnestly commended' to the attention of the House of Lord by 'the ardent military Imperialist', Lord Roberts.[1] To clarify the S.D.F. policy and to explain it further, Will Thorne, who was now a Member of Parliament, in 1908 undertook to introduce a Citizen Army Bill in the House of Commons. In this draft plan, the S.D.F. formulated a scheme for compulsory military training under democratic safeguards.[2] Naturally, however, the I.L.P.,

---

[1] *Labour Leader*, 16 Aug. 1907.
[2] For a summary of the bill, see Lee and Archbold, *Social-Democracy in Britain*, pp. 280–2.

which had condemned the S.D.F.'s policy on this question, now bitterly criticized the Bill and particularly the clause for democratic control which, it maintained, no capitalist government would accept: 'Yet, knowing this', said the *Labour Leader*, 'Mr. Thorne . . . deliberately put forward a compulsory military training scheme. . . . In the name of Social-Democracy, he would have the British working class led as lambs to the capitalist slaughter!'[1] It appears, however, that Thorne was dissuaded by his colleagues in the Labour Party from proceeding very far with the measure.

The S.D.F. had always distrusted proposals for disarmament made by despotic governments. Hyndman had organized a demonstration against the first Hague Peace Conference of 1899, and now it was Quelch who challenged the second Hague Conference of 1907. At the Stuttgart International Congress held in the same year he spoke of 'the thieves' supper at The Hague, miscalled a Peace Conference'. This utterance caused the Würtemberg Government to expel him from the country.[2] The expulsion certainly made him a hero to the Socialists; but it cannot be maintained that the International was able to formulate any more constructive programme than that discussed at The Hague. The resolution on militarism adopted at the full congress at Stuttgart amounted to no more than a compromise of various proposals and tendencies: Bebel's call for parliamentary agitation and for the creation of 'citizen armies', Lenin's advocacy of revolutionary war, Hervé's proposal for direct action against war, and above all Jaurès's optimism about the prospects of permanent peace. Hyndman and other British delegates took no part in the debate on the resolution, but it was clear that the S.D.F., in spite of its criticism of the German party, accepted Bebel's proposals while the I.L.P. shared the views expressed by Hervé and Jaurès. Quelch in

[1] *Labour Leader*, 4 Sept. 1908.
[2] *Justice*, 31 Aug. 1907; *Internationaler Sozialisten-Kongress zu Stuttgart* (Berlin, 1907), p. 32.

a letter to *The Times* had expressed disapproval of Hervé's anti-militarist campaign, which had a certain following in England not only in the I.L.P. but also among some of the S.D.F. members, notably Bax.[1] Although Bax and even Hervé later supported the war when it broke out, the discord in the Socialist movement between the anti-militarists and the advocates of national defence became further aggravated as the prospects of maintaining European peace began to dwindle.

5

One of the features of the era was the intensification of Anglo-German naval rivalry. In 1908 the German Emperor wrote to Lord Tweedmouth, First Lord of the Admiralty, that the German Fleet was not being built as a challenge to Britain's naval supremacy. Hyndman at least could not accept this disavowal; and so he wrote in *Justice*:

Germany . . . is preparing steadily for war, and every summer carries out a programme by land and by sea which is a dress rehearsal for a simultaneous attack on France and on Great Britain by land and by sea.[2]

During the great naval manœuvres in the summer of the same year both Hyndman and Blatchford agitated vigorously about the danger from Germany. Hyndman wrote an article in Blatchford's *Clarion* entitled 'The Coming German War against Great Britain', in which he said that 'the success of the German pan-Teutonic, anti-English, anti-French scheme of aggression would throw back Socialism in Europe for fully two generations'.[3] The attitude expressed by Hyndman and Blatchford naturally irritated the internationalist I.L.P. leaders. Hardie attacked Hyndman who, he said, 'has ransacked the columns of the gutter press for innuendo and insults levelled against the representatives of

[1] *The Times*, 17 Aug. 1907.   [2] *Justice*, 22 Feb. 1908.
[3] *Clarion*, 31 July 1908.

the German Empire, and dished these up with all the
assurance with which he is accustomed to predict the date of
the coming Social Revolution'.[1] This remark upset Hynd-
ham, who shortly afterwards refused to appear on the same
platform with Hardie at a proposed demonstration of
'Socialist unity'.[2]

In attempting to improve relations between Britain and
Germany, however, both sides of the British Socialist
movement could find a certain basis for collaboration. In
June 1908 Hyndman again proposed a meeting of the
International Socialist Bureau to deal with the mounting
tension between England and Germany; but his proposal,
like that of 1905, was not accepted. In July he joined with
Hardie and others in issuing an invitation to the leaders of
the German Social-Democratic Party to come to England so
that the British Section of the International could hold a
joint demonstration in favour of peace. The desire of the
British party to visit Berlin on a similar mission was also
communicated. In the following month Bebel sent a reply to
the *Labour Leader*, criticizing the proposal to send a British
deputation to Germany. 'It would look as if in England
people were afraid of Germany,' he said. '. . . Of the solidarity of the English and German working classes the rulers
on this side and on that side are convinced. Therefore, there
is no need of any fresh assurance.'[3] It may be that Bebel, for
all his emphasis on international solidarity, turned down the
proposal for fear of appearing too 'internationalist' in the
eyes of German popular opinion. It is certainly true that he
adopted an increasingly conservative attitude within the
Socialist International.[4] The basic policy of the German
Social-Democratic Party was in fact *mutatis mutandis* very
closely akin to that of the very much smaller S.D.F. in

[1] *Labour Leader*, 14 Aug. 1908.
[2] *Justice*, 28 Nov. 1908; *Labour Leader*, 11 Dec. 1908.
[3] *Labour Leader*, 28 Aug. 1908.
[4] C. E. Schorske, *German Social Democracy 1905–1917* (Cambridge, Mass.,
1955), pp. 75, 85.

Britain, though the latter, having no parliamentary representation, did not need to worry quite so often about the
reactions of the wider public.

It required a further invitation to persuade the German
party to send representatives to England. In September
Quelch, together with an I.L.P. delegate, attended the
Nuremberg congress of the German Social Democrats and
succeeded in inducing Kautsky and Ledebour to accept
their hospitality. In the following month the German
leaders arrived in London, and a public demonstration was
held for them in St. James's Hall. Kautsky spoke of the
danger of war, and made the following interesting prediction:

> The sufferings of a great war will immensely increase the ranks
> of the Labour Party, make it more revolutionary in its aims, its
> ways and means, and it is not impossible that through the war it
> may become at last the supreme political power in the Kingdom.[1]

Yet no great intimacy even with the Labour Party resulted
from this visit. In June 1909, the party sent its own delegation
headed by Ramsay MacDonald to Germany under the
auspices of a German-English Conciliation Committee,
which was composed of members of the Liberal trade unions
and various non-Socialist political leaders. Under these
circumstances the German Social-Democrats refused to take
any part in the reception of the Labour M.P.s.[2] Thus the
relations between the British and German movements
remained as remote as before, lacking mutual confidence or
even the understanding that could be derived from direct
contact.

6

Apart from the I.L.P. which pleaded consistently for
disarmament and peace, there were many Socialists including a fair proportion of the S.D.F. who objected to Hyndman's anti-German agitation. No doubt they sincerely

[1] *Social-Democrat*, xii (Nov. 1908), 494.
[2] *Justice*, 19 June 1909; R. MacDonald in *Socialist Review*, iii (1909), 324f.

believed in the solidarity of the international proletariat, and
consequently thought of the German party as a major
custodian of peace and fraternity. Under the leadership of
Theodore Rothstein, those of them who were S.D.F. members expressed criticism of Hyndman as he renewed his
campaign for rearmament.

When the Eastern Question again came to the fore, with
the Young Turk revolution and the Austrian annexation of
Bosnia and Herzegovina in 1908, *Justice* commented in an
editorial: '[Germany and Austria] control the destinies of
the Near East—and the Near West? . . . It is for the German
to speak and the Slav to hear—and obey.'[1] Rothstein,
amazed by 'the sudden enthusiasm for the downtrodden
Slav', declared that the editorial was 'word for word the
talk of the Harmsworth Press'. Zelda Kahan, also of Russian-
Jewish origin and now a schoolteacher in London, urged the
rank and file of the S.D.P. to repudiate Hyndman's anti-
German agitation. Askew, always sympathetic with the
German standpoint, denounced him as 'a bourgeois nationalist';[2] And a certain J. Finn wrote to *Justice*:

> Twenty-five years ago Hyndman taught me that we are not
> one nation but two, viz. the rich and the poor, and I believed it,
> and believe it still. . . . Why should Hyndman say 'we' and 'our'
> when the issue is British commercialism versus German com-
> mercialism?[3]

Meanwhile, Hyndman had been defending himself in *The
Times* correspondence columns from the charge brought
against him by various Liberal politicians of being a war-
monger. He pointed out that the Liberal Government itself
had lately discovered the danger from German naval
preparations.[4] The criticism from within his own party he
answered in an article in *Justice* entitled 'The Danger of
German Predominance':

[1] *Justice*, 10 April 1909.   [2] Ibid., 10 April, 17 April, 8 May 1909.
[3] Ibid., 8 May 1909.   [4] *The Times*, 23 March 1909.

Our Social-Democratic comrades in Germany have very little more influence in the matter of peace and war by land or by sea than we Social-Democrats here have in Great Britain. . . . Naval superiority in the narrow seas is to Great Britain a necessity: to Germany a luxury.[1]

It was difficult for his own colleagues to withstand his influence. 'Whenever Hyndman confronts the members, the latter quail', confessed Rothstein in a letter to Kautsky. Rothstein asked the German leader to convene a meeting of the International Socialist Bureau to discuss Anglo-German relations. 'The Bureau ought to try to influence Hyndman,' he said.[2] Kautsky's reply is unknown but it apparently stated 'grave' reasons why the German party was reluctant to hold a Bureau meeting.[3]

At the 1909 annual conference of the S.D.P., the opposition, in deference to Hyndman's authority, was 'simply . . . afraid to raise the question'.[4] A year later when the delegates again met, Hyndman rehearsed his arguments and urged the conference to support 'the provision of an adequate navy for the defence of our commerce and our coasts'.[5] Soon afterwards Rothstein wrote to Kautsky: 'I wonder if you could find time to write a letter to Quelch—Hyndman is past cure!—on the errors of his attitude?'[6] So Kautsky sent a May Day article to the editor of *Justice*, an article which however, contained as little internationalist sentiment as Hyndman's writings, for it stated as the reason for the futility of the 'big navy' propaganda that 'England's naval power could never be in a position to destroy the foundations of Germany's already flourishing trade.'[7]

Meanwhile, the Labour Party in the House of Commons on the whole took the I.L.P. attitude to defence, and

[1] *Justice*, 15 May 1909. Hyndman had used this last phrase a decade earlier with reference to France. See above p. 126.
[2] Rothstein to Kautsky, 18 May 1909, Kautsky Papers.
[3] Ibid., 27 May 1909.   [4] Ibid., 18 May 1909.
[5] S.D.P., *Conference Report*, 1910, p. 6.
[6] Rothstein to Kautsky, 7 April 1910, Kautsky Papers.
[7] *Justice*, 30 April 1910.

declared against the strengthening of the Navy. It seemed
to Hyndman that the party wanted only 'a sham defence'
which was 'worse than no defence at all'. In a letter to the
Morning Post he again advocated rearmament, even urging
the building of 'an aerial fleet'. He did not believe, as the
Labour Party did, that rearmament was an alternative to
social reform; he proposed that the additional expense
should be met by the cumulative taxation of all income
above £300 a year. An extra expenditure of as much as
£100,000,000 appeared to him to be 'a bagatelle for the
well-to-do to pay in order to secure a permanent superiority
in the narrow seas'.[1]

These new proposals by Hyndman were not well received
by the rank and file of the S.D.P. Zelda Kahan urged the
branches to protest against it, and a number of branches
actually did so. Rothstein wrote to Kautsky saying that
Hyndman's *Morning Post* letter was especially dangerous now
that the Liberal Government had 'capitulated' to the
Conservatives. A few days later *Vorwärts* attacked him, declaring that the author of such views should be 'shut out of
any Socialist party'.[2]

In these circumstances it was to be expected that
Hyndman would refuse to attend the 1910 congress of the
International at Copenhagen. The British delegation at the
congress, in which the I.L.P. contingent outnumbered that
of the S.D.P. by about two to one, decided by almost
exactly that proportion in votes not to re-elect him to the
International Bureau. Hardie now took the lead for Britain
at the congress, and the role of the I.L.P. increased as its
interest in foreign affairs grew in these years; the Hyndmanites, outnumbered at last, had to yield precedence. All the
same, the I.L.P.'s principal effort proved abortive. A
proposal made by the French Socialist Vaillant, and supported by Keir Hardie, to call an international general

[1] *Morning Post*, 6 July 1910.
[2] *Vorwärts*, 13 July 1910; Rothstein to Kautsky, 7 July 1910, Kautsky Papers.

strike in the event of war, was not carried, largely owing to German opposition.

Meanwhile Hyndman, regarded by his Socialist opponents as virtually hopeless on questions of defence and foreign policy, was still busy defending himself against the charge of having deserted the international principles of Socialism. Even while the Copenhagen congress was meeting he was explaining in *Justice* that he stood for

> . . . the right and the duty of this nationality to maintain its independence, even under capitalism. . . . There is no mistake about that. If this is to be a jingo, then I am a jingo; if this is to be a bourgeois, then I am a bourgeois; if this is to be an opponent of organized Socialist opinion, then I am an opponent of organized Socialist opinion.[1]

7

Gradually, the anti-militarists of the S.D.P. began to coalesce and to form a more determined faction in opposition to Hyndman. His defeat at the General Election in December 1910 gave Rothstein an opportunity to point out to the German Socialists how unpopular the 'big Navy' campaign was.[2] Early in 1911 Rothstein was given space in *Justice* to publish a series of articles on 'The German "Menace" '. He concluded that the campaign against Germany was due solely to the Teutonophobia bred by 'England's jealousy of a powerful rival in commerce and world finance'. His own attitude he declared in these words: 'I am not addicted to Anglophobia nor to any "phobia". But I am, I must confess, a strong "capitalistphobe".'[3]

The S.D.P. conference held at Coventry in April 1911 saw the first open clash between the Hyndmanites and their opponents. Zelda Kahan moved a resolution calling upon the entire party to 'combat' the demand for additional armaments. The resolution was seconded by W. P. Coates

---

[1] *Justice*, 3 Sept. 1910.   [2] *Neue Zeit*, 29 Jan. 1911.   [3] *Justice*, 15 April 1911.

of Sheffield, her future husband. Quelch moved an amendment on behalf of the executive which endorsed in principle the International resolutions in favour of peace, disarmament, and arbitration, but also demanded the maintenance of 'an adequate Navy' and the creation of 'a national citizen army'. He said: 'The small nations threatened by [Germany] regard the British Navy and the German Social-Democracy as their only hope.' The amendment was immediately attacked by a delegate from Southampton who denounced it as 'ultra-revisionist'. Hyndman, however, brought out his usual argument about the helplessness of the International, and the executive amendment was carried by 47 votes to 33.[1]

The immediate upshot of the armaments resolution passed at the Coventry conference was the resignation from the party of two senior members, Herbert Burrows and J. F. Green. 'The whole of the Executive Committee of the Party supported Hyndman', wrote Lenin shortly after the conference:

> You see how quickly those who step on the slippery slope of opportunism roll to the bottom! The British navy, which helps to enslave India . . . is [regarded] as champion of national liberty. . . . Zelda Kahan was right when she said that never had English Social Democracy so disgraced itself as it has now. Never has it so revealed its clearly sectarian character . . . as in the *facility* with which even men like Quelch *desert* to the side of the chauvinists.[2]

The summer of 1911 witnessed the second Moroccan crisis, and Franco-German relations seemed to be almost on the point of rupture. The crisis found the S.D.P. in the process of merging itself into the British Socialist Party. As we have seen, this brought various heterogeneous groups into precarious unity, and on questions of foreign policy the new party was divided from the start. Many of those who came from the I.L.P. supported the anti-militarist faction of the S.D.P., while the Clarion group allied itself with Hyndman

---

[1] *Justice*, 22 April 1911.   [2] *Lenin on Britain* (1934), pp. 112–13.

and his sympathizers. Since the Clarion group soon withdrew, it was on the whole the anti-militarists who benefited
from the merger. An executive meeting of the new party
held in December 1912 passed by five votes to three a resolution moved by Zelda Kahan in favour of disarmament; and
two of the five who voted for it were former members of the
I.L.P. This naturally irritated Hyndman's followers:
Hyndman himself threatened resignation from the chairmanship; Victor Fisher, a nationalist member of the executive,
did resign, denouncing 'Fräulein' Zelda Kahan and 'comrades alien in blood and race', but he was persuaded by
Hyndman to attend the following executive meeting held
two months later at which Hyndman succeeded in getting
the previous resolution suspended.[1]

The schism inside the executive, however, was followed by
a truce arranged at the party conference held at Blackpool
in May 1913. Zelda Kahan made a speech which was in the
main conciliatory and Hyndman promised not to raise
the question 'in any way that would prejudicially affect the
party'. After a resolution protesting mildly against an increase of armaments had been carried almost unanimously,
Zelda Kahan and Hyndman shook hands.[2] The internationalists and nationalists were thus reconciled, and the party
avoided the immediate danger of a split. It was, however,
significant that the conference was boycotted by three-
quarters of the Scottish branches, most of which were anti-
militarist. One young B.S.P. member, Willie Gallacher of the
Paisley branch, had attacked Quelch's 'citizen army'
proposals at the previous conference, and was now taking
an active part in a 'war against war' campaign in Scotland.

Meanwhile, Hyndman had been watching the development of German domestic politics with concern. When the
Reichstag elections in January 1912 resulted in further
successes for the German Social-Democrats, he declared that

---

[1] *Socialist Record*, Jan., March 1914; *Justice*, 4 Jan., 15 March 1913.
[2] B.S.P., *Conference Report*, 1913, pp. 17–18.

while Berlin and Hamburg had become 'virtually Social-Democratic cities', this very fact might bring the Hohenzollern Dynasty to the realization that 'foreign war, with all its horrible risks, is less hazardous than domestic peace with its certainty of approaching overthrow'.[1] His view was fully shared by Frederic Harrison, the Positivist, who had been issuing warnings against the 'German peril' for nearly half a century.[2] The two old Radicals, though they differed from each other on various other issues, were united in their friendly feeling towards France and in their fears of the danger from Germany.

On all these issues Hyndman had consistent support from his old colleague Quelch, who always painstakingly worked out his own views in terms of Marxist phraseology. Quelch's own special contribution seemed to be a pessimistic mood:

> The great bulk of bourgeois interests would suffer by war and are therefore favourable to peace. The proletariat . . . would certainly suffer from war, too—suffer terribly, worse than any other class; they, in any case, are victims. I know that. . . . The proletariat, my class, are the victims in either peace or war. War, undoubtedly, is 'hell' for them; but is peace . . . going to be so much better?[3]

Quelch's gloom may have been due in part to poor health: but in any case he did not share that 'perennial buoyancy of temperament' which Bax noted in Hyndman.[4] Although Hyndman was fully aware of the dangers of the international situation, it did not take much to bring out his optimism. Thus when a special conference of the International held at Basle in November 1912 struck a note of confidence, Hyndman, though he remained in London, shared it to the full:

> Peace between the peoples: war against the exploiters. That was the meaning of the great international gathering at Basle. No finer demonstration of Socialist solidarity could have been

[1] *Morning Post*, 19 Jan. 1912.
[2] F. Harrison, *The German Peril* (1915), p. 149.
[3] *British Socialist*, i (Jan. 1912), 5–6.
[4] E. B. Bax, *Reminiscences and Reflections* (1918), p. 96.

given. . . . It was to declare that war engineered by the militarists and capitalists abroad should be opposed to the utmost, and, if such opposition were unavailing, should be used to help on revolution at home.[1]

The passing of the years thus failed to dim his belief in the eventual triumph of Socialism throughout the world.

8

In spite of or in some quarters because of his hostility to Germany, Hyndman still commanded considerable respect as a national and international figure in the Socialist movement. On 7th March 1912 he celebrated his seventieth birthday; and letters of congratulations poured in, many of them from abroad, to pay tribute to the work of the 'most energetic embodiment of the British section of Marxism', as Kautsky both tactfully and accurately described him.[2]

Just over a year later, on 27th June 1913, Matilda Hyndman died after a long illness. They had had many years of happy married life, and Mrs. Hyndman had accepted and joined in her husband's enthusiasm for Socialism, playing a part herself in the work of the S.D.F. Hyndman felt the loss severely. He was not a widower for long, however: by December he was courting a middle-aged lady called Rosalind Travers, and wrote her letters of tender affection from Bax's villa at Nice, where he spent Christmas.[3] He told her of his prospects of wealth from investments in fields as far apart as Galicia and Assam, but warned her that he would spend it as usual on the Socialist cause. He went as far as to say that his 'dead elder wife' had had her 'comfort and happiness . . . sacrificed by my foolishness and fanaticism'.

[1] *Justice*, 18 Jan. 1913.
[2] Kautsky to F. H. Gorle, 3 March 1912, Hyndman, *Further Reminiscences*, p. 518.
[3] See letters from Hyndman to Rosalind Travers published in Gould, *Hyndman, Prophet of Socialism*, pp. 163ff.

PH

Originally Hyndman had plans to travel on into Italy, where various friends, including the Countess of Warwick, were spending part of the winter. But after a rapid exchange of correspondence with Rosalind Travers, culminating in a telegram from her—'ICH LIEBE DICH'—he hastened home in January. They were married on 14th May 1914, and Hyndman once again had domestic happiness and also an added political interest, because of his wife's special enthusiasm for Eastern European nationalisms.

Rosalind Travers was thirty-nine at the time of her marriage. She had been born in comfortable circumstances, her father being an Army officer who rose to the rank of colonel, and her maternal grandfather a bishop. She had lively literary interests, and published a book of verse and a play. The women's suffrage movement drew her into politics, and in 1908 on a visit to Finland she developed a strong sympathy for the Finnish national struggle against Russian domination.[1] In 1909 at an S.D.P. demonstration held in Trafalgar Square to protest against the Czar's proposed visit to England, she met Hyndman, 'a short, stout, bearded gentleman in a frock-coat and top-hat', and discussed with him the plight of the nascent social-democratic movement in Finland.[2] At a meeting of a 'Nationalities and Subject Races Committee' held in London in 1910 she spoke on the democratic constitution of the Finnish Diet, now threatened by the Russian government.[3] In 1912 and again in 1913 she visited the Balkan countries and made the acquaintance of several leading nationalists. After war broke out in 1914 Hyndman was able to make much use of her first-hand knowledge of Eastern Europe in his suggestions for the redrawing of the boundaries.

Before the war broke out, however, Hyndman and his bride were able to enjoy a happy holiday together without

[1] R. Travers, *Letters from Finland* (1911).
[2] R. T. Hyndman, *The Last Years of H. M. Hyndman*, p. 2.
[3] Nationalities and Subject Races Committee, *Report* of the conference held in the Caxton Hall, Westminster, 28–30 June 1910, p. 57.

much thought of politics. She has recorded how they spent a few weeks of relaxation sauntering in the yet unspoiled valleys of the North Downs and on the rugged Cornish coast, talking about literature and about the countryside that they visited, and putting aside for a time the cares of Britain, Europe, and the World.

XI ⁓ WORLD WAR AND
REVOLUTION

I

WHEN the Archduke Franz Ferdinand was assassinated
at Sarajevo at the end of June 1914, there were few who
thought that the incident would lead to a general war.
By the time of the Austrian declaration of war against
Serbia on 28th July, however, the Socialists at least had
awakened to the importance of the crisis and were actively
campaigning through the Press and with mass demonstrations against the threatened war. This was in accordance
with the programme for emergencies laid down by the
resolutions of the international conferences at Stuttgart and
Copenhagen. The executive of the B.S.P. for its part held a
meeting at short notice and passed a resolution declaring
that it 'heartily congratulates the Social-Democrats of
Vienna, Berlin, Paris, and other centres upon their vigorous
efforts to prevent the outbreak of war, and pledges its
members to do their utmost to support similar pacific
efforts in Great Britain'.[1] Dan Irving, then the B.S.P.
representative on the International Socialist Bureau, together with Keir Hardie and Bruce Glasier attended the
specially summoned meeting of the Bureau in Brussels on
29th July, but could do no more than pass a fresh resolution
urging the workers of all nations to 'strengthen their demonstration against war'.[2]

[1] *Justice*, 30 July 1914.
[2] W. E. Walling (ed.), *Socialists and the War* (New York, 1914), p. 125.

On Friday 31st July when news of the general mobilization of Russian troops reached London, the British Section of the Bureau held a meeting at the House of Commons and adopted a manifesto drafted by Hyndman and signed by Keir Hardie and Arthur Henderson warning against any Government action to support Russia. The manifesto also declared that

as we have no interest, direct or indirect, in the threatened quarrels which may result from the action of Austria in Serbia, the Government of Great Britain should rigidly decline to engage in war, but should confine itself to efforts to bring about peace as speedily as possible.[1]

On the following Sunday (2nd August) a huge 'Stop the War' demonstration took place in Trafalgar Square with Hyndman, Hardie, and George Lansbury presiding at three separate platforms. The crowd paid a silent tribute to Jean Jaurès whose assassination two days before Hyndman called 'a disaster to civilization'.[2] Thus in spite of his much-criticized nationalistic tendencies, Hyndman, like the other British Socialists, had so far scrupulously observed the peace resolutions of the International.

On 4th August Belgium was invaded, and late that night Britain declared war against Germany. Now the united peace campaign came to an end. On the same day, the French and German Socialists approved emergency war credits for their respective governments. In Britain, although the I.L.P. adhered to its anti-war policy, the labour movement as a whole quickly fell in line with the popular sentiment in favour of intervention. As for the B.S.P., the internal struggle over the issue of the 'German Menace' that had nearly wrecked the party a few years before had to be fought out all over again and much more urgently. Hyndman, himself, as was to be expected, threw himself into a vigorous campaign of support for the Allied cause.

[1] *Daily Citizen*, 1 Aug. 1914; *Socialist Review*, xii (Oct.–Dec. 1914), 313.
[2] *Justice*, 6 Aug. 1914.

The B.S.P. executive, which had been reorganized on the basis of district representation in 1913 after the withdrawal of the Syndicalist members, was still dominated by Hyndman's followers. Zelda Kahan, the foremost critic of his 'big navy' campaign, had lost her seat on the executive in that year, and E. C. Fairchild, a London member who was elected in April 1914, was practically the only outspoken opponent of Hyndman among the nine executive members. It was therefore rather remarkable that the manifesto adopted by such an executive and published in the 13th August issue of *Justice* did not go further than a qualified support of the war. It began with a condemnation of secret diplomacy as chiefly responsible for the disaster, but it suggested a programme of wartime 'palliatives' which was followed by a warning on the prospect of a war in which 'wives will lose their husbands and mothers their sons in tens of thousands before the power of Prussian militarism is broken'.

While the executive still remained cautious in its utterances, probably in order not to excite the opposition, Hyndman was trying to reconcile his attitude with Marxist theory and thereby to provide an apologia for the pro-war policy of his faction. When Austin Harrison, son of Frederic Harrison and editor of the *English Review*, sought to attribute part of the war guilt to the Marxist influence in Germany—the 'materialistic fanaticism' as he called it—Hyndman, in collaboration with Bax, wrote a reply pointing out that Marx had been 'the most powerful opponent in Europe of all that German Prussianized militarism stands for'. But he rejected the common Marxist interpretation that the war against Germany was a capitalist war in its origins, for, in his view, this was to make the mistake of 'omitting the mental factor'. Hyndman and Bax now declared that 'all wars are no more of necessity economic wars than all internal national conflicts are of necessity class struggles', and that the European war was 'the final effort of Prussian militarism to retain its predominance at home by conquest and annexation abroad'.[1]

At least the Socialists had done their best to prevent the war, although they were not powerful enough to succeed, said Hyndman:

Yet we Socialists, whose international organization . . . is anyhow but a child of yesterday, are blamed for not achieving, after half a century of tentative effort, what the followers of Christ have been wholly unable to accomplish by centuries of intellectual domination in Europe!

It was true, he conceded, that militant nationalism now obscured the ideal of international Socialism; but Socialism —'the industrial evolution of humanity'—could not be 'definitely arrested by the mutual slaughter of human beings'.[2] He made a similar point in a letter to *The Times*: the German workers could not stop the war, but 'they hate it and I venture to predict that they will give abundant evidence of the truth, both during and after this abominable campaign'.[3] Early in 1915 he refused to join a newly-founded 'Anti-German League', saying: 'I should advocate a thorough entente with the German Republic to-morrow. Nations cannot afford to indulge in permanent hatred.'[4] Thus Hyndman showed that he was not a mere Germanophobe, and if he later appeared in that light, it was only through years of anxiety about the outcome of the war and concern about the suffering that it entailed.

Meanwhile, Hyndman was encouraged by the thought that wartime conditions might facilitate the establishment of a Socialist society, as the needs of war brought about

[1] A. Harrison, 'The Materialist Conception of History', *English Review*, xviii (Nov. 1914), 443–55; Hyndman and Bax, 'Socialism, Materialism, and the War', *English Review*, xix (Dec. 1914), 52–69, reprinted in Hyndman, *Future of Democracy* (1915), pp. 17–48.
[2] Hyndman, 'The Coming Triumph of Marxist Socialism', *English Review*, xix (Feb. 1915), 290–304, reprinted in Hyndman, *Future of Democracy*, pp. 178–201.
[3] *The Times*, 18 Aug. 1914.
[4] Hyndman to Makgill, 1 May 1915, *Justice*, 6 May 1915.

some degree of state intervention in industry. 'I wonder how many years have passed', he wrote in *Justice* in October 1914:

since I ventured to say that we should never make a great stride towards Socialism in Great Britain until we had a shock from without. . . . The shock from without has come upon us suddenly in the shape of the greatest war ever waged on this planet. . . . And then what a change! . . . The old individualist, happy-go-lucky, laissez-faire, devil-take-the-hindmost conception of remedies for the position created by the war was swept aside with contempt.[1]

Moreover, the work of the War Emergency Workers' National Committee, on which almost all shades of labour and Socialist opinion—both pro-war and anti-war—were represented, seemed to encourage the prospect of social change. This body, which had originally been planned as a National Labour Peace Emergency Committee, had come into existence at a special conference held less than twenty-four hours after Britain's entry into the war, and Hyndman, as the B.S.P. representative, devoted all his energy and enthusiasm to its work, which was aimed at protecting the workers' interests in wartime.

The Committee met at least once—sometimes three times —each week, and Hyndman attended most of the meetings during its existence. It published a manifesto entitled 'The Workers and the War' calling for Government control of war relief, urging the need for strong labour representation on all national and local committees established in con-nexion with the war, and demanding adequate allowances for soldiers' dependants. Hyndman conducted a general investigation into War Office and Admiralty contracts, proposed, in conjunction with Sidney Webb, that the Government should control the shipping used for the trans-port of wheat across the Atlantic, worked on a Food Price Sub-Committee together with Ramsay MacDonald and

[1] *Justice*, 22 Oct. 1914.

Sidney Webb, and joined in a nation-wide campaign to demand the control of food prices.[1]

Probably inspired by Hyndman, the War Emergency Committee decided to consider the problem of the 'Confiscation of Riches', but the memorandum finally adopted by a sub-committee consisting among others of Hyndman, Sidney Webb, and Ramsay MacDonald, recommended only the raising of money for the war by taxation rather than by loans, and the sequestration of all unearned incomes.[2] Indeed, Hyndman's Socialism had long been losing its revolutionary edge, and as he became absorbed in the problems of the war, it seemed to merge into Fabian gradualism, although he still asserted the authority of Marx and even continued to use revolutionary phrases. In fact, he and Sidney Webb worked together very well on the Workers' National Committee through an 'unholy little compact'. 'When anything important comes up', said Hyndman to his wife, 'I bring out a root-and-ground revolutionary proposal, and set it well before them. That puts them in a fright; and then Webb comes in with his proposal, only a few degrees milder than mine; and they are so relieved that they pass Webb's motion unanimously.'[3]

Deeply involved as he was in the work of the Committee, Hyndman still had time for propaganda on behalf of the Allied cause. When the American Socialists suggested mediation by the U.S. Government, he replied in an open letter to the effect that 'our French and Belgian and British anti-Prussian Socialists are absolutely in the right, and if I were not seventy-two years old I would go out and fight myself'.[4] He also wrote an article for the *New Review* of New York in which he spoke of the Allies fighting 'a people's war'.[5] For Hyndman, the Allies were fighting a war of liberation,

[1] War Emergency Workers' National Committee, *Executive Report*, 9 Nov. 1914, 21 Jan., 18 Feb. 1915.
[2] Ibid., 4 Oct. 1917.   [3] R. T. Hyndman, op. cit., p. 87.
[4] *New York Times*, 21 Oct. 1914, quoted in Walling, op. cit., pp. 324–5.
[5] *New Review*, Feb. 1915, quoted in Walling, op. cit., pp. 325–6.

a war for the workers, and even a war for Socialism. But it was precisely on this question that he had to face an increasingly strong challenge from inside his own party.

2

In September 1914 the B.S.P. executive, which still predominantly consisted of Hyndman's supporters, issued a carefully worded manifesto in favour of Socialist participation in the recruiting campaign. There were, however, widespread protests from the rank and file, especially from the branches in London and Scotland where the internationalists had a large following. The leader of the Scottish internationalists was John Maclean, a Glasgow schoolmaster. Maclean had, it was true, advocated the policy of the 'citizen army', but he had done this not for any purpose of national defence but solely for the sake of facilitating an armed revolution. He now engaged in anti-war agitation on Clydeside, in which he was assisted by Willie Gallacher. At the time of an engineers' strike in February 1915, Gallacher played a leading part in setting up a 'Labour Withholding Committee', out of which later emerged a semi-permanent revolutionary organization known as the Clyde Workers' Committee. The growing unrest in the Glasgow area was to bring Maclean's anti-war propaganda to national prominence.

In London the opposition had begun to encroach upon the party leadership. Albert Inkpin, a young man who had succeeded Lee as general secretary in 1913, was inclined to sympathize with the internationalists. Furthermore, both London executive seats fell into the hands of the internationalists, although this was only because one of the existing executive members, who supported the war, volunteered for military service. J. Fineberg, a Russian Jew, was elected with an overwhelming majority to fill the vacancy, and he joined E. C. Fairchild, the other member, in

supporting the internationalist faction. This led to angry
protests from Hyndman's followers who deplored 'the
pro-German attitude of several Russo-Jewish refugees';
and Victor Fisher, who had been defeated in the executive
by-election, went so far as to repudiate the Socialist movement altogether as being dominated by the internationalist,
and therefore unpatriotic, outlook of exiles.[1]

The rivalry between the two factions was further exacer-
bated as the 1915 party conference drew near. Instead of a
national conference, which had to be abandoned on account
of wartime difficulties, the party held divisional conferences
in February in five main cities—Glasgow, London, Bristol,
Leeds, and Manchester—and the aggregate result of the
voting that took place at each conference was later announced
in *Justice*.[2] On the crucial issue of policy towards the war,
the party as a whole rejected both nationalist and internationalist resolutions and approved a compromise which
called for a speedy termination of the war but expressed
confidence in the editor of *Justice* (now Lee, the former
secretary, who was one of Hyndman's followers). On the
whole, however, the internationalists fared better than their
opponents: a Central Hackney resolution against Socialist
participation in a recruiting campaign was carried, though
by the small majority of 59 votes to 56. An amendment from
the Central Branch in favour of a fight 'to the point when
the Central European autocracies will have been destroyed'
was defeated by 81 votes to 46, and a resolution urging the
International Socialist Bureau to prepare a peace proposal
was carried by 114 votes to 24. A resolution to make the
policies adopted at the conferences binding upon all party
speakers was lost, the vote being a tie, and thus the party
narrowly managed to avoid an open split. Yet the internationalists secured a slight—five to four—majority on the
new executive, and it became clear that Hyndman and his
followers would be in a difficult position in the future. They

[1] *Justice*, 22 Oct. 1914, 14 Jan. 1915.   [2] Ibid., 4 March 1915.

had no intention of meekly accepting a minority status, however: they consolidated themselves effectively in the B.S.P. Central Branch and through their control of *Justice* continued to put forward their views to the membership as a whole.

3

The Socialist International now had little reality, for the majority of Socialists of most of the belligerent countries supported the war. 'To bring about international action after the war', wrote Hyndman at the time, 'we must discard all theoretical international jargon during the war.' He looked forward to rebuilding the International on the more realistic basis which he had always favoured: 'To be a useful Internationalist a man must be a Nationalist first.'[1]

European Socialists may be grouped roughly into three schools of thought according to their attitude towards the war and Socialism. One was constituted by those who saw in the defence of their fatherland nothing incompatible with their Socialist convictions. On both sides of the fighting lines they showed great reluctance to come into contact with any 'enemy' Socialists. Quite distinct from them were those who, as Lenin put it, recognized only 'the necessity of a revolutionary war of the proletarians of all countries against the bourgeois of all countries'.[2] They were completely opposed both to reformism and to any concessions to the principle of nationality. Between these two schools there was another group of Socialists who opposed participation in the war, but who equally could not accept 'revolutionary war' as desirable. Among the British Socialists, Hyndman of course belonged to the first school, the B.S.P. internationalists on the whole inclined to the second, and the I.L.P. to the third.

In February 1915 a conference of Allied Socialists was held

[1] Hyndman, *The Future of Democracy*, p. 64.   [2] Lenin, *Works*, xviii, p. 62.

in London under the sponsorship of the I.L.P. The B.S.P.
was represented by three pro-war delegates, Irving, Fisher,
and Hunter Watts, and the conference ended with an
awkward compromise between the pro-war element and the
anti-war moderates, as was shown by the passing of a
resolution which endorsed the war against German Imperialism while blaming 'every government' for its share of
imperialist policies.[1] The Socialist outlook for the First of
May 1915 was, as Hyndman said, 'gloomy indeed':

> Internationalism has gone by the board. . . . What is the use of
> reciting the old sentimental patter of brotherhood and comrade-
> ship under such circumstances as these? . . . The Germans had
> virtual control of International Congresses from 1900 to 1914
> because the majority of Socialists trusted their superior ability,
> organization, and discipline. This leadership is now finally at an
> end: destroyed by the Germans themselves.[2]

Meanwhile, the I.L.P. was carrying on a vigorous peace
agitation in the face of a bitterly hostile public opinion. It
was greatly assisted in this campaign by the newly-formed
Union of Democratic Control, an anti-war body composed
of leading Radical intellectuals. Hyndman had been
waiting impatiently for an opportunity to attack the close
co-operation between these two anti-war organizations.
Early in 1915 the I.L.P. published a pamphlet entitled
How the War Came as the first number of its 'Labour and
War' series in order to provide 'some knowledge of reality
to supplement absurdity about Germany and silence about
Russia', and it was clear that the pamphlet was inspired by
the Union of Democratic Control and especially by its
secretary, E. D. Morel. Hyndman at once sent a copy of
this pamphlet to his friend Georges Clemenceau, the leading
French Radical politician and editor, who was taking a
strongly 'patriotic' line. Clemenceau published in his paper,

---

[1] *Labour Leader*, 18 Feb. 1915; *Justice*, 18 Feb. 1915; Lee and Archbold,
op. cit., pp. 232–3.
[2] *Justice*, 29 April 1915.

L'Homme Enchaîné, two letters from Hyndman dated respectively 1st and 6th March. In the second letter which was also published in *L'Humanité* Hyndman wrote: 'This pamphlet is full of revolting lies. . . . We are curious to know where the money comes from for all its publications in favour of the Germans against the Allies.'[1]

The letter and its obvious insinuation caused a stir in the Socialist world. Emile Vandervelde, the pro-war chairman of the International Socialist Bureau, supported Hyndman's 'ill humour' which, he said, could be explained by 'the attitude of certain elements in the English working class. . . . Some of them go on strike; others refuse to work overtime.'[2] The B.S.P. executive, however, dissociated itself from Hyndman's views and a number of branches also protested strongly against them. Hyndman excused himself by stating that what he had really meant was that the I.L.P. was receiving money from the Union of Democratic Control though not necessarily from the Wilhelmstrasse, but this did not sound convincing to his critics. E. D. Morel was then writing a series of articles in the I.L.P.'s *Labour Leader* entitled 'The Charge of being "Pro-German" ', and it was indeed the commonest charge against the Union of Democratic Control that the body was in the pay of Germany.[3]

The initiative for a genuinely non-partisan Socialist conference could hardly come from the International Socialist Bureau itself, as so many of its leading members had taken a 'pro-war' line. It was consequently the Italian Socialist Party, the one major party to oppose the war, together with the Swiss and *émigré* Russian parties, which took the initiative. The international conference that they summoned finally met at Zimmerwald, a village in Switzerland, early in September 1915. Fairchild was delegated to attend the conference for the B.S.P., and there were to be two I.L.P.

---

[1] *L'Humanité*, 18 March 1915.   [2] Ibid., 28 March 1915.
[3] *Justice*, 1, 29 April 1915; *Labour Leader*, 25 March–22 July 1915; H. M. Swanwick, *Builders of Peace* (1924), pp. 91–92.

delegates, Glasier and Fred Jowett, but all were denied
passports. In the wider field of European Socialism, however,
Zimmerwald marked a new epoch which culminated in the
formation of the Third International. At the conference,
itself a result of co-operation between the centre and the
revolutionary elements, an ideological struggle was waged
between the two main participating groups. A compromise
which rather favoured the revolutionaries was reached in a
manifesto which declared for a peace without annexations
but which also urged the workers to 'stand up . . . for the
emancipation of the oppressed nations as well as of the en-
slaved classes, by means of the irreconcilable proletarian
class struggle'.[1] The B.S.P. executive decided by 5 votes to 3
to accept the manifesto, but even the internationalists did
not fully accept the Zimmerwald resolutions; Mrs. Zelda
Kahan Coates who had led the opposition to Hyndman
before the war criticized the Zimmerwald Left for having
declined into what she called an 'international impossibilist'
position by failing to consider the question of how to stop
wars under the existing capitalist system.[2]

All the same, the B.S.P. certainly had its 'international
impossibilists' who greeted the Zimmerwald decisions with
enthusiasm. One of the most prominent was John Maclean,
who now revived the *Vanguard*, an organ of the Scottish
section of the B.S.P., as the monthly journal of the party's
Glasgow District Council. In the first issue, which sold
3,000 copies, Maclean launched a fierce attack on the
Hyndmanites.[3] His energetic anti-war propaganda soon
led to his arrest, and the District Council then invited Peter
Petrov, a Russian refugee and a member of the Kentish
Town B.S.P., to come to Clydeside to help in the work.
Petrov, who was connected with the 'Groups Abroad' of the
Russian Social Democratic Labour Party, addressed a

[1] Lenin, *Works*, xviii, pp. 274–6.   [2] *Call*, 22 June 1916.
[3] *Vanguard*, Sept. 1915, quoted in T. Bell, *Maclean* (Glasgow, 1944), pp.
40–42.

number of meetings—some organized by the Clyde Workers'
Committee—to spread the gospel of Zimmerwald. Maclean
was soon out of prison, but both leaders were closely watched
by the police. In February 1916 Maclean was arrested for
the second time, and was tried and sentenced to three years'
penal servitude.[1] Willie Gallacher, who was the chairman
of the Clyde Workers' Committee, was also sent to prison
as the result of his own agitation on the platform and in the
Committee's organ, the *Worker*.

With the Glasgow B.S.P. thus deprived of its leaders, the
focus of the struggle of the internationalists against the
Hyndmanites shifted to London, where Fairchild acted as
their spokesman. In February 1916 he founded a penny
weekly, the *Call*, as an unofficial organ of the B.S.P. He
demanded in its first issue that the International Socialist
Bureau should endeavour to reconcile the workers now in
conflict.[2] Fairchild and H. Alexander, then the B.S.P.
representatives on the British section of the Bureau, closely
co-operated with the I.L.P., whose influence had been
predominant in the British section. They, unlike the Glasgow
men who seemed to have committed themselves to the
Zimmerwald position, were increasingly drawn to share
the views of the Socialist Centre. Yet the difference among
the B.S.P. internationalists remained concealed for the time
being in their joint effort to get rid of Hyndman.

4

Hyndman was, meanwhile, serving the cause of the Allies
with enthusiasm. He wrote a vigorous leader in *Justice*,
'The Immolation of Serbia', when the German-Austrian
army pushed through that country, and another, 'Vive la
France', when the Germans continued a fierce attack on
Verdun. At home, he welcomed the formation of the
Coalition Government in May 1915, and approved of

[1] *Justice*, 23 Dec. 1915–13 April 1916, *passim*.   [2] *Call*, 24 Feb. 1916.

Labour's entry into the ministry, hoping that it would fight on to the bitter end. He was the advocate of a more energetic foreign economic policy, and deplored the Declaration of London which was designed to protect the interests of neutrals. He also accused Bonar Law of being involved in a wartime business transaction to send iron ore to Krupps; stung by the accusation, the future Prime Minister, who was innocent of the charge, felt obliged to make a personal statement in the House of Commons exonerating himself.[1] Hyndman then demanded a stricter naval blockade against Germany; and finding the Foreign Office reluctant to risk conflict with the United States, the most important neutral, he wrote again and again on 'the unheard-of pro-German policy of our Foreign Office against our Navy'.[2] He resented 'America's moral reprobation and material hostility', and went so far as to declare that 'in conjunction with the Allies Japan could … carry out a campaign against the Philippines, Hawaii, and the Pacific slope of the United States'.[3]

Yet amidst his campaign for a more vigorous prosecution of the war, Hyndman's thoughts often returned to the special problems of the working class. 'What share have these fighters, and their fellows . . . in the country which is called, by courtesy, theirs?' he asked, for 'they are merely food for powder abroad: food for plunder at home'.[4] He also took a keen interest in the extension of public control of industry. Government control of the railways, introduced soon after the outbreak of the war, gave him an opportunity to point out the shortcomings of the transport system: he advocated complete nationalization and technical improvement of the existing railways and wrote in favour of a proposal to set up a central clearing station for all goods wagons handled by different lines operating in London.[5] In his opinion the

[1] R. Blake, *The Unknown Prime Minister* (1955), pp. 258–9; *Justice*, 6 May 1915.
[2] *Justice*, 11 Nov. 1915.   [3] Ibid., 14 Oct. 1915.   [4] Ibid., 16 Dec. 1915.
[5] 'National Railways after the War', *Nineteenth Century and After*, lxxix (Feb. 1916), 461-77; 'The Railway Problem Solved', ibid., lxxx (Nov. 1916), 1023-39.

wartime control of railways and shipping was only a first
step, creating as it did 'a supreme bureaucracy of Class-
State-Socialism'. The object of the future, he declared at a
meeting organized by the Sheffield B.S.P., was to transform
this State Socialism into Social Democracy for the people.[1]

Although Hyndman supported the recruiting campaigns,
he was opposed to conscription for 'our upper-class-officered
Army'.[2] At a meeting organized by the Bristol B.S.P. during
the Trades Union Congress at Bristol in September 1915, he
declared that 'if an attempt were made to force conscription
upon the workers of this country, who are doing 96 per cent.
of the fighting, all the producing, and the greater part of the
paying, there will be civil war'.[3] Meanwhile, however, the
parliamentary Labour Party which had always opposed
conscription was gradually being persuaded to accept the
need for such a measure. In May 1916 Hyndman wrote to
Clemenceau:

Now many of the same Labour leaders who sneered at us are
voting for conscription without any safeguards whatever for
their class. We oppose the blind militarist infatuation of these
men today as we denounced their blind pacifism yesterday.[4]

Thus, although he was definitely a 'pro-war' Socialist,
Hyndman did not allow his support of the war to make him
forget his Socialist standpoint on domestic questions. He was
never officially associated with the extreme 'patriotic'
element led by Victor Fisher, who founded a Socialist
National Defence Committee in April 1915. This body
included among its members the Clarion leaders Blatchford
and A. M. Thompson, 'patriotic' executive members of the
B.S.P. such as Irving and Bert Killip, Labour M.P.s such as
John Hodge and G. H. Roberts, and independent Socialists

[1] 'Cromwellism without Cromwell', *English Review*, xx (May 1915), 204–14;
Justice, 22 April 1915.
[2] 'The Armed Nation', *Fortnightly Review*, n.s. xcviii (Sept. 1915), 531.
[3] *Justice*, 23 Sept. 1915.
[4] Quoted in R. T. Hyndman, *Last Years*, p. 112.

such as H. G. Wells and Stewart Headlam. Its aim was 'to
assert the claims of "Britain for the British" ', a reminder of
Blatchford's well-known pamphlet of 1902, and to expose the
'error' of the anti-war 'pseudo-Socialists' who were 'aliens
by birth, blood, or sentiment'.[1] As time went on, this body
abandoned all real effort to present a distinctively Socialist
point of view; and most of the B.S.P. members who participated in its activities soon broke away. It presently changed
its name to 'British Workers' National League' and then to
'National Democratic Party', by which time it was avowedly
critical of Socialism.[2]

5

Although Hyndman and the pro-war B.S.P. members
can thus be distinguished from the extreme 'patriots', they
differed even more widely from the revolutionary element
and even from the Centre. Compromise with the anti-war
leaders of their own party became more and more difficult,
especially as the anti-war groups grew in relative strength.
In March 1916 forty-eight pro-war members issued a circular
calling for the reorganization of the executive on a national
basis, for it had been dominated by anti-war members
elected on the local basis. Challenged by Hyndman and
his followers, the anti-war candidates for the new executive
now declared their hostility to 'a spurious "national"
Socialism, symbol of a fictitious class unity'.[3] For the past
two years the B.S.P. had managed to avoid a split on this
issue solely because there was no occasion for the two
sections to meet each other. But the split now appeared
inevitable as the first national conference of wartime drew
nigh.

This conference, the B.S.P.'s fifth, was held in Salford on
23rd April 1916—ironically enough, St. George's Day. It

---

[1] *Clarion*, 14, 28 May 1915.
[2] For its activities, see *Clarion* and *British Citizen and Empire Worker*.
[3] *Justice*, 2 March 1916; *Call*, 23 March 1916.

was attended by 106 delegates representing ninety-one branches. At the opening of the conference, Albert Inkpin, the party secretary, announced that the executive had recommended that the proceedings should be held 'in camera' in order to secure free discussion. Dan Irving and Jack Jones opposed the proposal, and Hyndman demanded to speak; but the delegates booed him down, then refused him a hearing by 56 votes to 39, and finally adopted the executive recommendation by 76 votes to 28. Thereupon twenty-two pro-war delegates representing eighteen branches left the conference in a body in accordance with a pre-arranged plan. The battle was brief but decisive; the triumphant internationalist delegates swiftly carried through the remainder of the proceedings, passing several anti-war resolutions with an overwhelming majority; and 'an immediate peace' and 'the international working-class struggle against the whole capitalist régime' now became the official policy of the B.S.P.[1]

The twenty-two Hyndmanites, with the addition of two more who left the conference later, met afterwards at the Deansgate Hotel, Manchester, and decided to form a National Socialist Advisory Committee with headquarters in the premises of the Twentieth Century Press at Clerkenwell Green. The press, which owned *Justice* as its property, now declared that the paper was no longer the organ of the B.S.P. The Committee rejected an offer of fusion with Victor Fisher's organization, and in June changed its name to 'National Socialist Party', which was readily abbreviated to N.S.P. Joseph Burgess, the old I.L.P. rebel, who had originally suggested the new party name, became the party's organizer and largely as a result of his work the number of its branches reached forty-three by the end of the year.[2]

As we have seen, a party crisis was no new thing to Hyndman, but this was the first time that he had been forced

[1] *Call*, 4 May 1916; B.S.P., *Conference Report*, 1916, p. 3.
[2] *Justice*, 27 April–7 Dec. 1916, *passim*.

to withdraw from an organization with which he had been intimately associated. Yet his new party, the N.S.P., effectively maintained continuity with the old S.D.F., for practically all the 'Old Guard' who were still active in the movement, such as Bax, Headingley, Hunter Watts, Thorne, and Irving, followed his lead throughout the crisis. Moreover, the N.S.P. was a very small body, probably as small as the S.D.F. in the eighties, and its existence seemed dependent upon Hyndman's personal leadership. It was said at the time of the split, however, that the Hyndmanites were in an 'accidental' minority in the B.S.P. 'due to the fact that our own supporters are engaged at the front, and occupied in military training, or are scattered through the country working overtime in munition works'.[1] Hyndman hoped that his party would 'shortly' be transformed into the old S.D.F. at its best 'with the help of very heavy numbers from the front'.[2]

The separation of the N.S.P. from the B.S.P. was inevitable, given the policy differences involved. The surprising thing is that it took so long. At any rate, the two main groups of British Marxists were now in a position to pursue their separate goals independently of one another. While the younger element of Hyndman's following served in the forces, many of the B.S.P. suffered imprisonment as objectors to military service—in the Huddersfield branch, for instance, of its active members there were at one time no less than twenty-five in prison.[3] In January 1917 the B.S.P. summoned up enough support to fight a by-election at Rossendale on a programme of 'Peace by Negotiation', and obtained 1,804 votes.[4] All this was anathema to the Hyndmanites; and in the course of 1917 the Russian Revolution raised fresh issues to reveal the continuing deep divergence of viewpoint between the two Marxist groups.

[1] *Justice*, 27 April 1916.
[2] Hyndman to Seton-Watson, 20 Oct. 1917, Seton-Watson Papers.
[3] B.S.P., *Conference Report*, 1917, p. 17.   [4] *Call*, 18, 25 Jan. 1917.

6

The first Russian Revolution of March 1917 was greeted with universal enthusiasm by all the British Socialists, who had regarded Czarist Russia as the worst enemy of democracy. There were, however, differences of attitude already at this stage. The B.S.P. regarded the overthrow of the old régime as the first stage of the revolutionary struggle to be fought against capitalism inside Russia.[1] Hyndman, on the other hand, saw it as an attempt to revitalize Russia's war effort, which had been weakened by the intrigue of the old Imperial court. In an article published in the *Evening News* he pointed out that the ascendancy of Kerensky, a Social Revolutionary, and Miliukov, a Liberal —both of whom he called 'Social-Democrats'—would bring Russia closer to Western Europe.[2] He sent a cablegram to Kerensky through British official channels urging the leader of the Provisional Government to strengthen 'the Russian democracy in arms'.[3]

In March when Plekhanov passed through London on his way to Petrograd he asked Hyndman to visit Russia. Hyndman wrote to C. E. Russell, an American pro-war Socialist:

There is a general feeling that, under all circumstances, I ought to go to Petrograd and Moscow. In fact, some of the papers are pressing me to do so, and the War Cabinet would be glad for me to go. But I am not at all convinced that British influence in Russia would gain by further efforts. It would look too eager, too anxious to lead, or even to dictate, and the Slav is very touchy. . . . Moreover, we may have a revolution here, as I have said, before we expect it, and then I ought to be present.[4]

The N.S.P. executive, however, decided to recommend against the trip, apparently on the realistic grounds that a

[1] *Justice*, 29 March 1917.   [2] *Evening News*, 16 March 1917.
[3] 30 April 1917: copy in Russell Papers.
[4] Hyndman to Russell, 13 May 1917, Russell Papers.

man of seventy-five should not risk his life and health in a rough sea voyage on board a destroyer.

Hyndman's remark about the possibility of a revolution in Britain was not entirely unreasonable. War-weariness among all the European belligerents had combined with the influence of the March Revolution in Russia to bring about a quick growth of hostility towards existing governments. In Britain, a special conference of sympathizers with the Russian Revolution was called by the United Socialist Council, of which the I.L.P. and the B.S.P. were the main components. The conference was held at Leeds in June 1917, and was attended by well over a thousand delegates. It adopted a resolution urging the establishment in Britain of 'Councils of Workers' and Soldiers' Delegates' for 'the complete political and economic emancipation of international Labour'. The excitement at the conference was such that every speaker spoke with revolutionary fervour; and a few genuinely extreme delegates from the Clydeside, including Gallacher, regretted that the opportunity was not taken to recommend precise ways and means of enabling the working class to seize power through industrial action. In fact 'the rush and the wonder of Leeds', as Mrs. Charlotte Despard, the former suffragette leader, called it, soon passed away: and when the Provisional Committee which was set up at the conference first met in London, in October, the Workers' and Soldiers' Councils movement had become one of many propagandists organizations whose influence could easily be ignored by the Government.[1]

Meanwhile, Arthur Henderson had paid a visit to St. Petersburg, now known as Petrograd, and had become convinced that steps must be taken to secure, or at least try to secure, a negotiated peace. He expressed his support for a proposed conference of Allied, neutral, and enemy Socialists

[1] For the Leeds conference, see *Call*, 7 June 1917; *Labour Leader*, 7 June, 1917; *Herald*, 9 June 1917. See also *Call*, 5 July–25 Oct. 1917; *The Times*, 30 July, 10, 16, 22 Aug. 1917; Mrs. Despard to Lansbury, 7 June 1917, Lansbury Collection.

at Stockholm; and he carried the Labour Party with him on this question. Hyndman could not accept this, and he was soon at work, as he said, 'endeavouring to influence him against the Stockholm Conference, which he is so foolishly and so dangerously backing'.[1] Hyndman failed to persuade Henderson, but the Government refused passports to Stockholm. Hyndman claimed some credit for this 'success': 'We have killed the Stockholm Conference', he wrote, 'and I rejoice to think I have done my full share of the slaying.'[2] As for Henderson, the result was his resignation from the Government after the celebrated 'door-mat' incident, and then his development of an alternative foreign policy, which was to be of great importance in 1918.

7

For most of 1917, however, the fate of Russia's war effort still remained in the balance. Hyndman, who had been puzzled by the nature of the March Revolution, not knowing whether it was merely political or whether it was also economic in character, was now arguing that since the real Russia was rural, the initiative for the reorganization of the country should be taken by the emancipated peasants assisted by the Socialists in the towns.[3] As we have seen in connexion with the 1905 revolution, he had greater sympathy for the Social Revolutionaries, mostly agrarian, than for the Russian Social-Democrats. It was, therefore, natural that he should take a hostile view of the Bolsheviks, who were also the most determined advocates of an immediate peace. In September, when a counter-revolution threatened the Provisional Government, *Justice* refused to condemn General Kornilov, its leader, and blamed left-wing extremism for the situation. In November, shortly after the Bolshevik *coup*

---

[1] Hyndman to R. W. Seton-Watson, 4 Aug. 1917, Seton-Watson Papers.
[2] Hyndman to Simons, n.d., Simons Papers.
[3] *Justice*, 22 March, 24 May, 2 Aug. 1917.

d'état, the journal expressed regret that Kerensky had failed to co-operate with Kornilov in his struggle against the Bolsheviks.[1]

According to Bernard Shaw, Hyndman's attitude to the Bolsheviks was one to 'out-Churchill Churchill'.[2] Although this was a typical Shavian exaggeration, there was as usual a kernel of truth. Hyndman's *Evolution of Revolution*, published in 1920, 'a survey of the development and martyrdom of man' as he himself called it,[3] is full of invective against the Soviet leaders. He condemned Lenin for having played the part of 'a Communist Ivan the Terrible in the new pseudo-Marxist Tsardom'. He described the new régime as anarchist and 'impossibilist' and said that its administration was 'autocratic, cruel, and butcherly to the last degree'. On orthodox Marxist lines he agreed that its policy could not work, for Russia, being economically backward, had yet to pass through the stage of highly developed capitalism which alone would render capitalists superfluous and the socialization of the means of production inevitable.[4] This argument, though certainly thoroughly Marxist, was hardly consistent with some of his other utterances, for he had already largely disavowed the materialist interpretation of history, and had maintained in the case of Finland at least that Socialism could be achieved in an industrially backward country.[5] In reality it was opportunism rather than theory that led Hyndman to attack the Bolshevik leaders, and the cause of his opportunism was his commitment to the Allied war effort. For him, Britain was by far the most important country in the world, and as Shaw pointed out, Hyndman had 'set his heart on England being the Holy Land of the Communist faith: John Bull again'.[6]

The B.S.P. leaders, on the other hand, welcomed the Bolshevik Revolution as a display of 'a courageous loyalty

[1] *Justice*, 13 Sept., 29 Nov. 1917.   [2] R. T. Hyndman, *Last Years*, p. 293.
[3] Hyndman to Russell, 19 Dec. 1919, Russell Papers.
[4] Hyndman, *Evolution of Revolution* (1920), pp. 382-6.
[5] *Justice*, 12 April 1917.   [6] R. T. Hyndman, op. cit., p. 296.

to the principles of International Socialism'. They were in close contact with Maxim Litvinov, the Soviet representative in Britain, who now in the face of Allied intervention appealed to the British workers to do what they could to save the Revolution. 'Russia's Appeal—Will British workers remain silent?' read a B.S.P. manifesto, copies of which would have been distributed among the delegates of the Labour Party conference in January 1918 if they had not been confiscated by the police.[1] Litvinov himself, however, was allowed to speak at the conference, although he met with only limited support for his views.[2] Among the Socialist bodies affiliated to the Labour Party it was only the B.S.P. that expressed general approval of the new revolutionary government in Russia. In February 1918 Litvinov actually appointed John Maclean as Russian Consul in Glasgow—a move which showed already whom the Bolsheviks regarded as their friends in Britain. The arrangement did not, however, prove very satisfactory, for two months later Maclean was arrested for causing disaffection, and was sentenced to five years' penal servitude. But Litvinov also for that matter was soon arrested and sent back to Russia.

Hyndman wrote an article in the *Sunday Pictorial* criticizing the Labour Party for giving a hearing at its conference to Litvinov, 'the representative of these Petrograd butchers'.[3] Hyndman had been in close touch with J. O. Gavronsky, the representative of the Russian Constituent Assembly in England and a Social Revolutionary. In December 1917 he had written to the War Cabinet to advocate a policy of intervention, proposed originally by Gavronsky, by which the British Government was to equip and transport about 30,000 Russian troops then stationed in Western Europe in order to fight against the Bolsheviks and to strengthen the Eastern Front and thereby 'help Russian democrats to help

[1] *Call*, 15 Nov. 1917–24 Jan. 1918.
[2] Labour Party, *Conference Report*, Jan. 1918, p. 92, June 1918, p. 59.
[3] *Sunday Pictorial*, 27 Jan. 1918.

themselves'. He received a reply from the Foreign Office later in January 1918, upholding the principle of non-intervention in Russian internal affairs;[1] but soon after-wards, when the Bolshevik Government concluded peace with Germany at Brest-Litovsk, the British Government revised its policy. Allied intervention began in April, and a few months later Hyndman was writing in *Justice* that the Allies should support only those elements in Russia which were hostile both to the Bolsheviks and to Czarism.[2] 'Keren-sky has not played his cards at all well', he wrote to Russell. 'I have vainly tried to get him to make a vigorous public appeal against the Monarchist intrigues here and in Paris and the support being given to Monarchists in Russia.'[3]

It was, however, only after the armistice that Hyndman in any way regretted that British troops had been sent to Russia. 'It is a very bad business indeed', he then said. 'What makes the matter worse is that an ugly but, sad to say, a justifiable rumour connects this whole British manœuvre with the demands of international finance.'[4] His attitude towards intervention, though not free from the charge of opportunism, was not untypical of British labour, for apart from the B.S.P. and the I.L.P. which had condemned the intervention from the beginning, the British labour move-ment largely held aloof from criticism until after the armis-tice, which of course removed the military justification of the Allies' action. The post-war 'Hands Off Russia' move-ment soon became a powerful force in the country, taking full advantage of the industrial unrest at the time, but it was only after two years of strenuous agitation that the Govern-ment finally complied with its demand.

The Bolshevik revolution was soon to divide the Socialist world into two hostile camps—and the division was to be as complete as that between 'Allied' and 'Central Power'

---

[1] *Justice*, 9 Jan. 1919.   [2] Ibid., 12 Sept. 1918.
[3] Hyndman to Russell, 21 Oct. 1918, Russell Papers.
[4] *Justice*, 29 May 1919.

Socialists during the war. Soviet Russia, suffering as she was from civil war and the Allied intervention, appealed desperately to the forces of revolution in the belligerent countries. Moscow became the focus of the loyalties of the left-wing Socialists, and was soon to set up an International of its own. As we shall see, however, the B.S.P., the strongest among the British bodies that had supported the Russian revolution, was by no means unanimous in accepting the Bolshevik leadership, and an internal struggle had already begun. Meanwhile, the movement for the Stockholm conference had, in spite of its failure, strengthened the centre group Socialists of the Allied countries, and they pressed hard for negotiations with their counterparts in the enemy countries. Hyndman, however, who remained an advocate of Allied victory, not only deplored the growing importance of the Bolsheviks in the international movement, but also expressed determination to do all he could to prevent any attempts at peace by negotiation.

XII ∿ LAST YEARS

I

In 1917 Hyndman attained the age of seventy-five. The war was at too serious a stage for him to spend much time in celebration; he still remained astonishingly vigorous, and he devoted a high proportion of his energy to politics, as he had done with hardly a break for thirty-seven years. In 1917 he and his wife moved to 13 Well Walk, Hampstead, where the air was better and where he could do a little gardening as a recreation. The N.S.P. executive could not conveniently meet there, as it had met at Queen Anne's Gate; but that was the only important change of routine that was involved. Somewhat straitened circumstances, however, necessitated the letting of some of the rooms of the new house to con-genial lodgers.[1]

Some of Hyndman's political activities at this time bor-dered on the hysterical, although these years of bitter warfare and the harsh censorship of news gave rise to all sorts of absurdities. He joined in the *Morning Post*'s campaign to root out enemy spies on the British home front, and himself volunteered to investigate the activities of 'German spy waiters' in London. Fortunately for his reputation, the police declined his co-operation in its security work.[2] He bitterly denounced the 'treachery' of government officials and de-manded a thorough overhaul of the Foreign Office. He got hold of a list of Foreign Office employees: 'What was my

---

[1] R. T. Hyndman, *Last Years*, pp. 146, 278.
[2] Hyndman to Simons, 12 Aug. 1917, Simons Papers.

amazement and horror to find among them the name of Th. Rothstein, a Russian-German Jew, who had been working here for years in and out of the Socialist movement . . . for and on behalf of Germany.' He took the necessary steps to get his old adversary discharged from his official post.[1]

Hyndman was also greatly annoyed by the strong current of pacifist opinion in French politics. He described Joseph Caillaux, the former French Prime Minister, who was a persistent advocate of peace with Germany, as 'a scoundrel in every way', and reviled Jean Longuet, the leader of the anti-war minority of the French Socialist Party, who was 'hand in glove with Caillaux'. 'I may say I have known Longuet (Marx's grandson) since he was a mere boy', he wrote in a letter to R. W. Seton-Watson, the expert on Slavonic affairs. 'Of late the Jewish blood in him has been manifesting itself chiefly in love for intrigue.'[2] Hyndman took a keen interest in the prosecution of Caillaux for espionage, which was initiated by Clemenceau when he was Prime Minister; and he wrote a chapter on 'the enemy within' in his biography of Clemenceau.[3]

Yet at the same time he continued happily in his work for the War Emergency Workers' National Committee, which met regularly in the House of Commons or at the offices of the T.U.C. Hyndman was always one of its most active delegates, demanding, for instance, a reduction in the price of bread, and giving publicity to this demand by writing a letter to *The Times*.[4] In November 1917 he sent a letter to Lord Rhondda attacking the 'hopeless imbecility' of his policy as Food Controller. Early in the following year, Lord Rhondda in conjunction with J. R. Clynes, the new Food Controller, set up a Food Consumers' Council as a consultative body. Hyndman represented the War Emergency

1 Hyndman to Russell, 13 May 1917, Russell Papers.
2 Hyndman to Seton-Watson, 9 May 1917, Seton-Watson Papers.
3 Hyndman, *Clemenceau* (1919), pp. 257ff.
4 War Emergency Workers' National Committee, *Executive Report*, 15 Feb., 29 March 1917; *The Times*, 7 Nov. 1916.

Workers' National Committee on the Consumers' Council, defended the workers' interests against 'parasites upon the community', and was often at loggerheads with Lady Selborne, one of three representatives of the unorganized consumers invited by Lord Rhondda.[1]

The Government at last began to intervene in the supply and pricing of food, but there was some confusion to begin with, and according to Hyndman, 'monstrous injustice has been done to the poor'. 'For example', he said in a letter to A. M. Simons, the American Socialist:

our own folk, at the Twentieth Century Press and elsewhere, could not get sugar at all. We at the same time . . . could obtain 28lb. or even 56 lb. a week for ourselves, my wife, myself and four servants. This we did to a considerable extent and passed the sugar on, at cost price of course, to our comrades.[2]

Hyndman wrote almost every week in *Justice* on his work for the Consumers' Council, on 'filthy English milk', on 'the bacon muddle', and on "the coming privation'. He gave close attention to the food problem, essential as it was to the war effort, and in a letter to *The Times* he urged the need to cultivate pasture and waste lands, and appealed to the sense of duty of landlords as 'trustees of the welfare of the people'.[3] In these and other ways he did his best to strengthen the Home Front and to pave the way for victory.

Meanwhile, the war dragged on with much suffering and little prospect of early success. The American declaration of war in April 1917 had brightened the long term perspective, but the French offensive in the spring soon collapsed, and British operations in Flanders made little headway, although expensive in lives. In the autumn, the Italians under General Cadorna were forced back with heavy loss; and Hyndman, being an 'Italianissimo' of long standing and now recollecting his own experiences of the *risorgimento*, wrote:

[1] *Justice*, 29 Nov. 1917, 7 March 1918; War Emergency Workers' National Committee, *Executive Report*, 9 Jan. 1918; R. T. Hyndman, op. cit., p. 171.
[2] Hyndman to Simons, n.d., Simons Papers.   [3] *The Times*, 3 Jan. 1918.

It was a heavy blow to me personally. I have always been with Italy and the Italians. I hoped they had become a nation. I appealed to them to join the Allies. I rejoiced in their great success last year. Now I hope against hope they may recover, but I doubt it.[1]

He had been hoping to visit Italy to appeal directly to the Italian workers. Indeed a suggestion to that effect had come through the British Embassy in Rome. But the Foreign Office for some reason—perhaps, as Mrs. Hyndman says, because of his 'subversive' career—did not favour the plan.[2]

Until at least the early summer of 1918, the outcome of the war remained in the balance. The Russian surrender at Brest-Litovsk was followed in the spring by a renewed German offensive on the Western Front. At this critical moment the N.S.P. executive sent a telegram to Sir Douglas Haig, Commander-in-Chief of the British Army in France, expressing its confidence in final victory. The German offensive gradually weakened and was followed by Allied counter-attacks of increasing force, until at last on 11 November came the long-awaited victory. The N.S.P. executive passed a resolution to the effect that Hyndman should act as a representative of Great Britain at the Peace Conference, but it was supported only by the Conservative *Morning Post*, with which Hyndman had been associated both before and during the war and which now paid a tribute to the veteran Socialist as 'a sound Patriot—an Englishman who does not allow his Socialism or his democratic passion to produce anti-nationalism'.[3]

2

Hyndman's patriotism had always played an important part in deciding his attitude towards international affairs. He had convinced himself that the dawn of Socialism was

<hr />

[1] Hyndman to Russell, 7 Nov. 1917, Russell Papers.
[2] R. T. Hyndman, op. cit., p. 150.
[3] *Justice*, 28 Nov. 1918; *Morning Post*, 28 Nov. 1918.

nearest in Britain, where capitalism was most highly developed. It was true that his optimism had been shaken seriously by the continued weakness of the S.D.F., but the European war, which seemed to have forced the nation to recognize the power of labour, led him once more to entertain the hope of Britain becoming the first Socialist country. In his view, if only Britain were to lead the world in Socialism, then the breakdown of the Second International, dominated as it was by the German Social-Democrats, would by no means be a misfortune. Hyndman feared the resurgence of the German party just as he dreaded the ascendancy of the Bolsheviks because of their potential influence on the international Socialist movement.

At the Inter-Allied Socialist and Labour conference held in London in August 1917 Hyndman moved a resolution to the effect that no Allied Socialist should meet with the German Socialists 'so long as the Germans occupy the territories they have seized and carry on their campaign of murder, outrage, and piracy'. This resolution was heavily defeated, but he managed to have a 'Pro-Ally Socialist Manifesto' signed by Henderson, Sidney Webb, Vandervelde, Albert Thomas of the majority French Socialists, and several others.[1] 'As it is', he wrote to C. E. Russell, 'we have got an international pro-Ally group against the pacifists which I hope you will join.'[2]

Hyndman was now anxious to develop this group into an anti-German Socialist International. In another letter to Russell he said:

We are already on excellent terms with the French anti-German Socialists, Renaudel, Thomas, Bracke, and others and indeed with the Guesdists generally. . . . Now we want to get on terms of friendship with organized American Socialists. . . . We must act quickly. The Pro-Germans are already scheming to boycott all of us out of their International.[3]

[1] Labour Party, *Conference Report*, Jan. 1918, p. 9; *Justice* 6 Sept. 1917.
[2] Hyndman to Russell, n.d., Russell Papers.   [3] Ibid., n.d.

R H

Hyndman had been at odds with the French Marxists since the days of Engels and Aveling, but now he thought it necessary to come into close contact with the Guesdists who championed the cause of the 'Union Sacré'. But the French Socialists, even those who supported the war, appeared to be irritated by his continued association with Clemenceau, who was not a Socialist at all, and whose firm action against strikers in the past they had never forgiven. Furthermore, a general leftward swing was developing in the attitude of the French party, and so Hyndman made little headway in persuading the Guesdists to support his anti-German International. Across the Atlantic, on the other hand, a group of pro-war Socialists such as Russell, Simons, William English Walling, and John Spargo, who had seceded from the American Socialist Party, set up a 'Social Democratic League' of their own. The prospects of Hyndman's anti-German International seemed solely dependent on links with this small American body, for which the best that could be said was that it was no weaker than his own little National Socialist Party.

At this time the great bulk of Labour Party opinion, under the lead of Arthur Henderson, was moving towards a policy of peace by negotiation, thus threatening a conflict with the Government. On Henderson's initiative the Labour Party took an active part in the Inter-Allied Labour and Socialist conference held in London in February 1918, which declared in favour of an international conference including German Socialists. Shortly after the conference, Camille Huysmans of the International Socialist Bureau, who had been striving to the same end, visited Hyndman at his new residence in Hampstead. They talked for two hours, but Hyndman could not see eye to eye with his guest, and he still regarded the proposal to meet the Germans as 'utterly treacherous' and 'contemptible'.[1] After Huysmans had gone, he sat down and wrote a series of letters in order

---

[1] Hyndman to Simons, 26 Feb. 1918, Simons Papers.

to try to upset the plan. To Russell, for instance, he wrote:

Somehow or other, he [Huysmans] has become quite pro-German. . . . He has convinced himself that the war, even with America on the side of the Allies, must end in a stalemate. . . . In short, if he were an agent of the German Government—which I do not actually believe him to be—he could not be doing more mischief.[1]

He also warned Russell of a project to send an Allied Socialist mission including Huysmans to America—a project in the end abandoned owing to objections from the American side.

The main purpose of averting a conference with enemy Socialists brought Hyndman into line with Samuel Gompers, the President of the American Federation of Labor, who had never been a Socialist, but who now earned Hyndman's approval for having 'done good work in exposing the cowardly pro-Germanism of so many European Socialist "leaders" '.[2] Hyndman went to meet a delegation of the A.F.L. on its arrival in London in April 1918, but much to his annoyance the Americans in their consultations with British labour entirely ignored the N.S.P. In July, however, his repeated appeals for an anti-German International seemed to bear fruit. In that month an American delegation of pro-war Socialists including Simons and Spargo came to Europe. Some of them took part in a demonstration held in Trafalgar Square on 14th July—'Le Quatorze Juillet'—at which Hyndman declared:

The fall of the Bastille rang the deathknell of Feudalism. The fall of Germany will ring the death-knell of Militarism and Capitalism. The French in their great Revolution declared for the Rights of Man. The Allies now declare together for the Rights of Nations.[3]

The Americans naturally approached the other Allied

[1] Hyndman to Russell, 2 March 1918, Russell Papers.
[2] Hyndman to Simons, 26 Feb. 1918, Simons Papers.
[3] *Justice*, 18 July 1918.

Socialist leaders for consultations, and soon found themselves obliged to make certain concessions to the views held by the peace-by-negotiation groups. Hyndman strongly objected to the joint statement issued by the Socialists as a result of the visit. He said in a letter to Simons:

> It seems to me to give away the position to the German Socialist traitors quite unnecessarily. We of the N.S.P., of course, reserve the right to openly refuse to meet the German Social-Democrats at all . . . I shall not pass away with the German still in possession of the International.[1]

A few days later he wrote: 'This "International" has become a fetish. Weak men cultivate fetishes and distrust common sense.'[2]

Even after the end of the war Hyndman remained hostile to the resumption of contacts with the German Socialists. In this he was only equalled by Gompers and the A.F.L. who refused to accept an invitation to the international Socialist conference held at Berne in February 1919. 'No, I don't believe an International is possible at present', Hyndman wrote to Russell. '. . . The new International of Berne will be entirely under German influence again.'[3] A conference held at Geneva in the following year formally re-established the International, and it was decided to place the permanent seat in London for the reason that 'the final struggle for Socialism will not be decided in Russia, but in those countries where capitalism is most advanced and most powerful'.[4] Hyndman was not entirely satisfied by this: he still nursed the idea of forming an International to his own taste. But the N.S.P. officially welcomed the Geneva decision, declaring that the Socialist International with its headquarters now in London formed 'the best medium for

[1] Hyndman to Simons, 31 July 1918, Simons Papers.
[2] Ibid., 8 Aug. 1918.
[3] Hyndman to Russell, n.d., Russell Papers.
[4] 'Social Democracy v. Bolshevism', a manifesto of the Geneva International, *Justice*, 11 Nov. 1920.

the resumption of international Socialist relations'.[1] By this
time, however, the Bolsheviks had formed an International
of their own, and the gulf between the two rival Inter-
nationals had become too wide to bridge: the Geneva
International was dominated by the British and other
reformist parties, whereas the Communist International
consisted of revolutionary Socialists under Russian leadership.

3

The N.S.P. was, as we have seen, bitterly hostile to the
Bolsheviks, and the Twentieth Century Press produced a
series of anti-Bolshevik pamphlets such as Kerensky's *Allied
Policy in Russia* and Martov's *Down With Executions*. In
Justice Hyndman gave flattering reviews to such books as
Spargo's *Bolshevism: The Enemy of Political and Industrial
Democracy* and M. A. Landau-Aldanov's *Lenin*, a hostile
account of the revolutionary leader. Meanwhile, Professor
V. I. Isaiev, an old friend of Hyndman's, openly advocated
British support for 'the Russian democracy which is rallying
round Koltchak'.[2]

Yet Hyndman, though he never missed an opportunity
to attack the Bolshevik dictatorship, seemed by now to have
recovered from wartime excesses, and refused to support the
cries for revenge raised by Russian refugees in England. In
the summer of 1920, at a time when the Red Army was
driving back the Polish invaders, a Council of Action of
British Labour prepared a general strike in order to prevent
Government intervention against Russia. At this juncture
Hyndman declared at the annual conference of the N.S.P.:
'We have no right to go to war as a nation, however much we
dislike the Government of a country', and the conference
decided to support the projected strike provided that the
independence of Poland was assured.[3]

[1] *Justice*, 11 Nov. 1920; Hyndman to Russell, 9 Oct. 1920, Russell Papers.
[2] *Justice*, 20 Feb. 1919–22 April 1920, *passim*.   [3] Ibid., 29 Aug. 1920.

In the course of 1920 and early 1921 the B.S.P., the Socialist Labour Party and other elements united into the Communist Party of Great Britain. Naturally the N.S.P. had no sympathy with this development, but it was noteworthy that when in 1921 the Communist headquarters were raided by the police and their documents seized, the N.S.P. protested against 'a distinct and unwarranted infringement of the freedom of opinion'.[1] Hyndman regarded the Communist tactics of 'pushing the unfortunate unemployed into acts of violence' as detrimental to working-class interests, but he declared that the responsibility for post-war difficulties lay more with the Government than with 'the small minority which thus misconducted themselves'.[2] He criticized the 'monstrous' Emergency Powers Act which had been rushed through Parliament to meet the situation created by a coal dispute at the time. The Common Law was quite sufficient to deal with treason, he said:

But what is treason? Do analysis and criticism of capitalism and profiteering come under that ugly heading? . . . To suppress, in any way, vigorous and thoroughgoing public discussion of economic and social conditions, at such a critical juncture as this would be to destroy the only hope of a peaceful solution of the difficult and dangerous problems ahead of us.[3]

At least in public, Hyndman refrained from attacking the British Communists, and he assumed the same attitude of aloofness as he had shown to the S.L.P. and the B.S.P. after their splits. He may have thought it wise to ignore them: at any rate he would rather allow their criticism of capitalism than have it suppressed by the Government. His own propaganda was now mainly directed against the Russian Bolsheviks who, he said, had 'done much to retard the advance of Social-Democracy by enabling the reactionary classes in other countries to point to the effect of Lenin's anarchical methods as condemning Socialism under far

---

[1] *Justice*, 19 May 1921.   [2] *The Times*, 13 Oct. 1921.   [3] Ibid.

different economic conditions from those existing in Russia'.[1]
Indeed, he repeatedly emphasized that Britain was different
from Russia, and maintained that Russia, being backward
in her economy, was not ready for Socialism. He was thus
not less hostile to Russia after 1917 than he had been before,
and his hopes of world progress remained rooted in the
West.

4

This did not mean, however, that Hyndman had very
much enthusiasm for the newly-created League of Nations.
Realistic as ever, he pointed out that in such an organization
there was no security against the sort of the betrayal by which
in August 1914 the German Social-Democrats ruined the
Second International, 'the Socialist League of Nations'.[2]
The only international arrangement in which he saw any
hope in the immediate future was what he called 'the
Grand Democratic Triple Alliance' of Britain, France, and
the United States. He had written to Simons at the time of
the last German offensive on the Western Front:

Even if the Germans do get the Channel Ports after defeating
our armies they can see, nevertheless, Nemesis glaring at them
close ahead under the Union Jack, the Tricolour and the Stars
and Stripes. That is the Alliance offensive and defensive in peace
and in war I want to see. That is the Alliance I hoped for and
worked for nearly fifty years ago. Let that be the League of
Nations to start with.[3]

Hyndman's enthusiasm for such an alliance did not evapor-
ate at the end of the war. In 1920, for instance, when there
was a serious rift in Anglo-American relations owing to
American dislike of Britain's post-war colonial policy, he
wrote to Russell:

Much of the criticism is quite true; but many of the misdeeds
are inheritance from the past. You, however, have your very weak

[1] *Justice*, 22 April 1920.   [2] Ibid., 13 March 1919.
[3] Hyndman to Simons, 15 Apr. 1918, Simons Papers.

places. Do we put our fingers into them? Practically never. Even while all this virulent abuse is poured upon us we say not a word about The Negro Question: not a word! I myself have a whole record of outrages and a summary of the growing and forcible negro press, which is terrible even in its moderation. . . . I keep silent. Why? Because, horrible as it all is, it is more important that our two nations should in some way sink their ill feelings and come to practical terms for joint action in the near future than enter upon a campaign of recrimination on such topics, monstrous as has been and is the behaviour of both of us. I want to see before I die a thoroughly good understanding between England, France, the United States, and I hope, China, on a basis of freedom, self-government and progress for all peoples.[1]

In the case of France, Hyndman's life-long sympathy was reinforced by his affection and admiration for her leader, Clemenceau. When the French Prime Minister visited London shortly after the armistice, he found time to see Hyndman and to have what the latter described as 'a long and personally delightful chat'.[2] In 1919 Hyndman published an appreciative study entitled *Clemenceau: The Man and His Time*, in which he hailed his old friend as 'the great statesman of the Great War' and as 'the human embodiment of a cause'.[3]

Hyndman had been watching with sympathy the growth of the nationalist movement in China since the Boxer Rising, but the inclusion of China in his democratic alliance was mainly as a result of his distrust of Japan's Continental Programme against China. *The Awakening of Asia*, a book by Hyndman dealing with the modern history of China, Japan, and India, was originally written in 1916, but was held up by the censor for more than two years largely on account of his critical comment on the Anglo-Japanese alliance.[4] He was deeply concerned about what he called

---

[1] Hyndman to Russell, 3 July 1920, in R. T. Hyndman, *Last Years*, p. 213.
[2] Hyndman to Seton-Watson, 5 Dec. 1918, Seton-Watson Papers.
[3] Hyndman, *Clemenceau*, p. 299.
[4] *Justice*, 19 June 1919; Hyndman, *The Awakening of Asia* (1919), pp. vii, 161. A German translation appeared in 1921: *Der Aufstieg des Morgenlandes*, tr. by Werner-Otto von Hentig (Leipzig, 1921).

The veteran agitator (1919)

'the wholesale aggression of Japan in China'[1] and wrote an article entitled 'Japan as Mistress of Asia' in which he said: 'I venture to predict that Japan will follow the course of the great aggressive Empire of Modern Europe', and if she were allowed to have her own in Asia, 'then a war more terrible than that which is now being concluded may easily confront our successors'.[2]

Meanwhile, Hyndman's distrust of the Germans had not been in the least allayed by the restoration of peace. The German people, 'hypnotized' as they were by the 'cult of scientific barbarism', he said, had failed to learn from the war, which had not directly affected their country. So he demanded harsh and unalterable terms for the defeated nation.[3] Perhaps most interesting in this respect was his observation of the American attitude to the defeated nation: he wrote shortly before the armistice: 'The Americans are really too good-natured and my fear is—or was—that if and when Germany is down they may be inclined to let her up.'[4]

Thus, having little faith in the future good intentions of Germany and Japan, the veteran Socialist pleaded strongly for a democratic alliance of Britain, U.S.A., France, and China, for he knew that the world had not yet been made safe for democracy. In 1919 he wrote privately to R. W. Seton-Watson: 'So we have a peace—at last. But we have by no means got rid of war, as nobody knows better than you do.'[5] The Washington Conference on disarmament in 1921 he simply regarded as an 'international thieves' kitchen'— the very observation that had led to Quelch's expulsion from Stuttgart in 1907.[6] By pointing out the fresh dangers and the difficulty of compromise in a world of tension and insecurity, Hyndman thus became a realistic prophet of future international strife, against which he advocated what was fundamentally a conservative and non-revolutionary policy.

[1] Hyndman to Seton-Watson, 5 Dec. 1918, Seton-Watson Papers.
[2] *New Europe*, xi (29 May 1919), 154–8.   [3] *Justice*, 14 Nov. 1919.
[4] Hyndman to Seton-Watson, 3 Oct. 1918, Seton-Watson Papers.
[5] Ibid., 30 June 1919.   [6] *Justice*, 7 Nov. 1921.

5

At the same time, where nations were struggling to be
free, Hyndman supported their cause. He was not dissatisfied
with developments in Eastern Europe, which allowed for
the emergence of several new nations. He and his wife
were especially pleased by the emancipation of Finland.
When Finnish independence seemed to have been secured
by the March Revolution in Russia, the Hyndmans were
invited to a small gathering of Finns in London. 'It was a
historic occasion', he wrote shortly afterwards. 'I spoke.
And I spoke out. I said . . . that we English entered into the
heritage with our Finnish and Russian brothers; that the
dawning of the day had come in the East.'[1] He was soon
disappointed by the Russians: but he strongly supported
the other nations of Eastern Europe which were freeing
themselves from the crumbling edifices of Hohenzollern
and Hapsburg power.

As early as October 1916 a group of East European experts
including R. W. Seton-Watson and H. W. Steed of *The
Times* had formed a 'Serbian Society of Great Britain' with
a journal, *New Europe*. The objects of the Society were to
assist the creation of 'a Southern State' in the Balkans and to
strive for the reconstruction of Europe on the basis of nationality and the rights of minorities.[2] Hyndman participated
in its work, and sought to develop the Society into an
independent Foreign Affairs Committee, which should
advocate his idea of the democratic alliance and even assist
in his attempt to form an anti-German International of
Allied workers. He therefore strongly recommended that
the Society should be fully independent from the Foreign
Office, from the 'second-rate persons who now control our
national policy'.[3] He wrote to Seton-Watson in the language

[1] Hyndman to Simons, 30 April 1917, Simons Papers.
[2] H. W. Steed, *Through Thirty Years* (1924), ii, pp. 124–6.
[3] Hyndman to Seton-Watson, 19 Feb. 1917, Seton-Watson Papers.

of the revolutionary, telling him that 'the present system is played out' and that '*our class*, the class to which you and I belong, is to all intents and purposes, "a back number" '.[1] He tried hard to bring Seton-Watson into contact with 'some of the more serious and intelligent workers'; and he pressed again and again for the reorganization of the Serbian Society, seeing in it (rather surprisingly) the nucleus of 'an active Committee of Public Safety'.[2] Unhappily for him, but not unnaturally, it failed to live up to his hopes. Not only did it form no effective link with the working-class movement but, as he said, it 'has been powerless throughout [and] has given the public neither a lead nor information'.[3] Hyndman, however continued to belong to it because of his support for the claims of the new Slav nations.

The three principal new Slav nations to emerge from the war were Poland, Yugoslavia, and Czechoslovakia. Hyndman was active on behalf of the claims of each of these new countries, even before they were born. In a lecture given at the Holborn Restaurant in January 1918 he gave his backing to the Polish demand for a free port at Danzig and command of the Vistula, on the ground that they were 'geographically necessary' for the permanent peace of Europe.[4] In the case of Yugoslavia it was a matter of supporting her claims against Italy's on the Fiume boundary question. Hyndman joined with other members of the Serbian Society in writing to *The Times* on this subject in November 1919.[5] He was sorry to be at odds with the Italians, whom he had always liked; but he felt that their policy in the Adriatic was 'imperialist'; and he especially disliked the activities of Benito Mussolini, who, though a Socialist, had become 'a most virulent champion of d'Annunzio's piratical raids on Fiume'.[6]

[1] Ibid., 15 July 1917.   [2] Ibid., 4 Feb., 5 May 1918.
[3] Ibid., 30 June 1919.
[4] H. M. Hyndman, *An Independent Poland* (1918), p. 12.
[5] *The Times*, 18 Nov. 1919.   [6] *Justice*, 15 Jan. 1920.

But Hyndman's greatest enthusiasm was for the Czechs, with whose leader, Professor Thomas Masaryk, he had become personally acquainted. Masaryk tried to draw Hyndman into an advisory post at the Versailles Conference, and although Hyndman would not serve, he formed a very favourable impression of the future prospects of Czechoslovakia under Masaryk's leadership.[1] In 1920 he wrote a preface to a pamphlet by Alexander Brož, secretary of the Czech Press Bureau, entitled *The First Year of the Czecho-Slovak Republic*. 'Never was a revolution carried out more thoroughly or more peacefully,' said Hyndman. 'All classes joined cordially in bringing about this splendid result. Even the expropriation of the German landlords, whose high-handed methods had exasperated the Czechs for ten generations, was . . . carried out without the loss of a life to the oppressor.'

The movement for national self-determination was also gathering strength within the British Empire. India and Ireland had gone through serious disturbances during the war and the situation in both countries reached a critical point in 1920–1. Hyndman, however, at least before the armistice, appeared reluctant to give open support to these movements.

Hyndman's attitude to the Irish question depended very much on the exigencies of the European War. On Easter Monday 1916, when the Irish Republican Army, under the leadership of James Connolly, made an abortive attempt to establish national independence by an armed rising in Dublin, he denounced these 'reckless fanatics' who took 'hopeless risks at a most serious crisis in our foreign and domestic affairs'.[2] After the war, however, when the Emerald Isle became the scene of warfare between the Republican Army and the Royal Irish Constabulary (and 'Black and Tans'), Hyndman was distressed by the 'Irish sore' and the atrocities committed by 'our Huns' in Ireland. He advocated

[1] R. T. Hyndman, *Last Years*, p. 184.   [2] *Justice*, 4 May, 1916.

a national convention representative of the two sides with a view to putting an end to the infamy.[1]

Similarly, during the war Hyndman paid little attention to the Indian Home Rule movement led by Mrs. Annie Besant and Tilak. After the war, however, when Tilak came to London to consult with the leaders of the Labour Party, Hyndman wrote: 'I am entirely in agreement with you that India must have the right to determine her political future. Why shouldn't she enjoy that right if other nations can?'[2] He took the chair at a joint meeting of Labour M.P.s and Indian delegates held in the House of Commons in the autumn of 1919 to consider the new Government measure of constitutional reform. The chapters on India in his book the *Awakening of Asia* were friendly to Indian nationalism, and were reproduced as a propaganda pamphlet in Madras.[3] But the self-government of India, for which he had worked for more than forty years, had to await the aftermath of another war before coming to complete fruition.

6

'No hope but in the Labour Party, and not much in that' was Hyndman's characteristic evaluation of the post-war labour movement.[4] Although he had advocated the affiliation of the S.D.F. and B.S.P. to the Labour Party prior to the war, his new organization the N.S.P., partly because of its small size, partly because of its objection to the anti-war elements inside the Labour Party, at first made no application to affiliate. But Hyndman welcomed the new constitution of the Labour Party adopted at its conference in January–February 1918, for it was accompanied by a policy statement called *Labour and the New Social Order* which

[1] *The Times*, 16 March 1921.
[2] D. V. Tahmankar, *Lokamanya Tilak* (1956), p. 284.
[3] Hyndman, *The Truth About India* (Madras, c. 1921).
[4] Hyndman to Seton-Watson, 28 March 1920, Seton-Watson Papers.

committed the Labour Party definitely to Socialism. He wrote to Russell at the time:

Here we have a series of Socialist measures for which my old friends and I of the Social-Democratic Party have agitated for nearly forty years put on record as the political and social programme of organized labour. True they are watered down and Fabianized almost beyond recognition. But it won't be long before the truth the whole truth and nothing but the truth of Socialism is forced to the front. That is part of our business.[1]

There was, however, another reason for his support of the new constitution: it reduced the power of the anti-war I.L.P. and B.S.P. by creating an individual membership of local Labour Parties, and it also deprived the Socialist Societies of the right to elect their own representatives to the party executive. The N.S.P. therefore, at once made application for affiliation to the Labour Party, which was duly accepted by the latter, and at their own annual conference in August 1918, Dan Irving, Jack Jones, and others discussed 'the necessity for forming a pro-Ally block' inside the Labour Party.[2]

In November, shortly after the armistice, Parliament was dissolved, and the nation was plunged into the 'khaki election' in December. The Labour Party put forward 361 candidates, of whom only fifty-seven, nearly all with a pro-war record, were returned. The well-known I.L.P. leaders as well as fourteen B.S.P. candidates were all defeated. Eleven N.S.P. members stood on a programme 'to kill—Bolshevism, Capitalism, Militarism', and six were successful: Dan Irving (Burnley), James O'Grady (Leeds South-West, unopposed), Arthur Hayday (Nottingham West), Ben Tillett (Salford North), Will Thorne (West Ham, Plaistow), and Jack Jones (West Ham, Silvertown). Thus Burnley was at last won by a Hyndmanite, if not by Hyndman. The N.S.P. group could now establish itself as a wing of the

[1] Hyndman to Russell, n.d., Russell Papers.
[2] *Justice*, 7 Feb., 22 Aug. 1918.

parliamentary Labour Party, although its representatives
were too old and too conservative to make very much
impact with their ideas.

The conservatism of the Hyndmanites in domestic affairs
was well illustrated by the attitude of their leader to the
post-war industrial unrest. Glasgow, Belfast, and London
were soon involved in engineers' strikes for shorter hours of
work; and troops were introduced to suppress a general
strike in Glasgow. The miners were also threatening a
national strike in order to enforce the nationalization of
their industry. Hyndman had always been opposed to
industrial direct action, and during the war he had denounced strikes as a 'treachery to the whole nation'.[1] He
regarded the threatened action by the 'Triple Alliance' of
the Miners, Railwaymen, and Transport Workers as a
desperate and hopeless resort. He wrote to Russell:

The old Chartists advocated the Holy Month with its cessation
of work for that period; but they could never get the workers to
save up for it, and the wiser heads saw, as I think we can see,
that a movement not in accord with the economics of the situation would break down. If tried with its resulting failure reaction
will, for the time being, gain ground. If partial success a cry will
arise for a military dictator. If wholly successful—to argue an
impossibility—then anarchy all round and general overthrow.[2]

In the autumn, when the railwaymen held a nine-day
national strike, Hyndman was critical of the move:

Unfortunately, they are in a hurry and talk as if you could
hustle unthinking men and women safely into the greatest social
revolution of all time! There are times in great affairs as in small
when what chess players call the *coup de repos* is the best policy.[3]

No one, however, was willing to accept Hyndman's advice
on this question; and the exacerbation of industrial unrest
in 1920-1 made him regard the situation as 'desperately
dangerous'. 'The more so', he wrote to Russell:

[1] *Justice*, 1 Aug. 1918.
[2] Hyndman to Russell, 26 July 1919, Russell Papers.
[3] Ibid., 19 Dec. 1919.

since neither Ministers nor people have any definite principles and live on from hand to mouth in the Micawberish hope that something will turn up. There are epochs in the life of a nation when rulers and people seem, as the Scotch say, 'fey'. . . . Government by its ineptitude, treachery and cowardice plays into the hands of the Bolshevists. The Bolshevists by their wild rebellion and anarchism play into the hands of the Government and its profiteering supporters. Thus we have reaction and anarchy face to face, while the great body of our people are stamped upon by both the extreme factions.[1]

Such a polarization in politics between the extreme right and left would mean an imminent danger of civil war. Hyndman was convinced that the Government was endeavouring to 'force a downright fight to a finish with the Trade Unions'.[2] The dreaded miners' strike began in April 1921; it took the form of a lock-out, and in this struggle it soon became clear that the workers were on the defensive. Shortly after 'Black Friday', 15th April, when the other unions 'deserted' the miners, Hyndman wrote to Russell saying that the whole thing was 'a plot' against organized labour hatched in the dark by Lloyd George, Winston Churchill, Bonar Law, and several others, and that 'George was furiously angry when the Triple Alliance did not come off'.[3] The lock-out dragged on for three months and ended in the defeat of the miners.

In June 1921 a debate was held in the House of Commons between Hyndman and the Duke of Northumberland on the cause of industrial unrest. Hyndman maintained that the Government and the mine owners were responsible for the whole crisis. The Duke insisted that the coal strike was a plot of the miners' executive, which was honeycombed by Communists. He denounced the Labour Party as an undisciplined and loose organization which 'shelters under its wings all the subversive elements of society', and condemned the whole Labour and Socialist movement as an accessory to the

[1] Hyndman to Russell, 9 Oct. 1920, Russell Papers.
[2] Ibid., 17 Nov. 1920.   [3] Ibid., n.d.

Moscow International. In his reply Hyndman simply
ignored the Duke's attack on the labour movement and
instead pleaded for the mutual understanding of gigantic
trusts and formidable trade unions so that Great Britain
might lead the world into a Co-operative Commonwealth
as she had done into capitalism.[1]

The miners' struggle had become a target of bitter
criticism from non-Socialist quarters. Frederic Harrison,
another veteran of nineteenth-century Radicalism, deplored
the 'suicidal folly' of the miners and declared that trade
unionism had been degraded into 'a cover of Communism',
which he considered to be 'treason to the whole men who
founded trade unions'.[2] Hyndman wrote a reply to Harrison
saying that things had changed since the days when Harrison
championed the cause of trade unions. 'Those were the days
of competitive Capitalism: these are the days of combining
Capitalism,' he said. 'The greatest of our productive and
distributive agencies are in company form—a form which,
as we saw during the war, lends itself most readily to
nationalization and socialization.'[3]

The peaceful transformation of industry into a Socialist
Commonwealth through some sort of co-operation and
arrangement between trade unions, co-operative societies,
companies, and trusts appears to have been the outcome that
Hyndman now hoped for. Such a transformation required
thorough democratization of the Government as a preliminary
step. His expectations of the Socialist future had undergone
many vicissitudes, but had never disappeared. Yet at the time
he had not lost his belief in the value of more immediate reforms. He therefore once more wrote on the need for such
constitutional changes as the introduction of proportional
representation and the popular initiative in legislation.[4]

[1] *The Cause of Industrial Unrest, Verbatim Report of Debate between Hyndman and the Duke of Northumberland* (1921).
[2] *The Times*, 1 April 1921.   [3] Ibid., 4 April 1921.
[4] Hyndman, 'An Antiquated Assembly', *Nineteenth Century and After*, lxxxix (June 1921), 979-92; *The Times*, 20 April 1921.

SH

Until the dissolution of the Food Consumers' Council in
December 1920 he worked hard for that body, which
he regarded as 'the Ministry of the People'. He took
a keen interest in the extension of home agriculture and
wrote frequently to *The Times* advocating home colonization
—'Back to Land'.[1] He envied the United States for her
self-supporting economy and pleaded for the achievement of
national autarky as a step towards a Co-operative Commonwealth in Britain.[2] At the end of 1920 he was once again
advocating the S.D.F. programme of forty years before for
dealing with the increasing problem of unemployment.[3]

Meanwhile, the N.S.P. had a new secretary, Thomas
Kennedy, who had returned from the Italian Front after
the armistice. To match its parliamentary successes it made
fresh efforts to build up its strength in the country. The
establishment of new branches was frequently reported in
the pages of *Justice*, but its official membership for purposes
of affiliation to the Labour Party remained at 2,000. In
February 1920 the party adopted for the first time since its
formation a definite programme of reforms, including the
social ownership of natural resources, democratic manage-
ment of basic industries, and a citizen army.[4]

In spite of Hyndman's 'nationalist' tendencies, the name
of 'National Socialist Party' had not commended itself to
him. He and his colleagues of the 'Old Guard' had a senti-
mental attachment to the old name of 'Social-Democratic
Federation'; and Joseph Burgess, who had proposed the new
name, had left the party when it decided to affiliate to the
Labour Party. At the 1920 annual conference, therefore, the
name was changed back to the old one. ' "National" has
outlived its wartime usefulness', wrote Lee.[5] It was not clear,
however, whether there was any place for the organization
under whatever name, in the new post-war world.

[1] *The Times*, 30 Aug., 10, 14, 19 Sept., 24 Oct. 1919.
[2] Hyndman, *The Evolution of Revolution*, p. 396.
[3] *The Times*, 29 Dec. 1920, 1 Jan. 1921.
[4] *Justice*, 5 Feb. 1920.   [5] Ibid., 29 July, 19 Aug. 1920.

7

Hyndman at least retained a surprising amount of his pristine vigour. He wrote innumerable letters, many for the private edification of his friends, but many also for the press. He also travelled round the country lecturing as he had always done. Early in 1921 he went up to Burnley once more to speak in favour of the confiscation of war wealth and the wiping out of the 8,000 million pounds of war debt. In March, as he was entering his eightieth year, a *Times* reporter found him 'in excellent health, and both physically and intellectually vigorous'. Late in the month he went to Chester to 'kick off' at a football match between Clarion Scouts and a team of French workers.

Hyndman and his wife had been invited to attend the Workers' 'Sokol' or Olympiad, held in Prague in the summer. They set off in June, travelling by way of Brussels and Cologne. 'I never had a more delightful time in all my long life', he wrote to Russell:

We were treated in princely fashion throughout, given the most prominent place at the huge Olympiad, which we went there to see, and when we went quite by chance to the Senate, the whole of the members rose from their seats to greet me and applauded vociferously.[1]

He delivered five speeches, three in Prague, one in Pilsen and one in Ostrava. In one of these speeches addressed to the Social Democrats of Czechoslovakia, he criticized both the Geneva and the Moscow International and said:

Every nation has its own historic growth and its own internal difficulties to reckon with. . . . The best any, or all, of us can do is to help one another in pressing forward, upwards, and onwards from the stage of development each of us has reached to a higher plane of industry and custom.

At the same time, however, in his characteristic way he made a special claim for his own country:

[1] Hyndman to Russell, 13 July 1921, Russell Papers.

It is my profound conviction that we Englishmen, owing to our geographical, social, economic, and political situation, are nearer to the realization of Social Democracy and the Co-operative Commonwealth than any other people in the world.[1]

In the autumn, Hyndman did more writing and continued his propaganda activities for the S.D.F. In October he went up to Kirkcaldy to speak for Thomas Kennedy, who had been elected to Parliament for the constituency at a by-election in the previous March. The meeting was held in the Adam Smith Hall, and Hyndman spoke on 'The Breakdown of the Capitalist System'. 'I gave them the full gospel', he wrote to Russell in America.[2] There were dangers, however, in such an active life for a man of almost eighty. On 9th November he went down to Enfield to speak on 'Industrial Ruin and the Way Out'. It was a chilly and foggy night, but his wife saw to it that he took all precautions, 'fur coat and closed motor car all the way'. All the same, he returned with a bad cold, which soon turned to pneumonia.

For several days Hyndman battled against the illness, and by 20th November he was apparently recovering, and already planning a holiday for himself and his very solicitous wife. But the strain had been too great: on 22nd November, as his wife put it, 'Quite suddenly and painlessly, in the early morning . . . his heart gave way. I am not sure if he knew it, but he died in my arms. . . .'

The funeral took place at Golders Green Crematorium. The coffin, covered with a red flag, was carried from the station by members of the S.D.F. executive, with a few members of the dwindling 'Old Guard' following behind. They marched to the strains of Chopin's Funeral March, played by the Musicians' Union Band. A few verses of 'The Red Flag' and 'England Arise' were sung at the crematorium and there were brief speeches by Lee, Kennedy, Clynes, Thorne, Irving, and Jack Jones—all but Lee being M.P.s.

[1] Quoted in R. T. Hyndman, *Last Years*, p. 319.
[2] Hyndman to Russell, 14 Oct. 1920, Russell Papers.

Two verses of the 'Marseillaise' followed, and then the mourners filed past the coffin in the chapel. As Rosalind Hyndman said:

With no religious ceremony, the speakers all being reasonable agnostics of a materialist type, they simply could not get away from the sense of the immortality of his work and being.[1]

[1] R. T. Hyndman to Russell, 13 Dec. 1921, Russell Papers.

XIII ∿ EPILOGUE

I

In March 1922 a 'Hyndman Memorial Committee' made its appearance, with an impressive membership including Lady St. Helier, the Countess of Warwick, Bernard Shaw, Sir James Frazer (the anthropologist), Wickham Steed (editor of *The Times*), R. W. Seton-Watson, and Thomas Hardy, whose acquaintance Hyndman had made during the war. The Committee arranged for a bronze bust of Hyndman, the work of the young sculptor Edward Lacey, to be presented to the National Portrait Gallery; and it sponsored two Hyndman Memorial Lectures, on successive anniversaries of his birthday. The earlier of these, in 1923, was delivered by R. W. Seton-Watson, and his subject was 'The Emancipation of South-Eastern Europe'. A year later, F. J. Gould spoke on 'Hyndman as Prophet of Socialism'.

Meanwhile, Rosalind Travers Hyndman had been completing her last work of devotion for her husband—the memoir of the last decade of his life, published in 1923 under the title *The Last Years of H. M. Hyndman*. A few days after sending the manuscript to the publishers, she took an overdose of sleeping tablets and died on 7th April 1923. By her will all her possessions were to go to such causes as would keep alive the memory of her husband's work, except for £600 in cash, to be divided among needy members of the S.D.F. All pecuniary benefits from his or her literary works were to finance a 'Hyndman Literary Trust', for the publication or republication of works by or about Hyndman;

and the remainder of her property was to support the general work of the S.D.F.

Two notable pieces of writing by Hyndman were published posthumously as a result. One of these was a pamphlet called *Introduction to 'The Life to Come'*. Hyndman had planned to write a utopian romance in the vein of Edward Bellamy's *Looking Backward* or Morris's *News from Nowhere*, and this was to be entitled *The Life to Come*: only a prefatory section, however, was completed before his death. The other work was 'Books of a Lifetime', an account of the four books which had influenced him most. This was published in the S.D.F. monthly the *Social Democrat* in 1925–6. The four books which Hyndman singled out were Morgan's *Ancient Society*, on which Engels had drawn for his *Origin of the Family*; Marx's *Capital*; Shelley's *Prometheus Unbound*, which he found a constant source of inspiration for his own struggle against authority; and Eugene Sue's *Le Juif Errant*, which he liked principally for its anti-clericalism.

2

Hyndman's long career provides a link connecting the last century to the present. He grew up with the Victorian belief in progress and prosperity, but he was one of the first to appreciate the threat to Britain's survival posed by foreign commercial and political rivalry. He was present at the inception of many great causes, and saw their growth and transformation in his own lifetime. His childhood memories went back to the great days of the Chartist movement, yet he lived to see the Labour Party coming to maturity. He sought the friendship of Marx when Marx was almost unknown in Britain, and in his old age he became one of the bitterest critics of Lenin. He knew Mazzini, admired Cavour, and kept up his sympathy with the Italian nationalist movement until Mussolini's influence perverted it. Two great landmarks of modern Indian history—the Mutiny and the beginning of Gandhi's 'Satyargraha' movement—fell in his lifetime, and his support for Indian self-government was consistent throughout. Thus the events and personalities that were woven into his life illustrate the extent to which his work and interests have relevance to our own time.

One of the unique features of Hyndman's character was his ability to reconcile his business activities, mostly of a very speculative character, with his role as a Socialist who aspired to lead the proletariat to its millennium. Yet the paradox is not so extraordinary as it seems. His knowledge of international finance gave him an insight into the weaknesses of the capitalist system, and this in part explains his conversion to Socialism. What wealth he had at his disposal he used to finance his political activities: the only trouble was that there was never enough of it. Frequently, lack of attention to business or too extravagant political expenditure left him in difficulties, and he and his wife had to cut their personal expenses.

The abiding impression of his political career, however, is not that he made great sacrifices for the cause, but rather that he fulfilled himself in fighting for it. A tremendously vigorous, restless, and loquacious man, he could dispose of much of his surplus energy by ceaseless political agitation. A reviewer of his first volume of memoirs pointed out that he gave 'the impression of a man who is always talking';[1] and H. S. Salt, a fellow-Socialist, has told how he travelled with him by train from Kent to London, 'and he talked and talked till between his oration and the swaying of the train I was actually dizzy'.[2] Another Socialist has described his platform method as follows:

His undisguised appreciation of his own talent for sarcastic witticism was highly infectious, and immensely delighted those who happened to agree with him. He, however, often repelled possible converts by his habit, fatal in a propagandist, of mistaking innocent inquirers for subtle adversaries and scoring off them unmercifully.[3]

[1] *The Times Literary Supplement*, 5 Oct. 1911.
[2] H. S. Salt, *Company I Have Kept* (1930), p. 92.
[3] W. S. Sanders, *Early Socialist Days* (1927), p. 34.

With these characteristics Hyndman was not likely to get on well with his colleagues or to enjoy the give and take of genuine collective decision. It was all too easy for him to take advantage of his wealth, education, and experience in order to guide the S.D.F. executive. This was dangerous in an organization dedicated to extreme democratic principles. Charges of 'dictatorship' were all too frequently brought against him from within the Federation, and undoubtedly Hyndman's personality was a major factor in the numerous schisms from which the Federation suffered throughout its life.

There was a strong element of paternalism in Hyndman's attitude to the working class: he felt almost towards them as he did towards the Fijians, the Africans, and the Indians. He was a different species, a member of the 'educated classes', and furthermore a 'City man'. He never refrained from dressing the part, looking for all the world like the Governor of the Bank of England.[1] He probably realized that this often aroused an initial hostility among his audience. He thought, however, that it was the best way to draw attention to himself and to his gospel of class consciousness. In any case, his upbringing and manners would have severely interfered with any attempt on his part to behave differently.

The fact that he was by family background and by political instinct a Tory rather than a Liberal marked him off from the great bulk of working-class Radicals. His early work for the *Pall Mall Gazette* in its days of independent Conservatism was paralleled later by his association with the *Morning Post*; and he always had a great dislike of Gladstonianism. Hostile to all religion, he retained a certain respect for what he called 'the Catholic International', but he never concealed his contempt for adherents of the 'silly and sickening prudery of the lower Nonconformist variety'.[2]

---

[1] The comparison was made by one who heard him speak in 1908. J. W. Robertson Scott, *Story of the Pall Mall Gazette* (Oxford, 1956), p. 436n.

[2] Hyndman to Hillquit, n.d. (Dec. 1907?), Hillquit Papers.

The most obviously Tory characteristic of Hyndman's belief was, of course, his emphasis upon the importance of maintaining British national power and on developing the Empire. For him, Socialism could not have the same implications as it had for its Continental exponents. 'Hyndman's Marxism', wrote Kautsky, 'is no imported product, "Made in Germany", but a genuine British growth.'[1] This did not necessarily mean a perversion of Marxism: in Bernstein's view Hyndman's patriotic feeling did not go 'beyond the degree to which it is still possible to combine with a good internationalism. He is by no means any more nationalist than Karl Marx and Giuseppe Mazzini whom he respects as his political masters'.[2] And on another occasion Bernstein said that Hyndman's apparent jingoism 'would have survived the strictest Socialist criticism'.[3] Thus the two most distinguished German Socialist theorists of Hyndman's own generation were both prepared to verify his credentials.

Like many another nineteenth-century English democrat, however, Hyndman's main Continental sympathies were with France. It was a characteristic which in his generation he shared with the Positivists and with Sir Charles Dilke. Hyndman's friendship with Clemenceau was very significant, for Clemenceau after all was not a Socialist but a Radical. Yet the two had much in common—anti-clericalism, hostility to aristocracy, zeal for the defence of free institutions. Undoubtedly Hyndman's identification with France, with Paris, and with Clemenceau increased his suspicions of Germany and even of German Socialism.

Hyndman was a true adventurer: he was prepared for anything. This made him at once a romantic and a realist. For most of the time, he was prepared to work on the

[1] Kautsky to F. H. Gorle, 3 March 1912, published in Hyndman, *Further Reminiscences*, p. 518.
[2] E. Bernstein, 'H. M. Hyndman's Erinnerungen', *Archiv für die Geschichte des Socialismus und der Arbeiterbewegung*, iv, 105-15.
[3] Bernstein, *My Years of Exile*, p. 257.

assumption that reform would come gradually, by piecemeal legislation. But he would not have been surprised by the onset of a revolution. As time went on, he was disappointed that progress towards the Socialist ideal was so slow: but this disappointment he shared with many of the leading Socialists of his time, including the very shrewd and cynical Bernard Shaw. At the end of his life he enjoyed collaboration with Sidney Webb in the humdrum work of the War Emergency Workers' National Committee: yet his last letters were full of talk about 'the approaching cataclysm' and even 'the opening of the Seventh Seal'.

Hyndman was a personally ambitious man, and yet he never got into Parliament. Was it his principles which kept him out? Hardly: he could be very opportunistic when occasion demanded. As much as anything, it was a matter of character. He lacked many of the essential political virtues, such as tact, a willingness to listen to other people, and a capacity to suffer fools gladly. As Shaw felicitously pointed out, he was a man 'without hypocrisy or any pretence of superiority to hearty illwill'.[1] Such a man may win the devotion of a minority, but he is not likely to win the approval of the British electorate.

3

The S.D.F. always bore the imprint of Hyndman's personality, and its weekly organ, *Justice*, spoke constantly with his voice—bitter, tactless, and narrow-minded in its support of 'the Cause', but also (as H. G. Wells said of Hyndman) possessed of a 'magnificent obstinacy'.[2] Even when Hyndman was no longer its editor it was the same: for in spite of occasional differences he had moulded Quelch's ideas in very much his own pattern. And so, while the Federation obtained the constant loyalty of a few enthusiasts, it never

[1] Quoted R. T. Hyndman, *Last Years*, p. 388.
[2] Quoted Hyndman, *Further Reminiscences*, p. 511.

secured wide approval among the mass of the British people.
S.D.F. propaganda may have made many recruits for
Socialism; it retained few, however, for its own organization.
Even apart from the I.L.P., the formation of so many
different left-wing groups, from the Socialist League to the
Communist Party, showed that the S.D.F. had failed to
provide one broad channel for the current of British
Socialism.

Yet the influence of the Federation must not be under-
estimated. In the trade union movement, for instance, it
eventually secured many important adherents. Although
Hyndman had been personally rather contemptuous of
trade unionism in the early 1880's, the members had often
played major roles in the development of 'new unionism',
and Will Thorne, the founder of the Gasworkers' Union,
retained his allegiance to the S.D.F. throughout his life. In
the 1890's the London Trades Council fell almost entirely
into the hands of the S.D.F., James Macdonald being its
secretary from 1896 and Quelch himself being its chairman
a few years later. The London Society of Compositors and
the Boot and Shoe Operatives were also considerably
influenced by the Federation. Although Hyndman himself
could not be a member of a union, the rank and file of the
Federation's membership were mostly actively trade unionists: cotton weavers in North-East Lancashire, compositors
and general labourers in London, engineers on the Clydeside,
bootmakers in Northampton, agricultural labourers in the
South and so on.

Much of this activity in the trade unions took place at a
local level; and it must be emphasized that at that level the
S.D.F. branches and their members had a great deal of
independence. They collaborated with the local I.L.P. to an
extent unheard of at the national level; they often remained
affiliated to local L.R.C.'s; and they engaged in joint
campaigns for representation on the municipalities. The visit
of Hyndman or any other nationally-known leader of the

S.D.F. would be a rare and special occasion, valuable for recruiting purposes, but not necessarily decisive for the shaping of branch policy.

All the same, by the time of Hyndman's death the S.D.F. had been through so many vicissitudes that it had altogether lost its strength at the 'grass-roots'. Those who followed Hyndman out of the B.S.P. were mostly the older generation, no longer active in the work of marshalling the support of the young. In the course of the 1920's death took its toll of them: Dan Irving died while still M.P. for Burnley in 1924; Bax lived only until November 1926.

Meanwhile, the S.D.F. organization remained in a moribund state. The money left to it by Rosalind Travers Hyndman may have helped to keep it alive, but little came in from any other source. On 22nd January 1925 the last issue of *Justice*, No. 2141, was published, and it was succeeded by a monthly journal called the *Social-Democrat*. This appeared in regular printed form until December 1933, after which date it was replaced by a duplicated bulletin. For a time in the 1920's, a Hyndman Club and Institute existed in North London, as a headquarters for the Hyndman Literary Trust, a home for Hyndman's library, and a social centre for London Socialists. In the 1930's, however, it proved impossible to keep it going as a social centre. In 1933 the affiliation fee to the Labour Party was paid on a basis of 1,000 members only, instead of 2,000; it remained at the lower figure until 1939, when it was further cut to a basis of 500. In that year the group still had a spark of life; it was able to reassert a traditional attitude by declaring its support for National Service and its opposition to the proposed Popular Front with the Communists.[1] A few local branches still survived, including one at Burnley. But the outbreak of war was the final blow to the organization: and on 12 October 1939, with Hitler and Stalin sharing Poland between them, a meeting of the executive was held and it

[1] S.D.F. Executive Minutes, 30 March 1939.

was 'agreed to wind up the S.D.F.' This process was not finally completed until 1941, by which time the Twentieth Century Press shares had been sold, the last headquarters in Islington vacated, and the record of executive meetings finally concluded.

4

When all of Hyndman's works had been published, and when the S.D.F. had gone out of existence, what was there left of his life's activity? There was, at least, an important tradition in the labour movement—a tradition which has been described as 'Anglo-Marxist', to distinguish it from the 'Russian-Marxist' or Marxist-Leninist tradition now embodied in the Communist Party.[1] Just after Hyndman's death, 'Anglo-Marxism' found a new channel of influence inside the labour movement in the work of the National Council of Labour Colleges. The Labour College movement, it is true, was originally at odds with the S.D.F., being led by members of the Socialist Labour Party and having strong leanings towards 'direct action' of which Hyndman disapproved. After the formation of the Communist Party, however, it took an independent line which led to a reassertion of Marxist as against Marxist-Leninist orthodoxy. Long is the list of labour leaders of the last few generations who have been influenced by its classes. Appropriately enough, it was to the National Council of Labour Colleges that Hyndman's library was presented by his executors; and it may still be seen, by permission of the general secretary, at Wortley Hall, the former home of the Earls of Wharncliffe which has been turned into a conference centre for the Yorkshire Labour Parties—itself a relic of the old order and a symbol of its transformation, as Hyndman himself was in his lifetime.

[1] I owe the expression 'Anglo-Marxist' to Denis Healey, M.P., who used it when speaking at Nuffield College, Oxford, in 1958.

APPENDIX A

S.D.F. Finances

IN the early eighties Hyndman seems to have paid most of the expenses for running the Federation, including the rent of its headquarters and the £2-a-week salary of its first Secretary. He was, however, not alone among the wealthy supporters of the Federation: there were Edward Carpenter, whose liberal donation had led to the foundation of *Justice*, William Morris, at the time Treasurer of the Federation, who sustained the weekly loss on the paper until he withdrew from the body, and many others, such as H. H. Champion, Belfort Bax, and Walter Crane. Donations from these middle-class members and sympathizers seem to have been the principal source of the Federation's income in the early years. In 1885 a sum of £100 was given by 'a friend' for the purpose of sending lecturers to the north.[1] The successful organization campaign in Lancashire in 1892 was financed by a Miss Howell, a member of the S.D.F.[2] Later important contributors were Lady Warwick and Joseph Fels, the American millionaire soap-manufacturer and apostle of Henry George.

In these circumstances it was natural that the S.D.F. should be most reluctant to publish full details of its finances. It was not until 1894 that it mentioned in its conference report so much as the bare totals of income and expenditure. According to these accounts the central office income stood at £579 in 1893–4 and increased to £1,554 by 1897–8; later during the set-backs of the South African War and the 'impossibilist revolt' there was silence even about the totals. When the S.D.F. finances recovered somewhat, exact figures were still withheld, and instead the total income of the whole S.D.F., i.e. branches and the head office, was given—£15,500 in 1906 and £19,000 in 1909. This may suggest that the increase in central office income lagged behind that in

[1] *Justice*, 7 Aug. 1886. [2] Ibid., 6 Aug. 1892.

branch revenue. In any case, the whole organization's financial structure was unsatisfactory, and it was significant that the annual conference in 1910 decided to appoint 'an outside auditor'. It was not until the S.D.P. merged into the B.S.P. that a real improvement took place.

For one year, 1898–9, some details of the S.D.F. central office finance are available as a result of a disclosure in the *Labour Leader*.[1] According to this the income consisted of £134 from branch dues, £106 from donations, £231 from contributions to the Central Election Fund, and £726 from the trading depot (for which see below). The expenditure amounted to £163 for lectures and meetings, £219 for the Central Election Fund, £688 for the trading depot, and £31 for the Welsh miners' relief fund. As the total revenue of the central office for that year was £1,640, there was a balance of more than £400 left unaccounted for. Branch dues in this period were assigned to the Propaganda Fund, and donations were usually devoted either to propaganda or to organizing. The day-to-day office expenses, therefore, must have come from other unspecified sources, though later when branch dues for the Propaganda Fund were replaced by the 1s. per member dues from branches, these were generally allocated to this purpose.[2]

With the formation of the B.S.P. a new period of open acccountancy began. The first complete financial statement was for the year 1912, and according to this the main items in the total revenue of £1,868 were branch dues, £565; lectures and meetings, £325; leaflet sales, £187; the Pioneer Boot Works, £110; the 'Clarion' Fund, £40; donations, £36; and trading profits, £28. Expenditure included £380 for lectures and meetings, £203 for the secretary's salary (58 weeks at £3 10s. a week), £84 for leaflets, and £80 for executive meetings.[3] If we compare the relative importance of dues and donations in 1898–9 and in 1912, it would appear that the S.D.F. was making some progress in the regularity of its working-class support, for dues which had constituted only 8 per cent. of the total income in 1898–9 increased to 30 per cent. in 1912, while donations which were 6–7 per cent. decreased to 1·9 per cent.

One item which played an important part in the S.D.F. finances was trading. At the annual conference in 1898 it was reported that 'a little trading' that had been carried on in con-

---

1 *Labour Leader*, 12 Aug. 1899.   2 S.D.P., *Conference Report*, 1910, p. 31.
3 B.S.P., *Conference Report*, 1913, pp. 42ff.

nexion with the central office had realized £108.[1] 'Liberty
blends of tea and coffee' or 'Loose and packet tobaccos. . . .
Profit to the Propaganda Fund'—these advertisements of the
S.D.F. trading department often appeared in *Justice*. Christmas
bazaars were also organized, usually with the active participation of an 'S.D.F. Band' under the conductorship of H. W. Lee,
and one in 1909 raised £250 for the 'Social-Democratic War
Chest'.[2] In 1913 there were donations of £438 from Leicester
and £137 from Reading to the Propaganda Fund:[3] these local
donations usually came from trading carried on by branches.
S.D.F. members at Leicester were making and selling ladies'
garments and shoes; those at Reading were trading in agricultural produce, and their activities led to the foundation
of a local co-operative farm which still exists today.[4] The
most important of these S.D.F. trading enterprises, however,
were the Twentieth Century Press and the Pioneer Boot
Works.

The Twentieth Century Press was formed in October 1891 as a
limited liability company with a nominal capital of £1,000.
This was in fact a firm of 'general and commercial printers', but
it did most of its work for Socialist and trade union organizations.
It purchased *Justice* from Hyndman for the sum of £350, which
was to be paid in shares (or £100 in cash and the rest in shares).
Seven hundred and twenty shares worth £180 were held by the
executive council of the S.D.F. in the names of Hyndman,
Quelch, and H. R. Taylor, as trustees appointed in 1893.[5]
A. A. Watts was appointed secretary, and Quelch, the editor of
Justice, became managing director. Later the authorized capital
was increased to £5,000, and by 1907 the press had contributed
no less than £1,000 to the support of *Justice*.[6] Having lost a libel
case, however, it went bankrupt in 1912, and a new company,
the 'Twentieth Century Press (1912) Ltd.', was immediately set
up to take its place. After the death of Quelch in 1913 W. A.
Woodroffe became manager. In spite of its own difficulties during
the war, the press met the loss on *Justice*, which rapidly increased
after the 'split' to £130 in 1917 and £235 in 1918.[7] The press
survived the S.D.F. and still exists as a commercial establishment,

[1] S.D.F., *Conference Report*, 1898, p. 8.
[2] S.D.P., *Conference Report*, 1910, p. 31.
[3] B.S.P., *Conference Report*, 1914, p. 42.
[4] Information from Mr. Frank Jackson.
[5] S.D.F., *Conference Report*, 1897, pp. 14-15.
[6] *Justice*, 15 June 1907.   [7] Ibid., 12 June 1919.

TH

and there remain a few old S.D.F. members among the share-holders of today.

The Pioneer Boot Works, a co-operative factory, was founded by James Gribble at Northampton in 1904, and made direct contributions to the S.D.F.'s propaganda fund. It was a success from the start and sent £180 to the 'War Chest' on its first year's trading.[1] By 1916 regular contributions from Gribble to the central office amounted to an accumulated total of £2,339, besides £1,036 paid to S.D.F. branches on the basis of purchases.[2] As with the press, the managing committee of the boot works consisted of Hyndmanites: and with the 'split' in 1916 their relation with the B.S.P. came to an end. They do not, however, appear to have given their support to the N.S.P. As a Socialist co-operative Gribble's enterprise went into decline and was liquidated in 1924.[3]

The first independent demonstration of the Federation held in Hyde Park in June 1882 against Irish coercion involved an ex-penditure of £72.[4] From then on, the cost of meetings and lect-ures seemd to have been the largest item of S.D.F. expenditure. Electoral campaigns, however, though much less frequent, were far more costly. For this purpose the S.D.F. set apart the Central Election Fund which later became the 'War Chest', and from these funds a grant of £200 was made to the four candidates at the 1895 General Election, £220 to the two candidates in 1900, and £840 to the nine candidates in 1906.[5] Naturally these grants met only a small part of the election expenses of each candidate. At the 1906 General Election, the Countess of Warwick seems to have 'quietly' given substantial assistance to S.D.F. candidates in addition to her contribution of £200 to the central election fund.[6] Quelch's election expenses at Southampton amounted to £350 of which £80 came from the War Chest, £62 from the local S.D.F., and £150 from Lady Warwick.[7] Hyndman did not disclose his own election expenses, but as he often admitted he found them 'costly'.

---

[1] S.D.F., *Conference Report*, 1905, p. 3.   [2] B.S.P., *Conference Report*, 1916, p. 34.
[3] Ibid., 1917, p. 17; A. Fox, *History of the National Union of Boot and Shoe Operatives* (1958), p. 544.
[4] *Justice*, 4 Aug. 1884.   [5] S.D.F., *Conference Report*, 1906, p. 17.
[6] *Northampton Independent*, 6 Jan. 1906.   [7] *Justice*, 7 March 1906.

APPENDIX B

S.D.F. Membership

THROUGHOUT its history the S.D.F. was extremely reluctant
to publish details of its membership. It is true that the Federation,
existing as it did in a hostile world, had to assume certain conspiratorial features, but there is little doubt that its secretiveness
was partly due to reluctance to disclose its real size for fear of
embarrassment. In the eighties, when the Federation went through
a series of internal crises, it kept complete silence about its
strength, though a few details transpired as a result of revelations
by Hyndman's opponents such as Morris, Champion, and Burns.

There was less aversion, however, to revealing the number of
branches in existence at any time; and from these figures it is
possible to estimate fluctuations in the total membership. Sometimes branch totals were mentioned in *Justice*; sometimes as in
1884 and in 1900 they can be estimated from a careful
reading of the reports of activity week by week. Only in 1894
did the S.D.F. begin to publish the reports of its annual conferences as separate brochures, apparently in imitation of the
I.L.P., which did so from its foundation in 1893. An estimate of
total membership was given in the 1894 report, but only rarely
did one appear thereafter.

Although it is not impossible for certain isolated years to
estimate the S.D.F. membership from the amount of dues paid
by members, the S.D.F. finances were confused, and usually the
conference reports published only the total income and expenditure of the central office. Moreover, the rule concerning
membership dues varied from time to time. In the eighties a
member was expected to pay 1d. a week to his or her branch,
and each branch was asked to contribute at least one quarter of
its dues income to the 'Propaganda Fund'.[1] This rule, which
meant a branch contribution of 1s. 1d. per member per year,
continued to operate until at least 1900 and most likely up to

[1] Rule 2, *S.D.F. Rules*, 1887.

1903 when the 'very critical' state of S.D.F. finances led to higher dues of 2*d*. per week per member, one half of which— 4*s*. 4*d*. per member per year—was to be sent by the branches to the central office.[1] This 2*d*. per week contribution was soon found too high, and the new rules published in 1906 stated that a member's contribution to his or her branch should be regulated by the branch and each branch was simply to pay 1*s*. per member per year to the central office.[2]

In addition to these regular membership dues, the S.D.F. for some time had a special levy on each member for the purpose of financing electoral campaigns. The 'Central Election Fund' which was founded in 1890 was at first based on voluntary contributions,[3] but the Baring crisis in the same year, which hit Hyndman very heavily, seems to have rendered the voluntary principle unworkable. The S.D.F. rules published in 1892 describe the Central Election Fund as based on an obligatory contribution of 1*s*. per member per year,[4] and this special levy continued until 1903 when it was replaced by a 'Social-Democratic War Chest' which was to be based on voluntary contributions.[5] The required annual payment of a member to his or her branch, therefore, was 4*s*. 4*d*. in the eighties, 5*s*. 4*d*. for ten years after 1892, 8*s*. 8*d*. from 1903 to 1905, and dependent upon branch discretion after 1906. These levies were rather high for a poor working-class membership, and there must have been many who were unable to keep up their contributions—apart from those who were unemployed or on strike or sick, for whom special exemption was possible. Moreover, many branches, actively engaged as they were in their local work, were often extremely lax in paying their required minimum contribution to the central office. The Coventry branch, for instance, had a membership of 320 in 1912, of which only 120 were due-paying members.[6] The 'paying membership' calculated on the basis of branch dues, therefore, would give only an inadequate estimate of the real strength of the S.D.F. On the other hand, the Central Election Fund from which there was no rule of exemption gives no better estimate of membership, for it was only 'in part' made up of obligatory contributions from members.[7]

The B.S.P., in which the S.D.P. merged with the Clarion

[1] Rules 3 and 9, *S.D.F. Rules*, 1903.   [2] Rules 3 and 9, ibid., 1906.
[3] *Justice*, 15 March 1890.   [4] Rule 27, *S.D.F. Rules*, 1892.
[5] S.D.F., *Conference Report*, 1904, pp. 18-19.
[6] Information from Mr. Frank Jackson.
[7] S.D.F, *Conference Report*, 1904, p. 19.

groups and the I.L.P. 'rebels', claimed a membership of 40,000 in its first year, and a branch directory published in the same year listed 343 branches.[1] Branch dues remained 1s. per member per year until 1917 when they were increased to 2s.; and in 1916 a 'Parliamentary Fund' was introduced, to which members had to pay a minimum contribution of 1s. a year.[2] Unlike the S.D.F., the B.S.P. published details of its financial accounts. From its reports of branch dues paid and outstanding it is possible to estimate its total and paying memberships which, as shown in the attached table, slowly but steadily decreased after 1912.

Altogether twenty-three branches withdrew at the time of the 'split' in 1916; some of them went over to the N.S.P., but some set up as independent Socialist Societies. The loss caused by the 'split' seems to have been compensated for by the affiliation of the 'Jewish Social-Democratic organization' with its central committee and branches in London, Manchester, Leeds, and Glasgow.[3] As the war went on, however, the B.S.P. must have lost members on balance. The government's prosecution of anti-war and pro-Bolshevik Socialists became more intense, and many of the B.S.P. activities became conspiratorial once more. Meanwhile, Hyndman's N.S.P. was able to set up a few new branches, but their number did not rise beyond fifty. In affiliating to the Labour Party, the N.S.P. claimed a membership of 2,000, while the B.S.P. claimed 10,000. The Communist Party of which the B.S.P. formed the largest element claimed the same total of 10,000 at its formation in 1920, but its 'real' strength was estimated by its national organizer, Tom Bell, at 2,000–2,500.[4]

[1] B.S.P., *Conference Report*, 1912, pp. 40f.
[2] B.S.P. Rules, 1912 and 1917, *Conference Report*, 1912, 1917.
[3] B.S.P., *Conference Report*, 1917, p. 17.
[4] Tom Bell, *Pioneering Days*, p. 195.

S.D.F. MEMBERSHIP AND BRANCHES

Year	Membership Claimed	Paying	Sources(a)	Branches	Sources(a)
1884	500		Morris quoted in Bernstein, *Briefe von Engels*, p. 161.	25	*Justice*, 1884, *passim*.
1885				17	*Justice*, 8 Aug. 1885.
1886				20	Ibid., 7 Aug. 1886.
1887		689	Champion in *Common Sense*, 15 Sept. 1887	24	Ibid., 13 Aug. 1887.
				48	Ibid., 11 Aug. 1888.
				66(*b*)	Ibid., 24 June 1893.
1888				43	Ibid., 11 Aug. 1888.
1889	1,926(*c*)				
1893				62	Ibid., 24 June 1893.
1894	4,000		S.D.F. *CR*, 1894, p. 16	91	Ibid., 11 Aug. 1894.
1896	10,536		*Justice*, 19 Sept. 1896	134	S.D.F. *CR*, 1896, p. 20.
1897		1,216(*d*)			
1898				137	S.D.F. *CR*, 1898, p. 8.
1899		2,483(*e*)		136	*Labour Annual*, 1900, p.8
1900	9,000		*Justice*, 3 March 1900	96	*Justice*, 1900, *passim*.
1903	9,000		*Reformers' Year Book*, 1904, p. 132.		
1904				108	*Justice*, 13 Aug. 1904.
1905				143	*Socialist Annual*, 1906, p. 59.
1906				151	S.D.F. *CR*, 1906, p. 15.
1907		6,000	Glasier in *Labour Leader*, 23 Aug. 1907.	186	S.D.F. *CR*, 1907, p. 11.
1908	12,000	10,040	S.D.P. *CR*, 1909, p. 13	232	*Socialist Annual*, 1909, p. 53.
1909	17,000		International Socialist Bureau *Bericht*, 1907–9, Vorrede, p. 3.		
1910				235	*Justice*, 2 April, 1910.
1911		8,220.	*Socialist Year Book*, 1912, p. 30.	189	Ibid., 29 July 1911.

B.S.P.

Year	Membership Claimed	Paying	Sources(a)	Branches	Sources(a)
1912	40,000		B.S.P. *CR*, 1912, pp. 4of.	343	B.S.P. *CR*, 1912, pp.4of.
1912–13					
	15,313	11,313	B.S.P. *CR*, 1913, p. 40		
1913—14					
	13,755	9,955.	B.S.P. *CR*, 1914, pp. 36, 39.		
1914	20,000		Labour Party *CR*, 1916, p. 10.		

Year	Membership Claimed	Paying	Sources(a)	Branches	Sources(a)
1915–16		7,335.	B.S.P. *CR*, 1916, p. 33.		
1916–17		6,435.	B.S.P. *CR*, 1917, p. 17.		
1917	10,000		Labour Party *CR*, 1917, p. 7.		

N.S.P. (later S.D.F.)

1917				50	*Justice*, 18 Jan. 1917.
1918				42	Ibid., 1 Aug. 1918.
1919	2,000		Labour Party *CR*, 1919, p. 93.		

S.D.F.

1921	2,000		Ibid., 1921.		
1933–8	1,000		S.D.F. *Executive Minutes*, 1933.		
1939	500		Ibid., 1939.		

(*a*) Conference Reports are cited as *CR*.

(*b*) This number includes branches of the North of England Socialist Federation which often existed only on paper. S.D.F. *CR*, 1896, p. 20.

(*c*) Reported to the Paris Possibilist congress as representing fifteen branches of the S.D.F. (Hyndman representing the General Council), but Burns claimed that the real membership was less than one half of this. *Labour Elector*, 3 Aug. 1889.

(*d*) Based on 'Parliamentary dues' of £60. 16s. S.D.F. *CR*, 1897, p. 17.

(*e*) Based on branch dues of £134. 8s. 9d. *Labour Leader*, 12 Aug. 1899.

APPENDIX C

Bibliography of Works by

H. M. Hyndman

━━━━━━

1. BOOKS AND PAMPHLETS:

The Nizam of Hyderabad: Indian Policy and English Justice. (1875)

The Indian Famine and the Crisis in India. (1877)

(With Henry Yule) *Mr. Henry M. Stanley and the Royal Geographical Society: Being the Record of a Protest.* (1878)

England for All: The Text-Book of Democracy. (1881)

Why Should India Pay for the Conquest of Egypt? (1882)

The Historical Basis of Socialism in England. (1883)

Socialism versus Smithism: An Open Letter to Samuel Smith, M.P. (1884)

Socialism and Slavery: Being an Answer to Mr. Herbert Spencer's Attack upon the Democratic Federation. (1884)

(With Charles Bradlaugh) *Will Socialism benefit the English People? Verbatim Report of a Debate between H.M. Hyndman and Charles Bradlaugh.* (1884)

(With William Morris) *A Summary of the Principles of Socialism* (1884)

The Social Reconstruction of England. (1884)

The Coming Revolution in England. (1884)

The Chicago Riots and the Class War in the United States. (1886)

The Bankruptcy of India: An Enquiry into the Administration of India under the Crown, including a chapter on the Silver Question. (1886)

A Commune for London. (1887)

The Emigration Fraud: A Reply to Lord Brabazon. (?1888)

(With Henry George) *The Single-Tax and Social-Democracy: Verbatim Report of the Debate between Henry George and H. M Hyndman held in St. James's Hall, 2nd July 1889.* (1889)

Marx's Theory of Value. (1889)

Draft of an Eight Hours Bill. (1890)

(With Charles Bradlaugh) *Eight Hours' Movements: Verbatim Report of a Debate between H. M. Hyndman and Charles Bradlaugh.* (1890)

General Booth's Book ('In Darkest England') Refuted. (1890)

Commercial Crises of the Nineteenth Century. (1892)

(With William Morris and George Bernard Shaw) *Manifesto of English Socialists.* (1893)

Mr. Gladstone and the Eight Hours' Law. (?1893)

Social Democrat's Ideal (?1893)

(With others) *How I Became a Socialist.* (?1894)

(With Henry Labouchere) *Debate on Socialism between H. Labouchere and H. M. Hyndman at the Temperance Hall, Northampton, on 8 February 1894: Verbatim Report.* (?1894)

The Final Futility of Final Utility. (1895)

The Economics of Socialism: Being a Series of Seven Lectures on Political Economy. (1896)

The Approaching Catastrophe in India. (?1897)

The Transvaal War and the Degradation of England. (?1899)

(With Harry Quelch and Belfort Bax) *Liberalism and Labour* (?1903)

Report on the Colonies and Dependencies to the International Socialist Congress, 1904. (1904)

Social-Democracy: The Basis of its Principles and the Causes of Its Success. (?1904)

The Unrest in India: Verbatim Report of the Speech delivered on 12th May 1907. (1907)

Darkness and Dawn of May Day. (1907)

Death and the Socialist Ideal. (?1907)

The Ruin of India by British Rule. (1907)

The Record of an Adventurous Life. (1911)

Socialism and Labour Unrest. (1912)

Further Reminiscences. (1912)

Tariff Reform and Imperialism, an Alternative Policy: An Address delivered by Hyndman at the Queen's Hall, Langham Place, London, on 18 April 1910. (1912)

The Murdering of British Seamen by Lloyd George, the Liberal Cabinet & the Board of Trade. (1913)

The Future of Democracy. (1915)

An Independent Poland, a Necessity for Democratic Europe. (1918)

The Only Way to Avert Anarchy. (1919)

Clemenceau: The Man and his Time. (1919)

The Awakening of Asia. (1919)

The Evolution of Revolution. (1920)

(With the Duke of Northumberland) *The Causes of Industrial Unrest: Verbatim Report of a Debate between H. M. Hyndman and the Duke of Northumberland on 8th June 1921 at the House of Commons.* (1921)

The Truth about India. (Madras, 1921)

An Introduction to the 'Life to Come'. (1926)

'Real Reform.' (Burnley, n.d.)

2. ARTICLES:[1]

'Cavour', *Fortnightly Review*, n.s. xxii (1 Aug. 1877), 219–43.

'The Bankruptcy of India', *Nineteenth Century*, v (March 1879), 443–62.

'Irish Needs and Irish Remedies', *Fortnightly Review*, n.s. xxvii (1 Feb. 1880), 208–26.

'Bleeding to Death', *Nineteenth Century*, viii (July 1880), 157–76.

'The Dawn of a Revolutionary Epoch', *Nineteenth Century*, ix (Jan. 1881), 1–18.

'Lights and Shades of American Politics', *Fortnightly Review*, xxix (1 March 1881), 340–57.

'The Coming Revolution in England', *North American Review*, cxxxv (Oct. 1882), 229–322.

'The Social Reconstruction of England', *International Review* (New York), xiv (Feb.–March 1883), 110–30.

'The Revolution of To-day', *To-day*, n.s. i (Jan. 1884) 3–24.

'Six Centuries of Work and Wages', a review of Thorold Rogers' book. *To-day*, n.s. ii (July 1884), 100–4.

'Revolution or Reform', *To-day*, n.s. ii (Aug. 1884), 180–98.

'Something Better than Emigration', *Nineteenth Century*, xvi (Dec. 1884), 991–8.

(With Henry George) 'Socialism and Rent-Appropriation: A Dialogue', *Nineteenth Century*, xvii (Feb. 1885), 369–80.

'The Radicals and Socialism', *Nineteenth Century*, xviii (Nov. 1885), 833–9.

'The Chicago Riots and the Class War in the United States', *Time*, n.s. vol. 3 (1886).

'Socialism in England', *North American Review*, cxliii (Sept. 1886), 225–36.

'The English Workers as They are', *Contemporary Review*, lii (July 1887), 122–36.

---

[1] Excluding newspaper articles, letters, and occasional notes.

'Marx's Theory of Value', *To-day*, xi (April 1889), 94–104; *International Review* (July 1889), 15–23.

'The International Congress of Workers', *International Review* (Aug. 1889), 33–44.

'Socialism', *Johnson's Universal Cyclopoedia*, vii (New York, 1895), 594–9.

'Social-Democrat or Socialist?', *Social-Democrat*, i (August 1897), 227–31.

'Henry George'. *Saturday Review*, lxxxiv (6 Nov. 1897), 485–6.

'Socialism and the Future of England', *Cosmopolis*, no. xxv (January 1898), 21–57.

'The Socialist Vote and the Liberal Party', *Social-Democrat*, ii (April 1898), 106–11.

'England and International Socialism', *International Socialist Review* (Chicago), i (July 1900), 17–22.

'Democracy', *Social-Democrat*, v (Feb. 1901), 38–41.

'Thoughts on Responsibility', *Social-Democrat*, v (Feb. 1901), 46–47.

'Zola's "Travail" and Jaurès' Criticism', *Social-Democrat*, v (July 1901), 207–8.

'The Fiscal Twaddle and Socialism', *Socialist Annual*, 1906, pp. 41–43.

'British India', *Socialist Annual*, 1906, pp. 52–54.

'The Scientific Investigation of History', *Social-Democrat*, x (Feb. 1906), 74–78.

'The Theories of Karl Marx', *Economist*, lxv (12 Oct. 1907), 1729–30. Reprinted in *Social-Democrat*, xi (Nov. 1907), 676–80.

'Socialism and Labourism in England', *International Socialist Review* (Chicago), x (Oct. 1909), 351–3.

'Peers and People', *Socialist Annual*, 1910, pp. 17–23.

'Trade Union Unrest and the Class War', *English Review*, vi (Oct. 1910), 539–53.

(With Gaylord Wilshire) 'Striking vs. Voting', *Wilshire's Magazine* (Nov. 1913–Jan. 1914). Reprinted from *Daily Herald*, 25 Sept.–30 Oct. 1913.

(With E. Belfort Bax) 'Socialism, Materialism, and the War', *English Review*, xix (Dec. 1914), 52–69.

'The Coming Triumph of Marxist Socialism', *English Review*, xix (Feb. 1915), 290–304.

'Social-Democracy and Peace', *Fortnightly Review*, n.s. xcvii (March 1915), 408–22.

'Cromwellism without Cromwell', *English Review*, xx (May 1915), 204–14.

'The Armed Nation', *Fortnightly Review*, n.s. xcviii (Sept, 1915), 529–41.

'Thrift no Panacea without Increased Production', *Nineteenth Century and After*, lxxviii (Sept. 1915), 714–28.

'Commercial Boycotts and Policies', *English Review*, xxi (Oct. 1915), 283–94.

'National Railways after the War', *Nineteenth Century and After*, lxxix (Feb. 1916), 461–77.

'The Emigration Madness', *English Review*, xxii (May 1916, 470–7.

'The Awakening of Asia', *Fortnightly Review*, n.s., c (Oct. 1916), 677–90.

'The Railway Problem Solved', *Nineteenth Century and After*, lxxx (Nov. 1916), 1023–39.

'British Policy and the Rights of the People', *New Europe*, i (28 Oct. 1916), 329–35.

'The Stockholm Conference', *Land and Water*, 14 June 1917.

'Clemenceau', *New Europe*, v (29 Nov. 1917), 216–17.

'The Evolution of Revolution', *Quarterly Review*, ccxcix (April 1918), 397–413.

'Japan as Mistress of China', *New Europe*, xi (29 May 1919), 154–8.

The Scandal of our Milk Supply', *Nineteenth Century and After*, lxxxvi (Sept. 1919), 554–66.

'An Antiquated Assembly', *Nineteenth Century and After*, lxxxix (June 1921), 979–92.

'Books of a Lifetime', *Social Democrat*, Sept. 1925–June 1926.

3. PREFACES, WORKS EDITED, TRANSLATED, ETC.:

The Nationalisation of the Land in 1775 and 1882: Being a Lecture delivered at Newcastle-on-Tyne by Thomas Spence, 1775. Reprinted and edited, with notes and introduction, by H. M. Hyndman. London, 1882.

Prince Kropotkin, *An Appeal to the Young*, translated by H. M. Hyndman. Reprinted from *To-Day* and *Justice*. London, 1885.

Memoir of William Morris in Morris, *How I Became a Socialist* (London, 1896).

Preface to F. J. Gould, *Pages for Young Socialists* (London, 1911).

Introduction to Joseph Burgess, *John Burns* (London, 1911).

Preface to Alexander Brož, *The First Year of the Czecho-Slovak Republic* (London, 1920).

APPENDIX D

List of Unpublished Sources Consulted

1. MANUSCRIPTS

N.B. The following abbreviations are used: B.M. Add. MSS for British Museum Additional Manuscripts; BLPES for British Library of Political and Economic Science, London; IISH for International Institute of Social History, Amsterdam; WSHS for Wisconsin State Historical Society, Madison, Wis., U.S.A. In several cases I have used microfilms or transcripts in the possession of Mr. Henry Pelling: these are indicated by an asterisk (*).

B.S.P. (Birmingham Section) Papers. BLPES.
John Burns Papers. B.M.Add.MSS. 46285–46288.
Thomas Davidson Correspondence. Yale University Library.*
Richard T. Ely Papers. WSHS.*
Friedrich Engels Correspondence. IISH.
Henry George Papers. New York Public Library.*
Jules Guesde Papers. IISH.
Morris Hillquit Papers. WSHS.*
Karl Kautsky Correspondence. IISH.
George Lansbury Collection. BLPES.
Henry Demarest Lloyd Papers. WSHS.*
Eleanor Marx Correspondence. IISH.
Karl Marx Correspondence. IISH.
Correspondence of John Stuart Mill and Helen Taylor. BLPES.
William Morris Papers. B.M.Add. MSS. 45345.
Charles E. Russell Papers. Library of Congress.*
Andreas Scheu Papers. IISH.
R. W. Seton-Watson Papers. By courtesy of Prof. Hugh and Mr. Christopher Seton-Watson.
Algernon M. Simons Papers. WSHS.*
Minute books of the Social-Democratic Federation, 1931–41. By courtesy of Secretary, National Council of Labour Colleges.*
Socialist Labor Party (American) Papers. WSHS*
Socialist League Papers. IISH.

Papers of Sidney and Beatrice Webb. BLPES.
H. Gaylord Wilshire Papers. By courtesy of Prof. H. H. Quint.*

2. UNPUBLISHED THESES AND ESSAYS

Burdick, Eugene. 'Syndicalism and Industrial Unionism in England until 1918.' D.Phil. Thesis, Oxford, 1950.
Neuall, Frank. 'The S.D.F., 1900–1910.' By courtesy of the author.
Solberg, C. T. 'The Independent Labour Party, 1893–1918.' B.Litt. Thesis, Oxford, 1939.
Tanner, Frank. 'The Social Democracy in Britain, 1900-1914.' By courtesy of the author.

INDEX

Uн

National Socialist Party (N.S.P.), 236, 243, 248, 249, 280, 283; foundation of, 234f.; attitude to European War, 246; to Second International, 250; to Bolsheviks, 251, 260; to Communist Party, 252; to Labour Party, 259f.; annual conferences, (1918) 260, (1920) 251, 264; becomes S.D.F., 264

National Union of Railwaymen, 187, 261

Nationalities and Subject Races Committee, 216

Nelson (Lancs.), 93, 95, 96

Nevill, Lady Dorothy, 150

Newcastle-on-Tyne, 37, 40, 81f., 169

New Europe, 256

New Review (New York), 223

News from Nowhere (Morris), 269

New South Wales, 13

New Unionism, 87–91, 274

New University Club, 73

New York, 15, 104, 133, 138, 223

New Zealand, 29, 103

Nicholas II, Czar, 197, 198, 216

Nicoll, David, 120

Nineteenth Century, 23, 24, 34

Nonconformist Protestantism, 14, 109, 271

Northampton, 99, 132, 135, 145, 147, 150, 155, 159, 160n., 171n., 274, 280

Northamptonshire, 150

Northumberland, 82

Northumberland, Duke of, 262

Nottingham, 48, 70, 71, 108, 260

Nutting, Sir J., 160

O'Grady, James, 105, 260

Openshaw Socialist Society, 174n.

Origin of the Family (Engels), 14, 60, 269

Osborne, W. V., 180

Osborne Judgment, 171, 180, 183

Overlookers' Association, 158

Owen, Robert, 38, 87

Oxburgh, 6, 7

Oxford, 53, 61, 181

Paisley, 213

Pall Mall Gazette, 9, 17, 18, 20f., 29, 37, 53, 71, 77, 79, 271

Palmer, Tom, 21f.

Pankhurst, Emmeline and Christabel, 190–3

Paris Commune, 17, 59, 112f.

Parnell, C. S., 28f., 44, 47

Parsons, Mrs., 85

Patriotic Club, 36

Pearson, Charles, 14

People (New York), 134

Perkins, Caroline S., 5

Perkins, John, 5

Petrograd (formerly St. Petersburg), 196, 236, 237, 240

Petite République, 126

Petrov, Peter, 229f.

Phoenix Park Murders (1882), 44f.

Pioneer Boot Works, 278, 280

Pius IX, Pope, 9

Plekhanov, George, 194, 197, 236

Plymouth, 104

Poland, 137, 251, 257, 275

Poplar Board of Guardians, 147

Popular Front, 275

Positivists, 17, 38, 272

Possibilists, 59, 84, 114–18

Poverty of India (Naoroji), 23

Primrose League, 8

Prometheus Unbound (Shelley), 269

Punjab, 195

Purcell, A. A., 175

Queensland (Australia), 13, 15

Quelch, Harry, 106, 109, 135, 146, 154, 185, 207, 255; early S.D.F. activities, 51f., 59, 66f., 78, 80, 107; editor of *Justice,* 79, 155, 160, 177, 273, 279; director of Twentieth Century Press, 279; trade union activities, 89, 91, 94, 274; election campaigns, 159, 160n., 280, 171n.; attitude to Liberal Party, 155, 160, 161; to Labour Party, 136, 155, 163, 165f., 177; to socialist unity, 152f.; to impossibilists, 136, 139, 140; to labour unrest, 184; to Irish Home Rule, 189; to suffragettes, 190, 192; on International Socialist Bureau, 125; views on defence and foreign policy, 203, 204, 209, 212, 214; death, 177

Radical, 36, 40

Railwaymen, National Union of, 187, 261

Railway Servants, Amalgamated Society of, 105, 110, 180, 181

Rand, 190

Ravachol, 120

Reading, 135, 279

Record of an Adventurous Life (Hyndman), 172

Reform Club, 73

Renaudel, Pierre, 247

Revue des Deux Mondes, 14

Reynolds's Newspaper, 75, 130, 146, 157

Rhondda, Lord, 244, 245

Roberts, G. H., 232

Printed in Great Britain by
The Camelot Press Ltd., London and Southampton